DISCOVERING ORIENTEERING

Skills, Techniques, and Activities

Orienteering USA
Editor

Charles Ferguson
Robert Turbyfill
Authors

HUMAN KINETICS

Library of Congress Cataloging-in-Publication Data

Ferguson, Charles.
   Orienteering USA / Charles Ferguson, Robert Turbyfill.
      pages cm. -- (Discovering orienteering)
   Includes index.
   1. Orienteering. I. Title.
   GV200.4.F46 2013
   796.58--dc23

                                     2012029282

ISBN-10: 0-7360-8423-1 (print)
ISBN-13: 978-0-7360-8423-9 (print)

The web addresses cited in this text were current as of October 10, 2012, unless otherwise noted.

Activity writer (appendix A): Mary Jo Childs; **Acquisitions Editor:** Gayle Kassing, PhD; **Developmental Editor:** Bethany J. Bentley; **Assistant Editor:** Derek Campbell; **Copyeditor:** Alisha Jeddeloh; **Indexer:** Sharon Duffy; **Permissions Manager:** Dalene Reeder; **Graphic Designer:** Keri Evans; **Graphic Artist:** Julie L. Denzer; **Cover Designer:** Keith Blomberg; **Photograph (cover):** Wil Smith; **Photographs (interior):** Courtesy of David Yee, NEOC (pp. 1, 43, 57, 71, 95, 121, 128, and 130); courtesy of Jerry Rhodes, CROC (pp. 3 and 13); courtesy of Martin and Erminia Farenfield, CIOR (p. 6); courtesy of Charlotte MacNaughton (pp. 8, 15, 19 [figure 2.3], 27, 36 [figure 3.9a], 38, 59, 64, 67, 91, 107, 110, and 119); courtesy of Julie Kiem, SVO (pp. 19 [figure 2.2], 20, 100, and 118 [figure 9.5b]); courtesy of Linda Ferguson (pp. 36 [figure 3.9b], 37, 46, 79, and 123); courtesy of Charles Ferguson (pp. 72, 88, 104, 118 [figure 9.5a], and 125); courtesy of Cory Peterson, CIOR (p. 85); **Photo Production Manager:** Jason Allen; **Art Manager:** Kelly Hendren; **Associate Art Manager:** Alan L. Wilborn; **Illustrations:** appendix A illustrations © Human Kinetics; map segments courtesy of Ed Hicks of Orienteering Unlimited (pp. 31, 33, and 34) and Bob Burg of Orienteering Unlimited (pp. 35, 48, 49, 50, 51, 52, 55, 59, 61, 63, 65, 66, 74, and 75); **Printer:** Versa Press

Printed in the United States of America   10   9   8   7   6   5   4   3   2   1

The paper in this book is certified under a sustainable forestry program.

Human Kinetics
Website: www.HumanKinetics.com

United States: Human Kinetics
P.O. Box 5076
Champaign, IL 61825-5076
800-747-4457
e-mail: humank@hkusa.com

Canada: Human Kinetics
475 Devonshire Road Unit 100
Windsor, ON N8Y 2L5
800-465-7301 (in Canada only)
e-mail: info@hkcanada.com

Europe: Human Kinetics
107 Bradford Road
Stanningley
Leeds LS28 6AT, United Kingdom
+44 (0) 113 255 5665
e-mail: hk@hkeurope.com

Australia: Human Kinetics
57A Price Avenue
Lower Mitcham, South Australia 5062
08 8372 0999
e-mail: info@hkaustralia.com

New Zealand: Human Kinetics
P.O. Box 80
Torrens Park, South Australia 5062
0800 222 062
e-mail: info@hknewzealand.com

E4879

We dedicate *Discovering Orienteering* to all desiring to learn and improve using a systematic approach to the art of navigation. We commend it to everyone with the patience, drive, and commitment to acquire, develop, or improve their navigation skills and abilities. Also, we thank all those coaches, teachers, orienteers, and especially the students in our classes, who taught us along the way. Finally, we especially appreciate our wives, Jo and Linda, for their patience and support in our many orienteering endeavors leading to this book.

Contents

Preface

Discover orienteering—a navigational sport that challenges your mind as much as your body. The book you hold is based on years of effort by top trainers from Orienteering USA who have created a simple plan for quickly developing the navigational skills that some take years to acquire. Bob Turbyfill, former Orienteering USA team coach, USA Champion, and North American Orienteering Champion, has been sharing this system with beginners, competitors, and coaches for decades and has now partnered with retired military orienteer and past Orienteering USA President Chuck Ferguson to bring this system to a wider audience. A foundation in the basic skills, techniques, and processes presented in this book can rapidly prepare someone with no previous navigational experience to be successful at intermediate-level land navigation and orienteering. Experienced orienteers and land navigators will find a wealth of assistance, too.

Orienteering is a sport for the 21st century. The modern world faces a variety of new challenges. Health issues are at the forefront of modern discourse, and the National Physical Activity Initiative aims to increase fitness levels across the United States. Stewardship of our natural resources will be increasingly important in the years to come. The sport of orienteering provides an excellent foray into the outdoors and develops a deeper appreciation and understanding of environmental issues in addition to providing excellent physical conditioning. Orienteering also requires critical-thinking and problem-solving skills, which are in high demand in our technologically advanced society. The confidence one develops by completing a course independently is a priceless resource for adults and children alike. Perhaps most importantly, orienteering is a lot of fun! It's a chance to exercise your mind and body, run off-trail, and test yourself against the land, the map, and yourself.

For those who get hooked on the sport, orienteering provides opportunities for exciting competition, from local events all the way up to world championships. Orienteers enjoy traveling to the wide variety of terrains used for such competitions and meeting fellow orienteers from all over the country and even around the world. Orienteering is a sport for everyone, with participants ranging in age from under 10 to over 80. Some compete seriously and are elite athletes, while others enjoy the chance for a unique recreational experience with friends or family. The older demographic benefits from the combined physical and mental challenges, both of which have been shown to increase the quality of life at advanced age.

A wide audience can benefit from the sport and the techniques presented. Learning orienteering and land navigation skills can be useful to those in the military and to search-and-rescue personnel. Anyone participating in an outdoor sport, such as hiking or hunting, should know the basic navigational methods used by orienteers. Anyone who relies on map information, such as drivers or delivery people, can benefit from improving their navigational skills. GPS systems have been known to send those ignorant of the map into dangerous situations. These techniques are equally useful for anyone competing in sports involving a navigational component, including both wild and urban adventure races. Experienced orienteers or coaches unfamiliar with this system will find it easy to understand and teach to others. Those with no previous orienteering experience will find that the method presented makes it easy to quickly become successful at cross-country navigation. If you have access to a local orienteering club, however, it is recommended that you use them as an additional resource to the book to get the most professional orienteering experiences.

ORGANIZATION

Chapter 1 introduces the basics of orienteering, and it establishes some historical perspective on the sport. This is especially important for beginners who have no frame of reference for the activities. Chapter 2 discusses fitness, nutrition, and safety practices pertaining to navigational sports. Chapter 3 details orienteering tools and equipment. The meat of the book is in chapters 4 through 6, which focus on orienteering skills, techniques, and processes. These chapters address the standard methodology used by Orienteering USA for teaching and coaching the sport of orienteering. The authors have spent many years developing and honing this system with a variety of audiences. It distills the sport into a small set of easy-to-remember skills and techniques that can be practiced through a variety of training exercises. Chapter 7 addresses sportsmanship and ethics in orienteering. Chapters 8 through 10 take a participant through the event experience, including preparation and postevent analysis. Appendix A presents activities in a simple lesson-plan format indicating the skills and techniques developed by the exercise, the expertise level of the intended audience, and the equipment needed for each activity. Appendix B provides reproducible forms in the preferred format for tracking the results of a series of competitions, which allow the coach to get a picture of competitive-weakness trends. With this trend sheet, any coach will be better equipped to make intelligent decisions about the type and quality of training needed to overcome weaknesses and bolster strengths.

This book has been developed in conjunction with Orienteering USA to address the methods, techniques, and types of orienteering that are commonly found throughout North America. The authors are highly experienced orienteers with expertise both as trainers and as elite competitors. Orienteering USA is excited to be a part of this book and to help bring the sport of orienteering to a new 21st-century audience prepared to tackle physical and environmental challenges. We hope you have as much fun learning and teaching orienteering as we do.

Clare Durand
Former President
Orienteering USA

Acknowledgments

Editors and Experts

Mary Jo Childs, Green Mountain Orienteering Club
Terra Walters, Editor and Writer
Capt. Chris Nelson, USMC

Photographs

Linda Ferguson, Photo Editor
David Yee, New England Orienteering Club
Charlotte MacNaughton, Orienteering Canada
Julie Kiem, Susquehanna Valley Orienteering
Jerry Rhodes, Columbia River Orienteering Club
Martin and Erminia Farenfield, CIOR Military Competitions Team
Cory Peterson, Team USA Military
Linda Ferguson, Quantico Orienteering Club & Georgia Orienteering Club
Vanessa Blake, Columbia River Orienteering Club

Maps and Graphics

Col. Mike Hendricks, USMA
Florida Orienteering Club
Les Stark, Columbia River Orienteering Club
Columbia River Orienteering Club

We would be remiss if we did not give special thanks to Orienteering Unlimited (OU) and to partners Bob Burg, perhaps one of the most creative map artists in the United States, and Ed Hicks, his friend and the senior business partner and owner of OU. They contributed the map legends, the terrain feature drawings, and the map segments, of which Bob's "simplify the map" series is particularly outstanding. Ed has championed orienteering locally, nationally, and internationally with outstanding results in adapting navigation activities for educational settings and objectives. Both took time from their busy lives to make the illustrations in *Discovering Orienteering* the best they could be.

Orienteering Activities

Mary Jo Childs, Editor and Author, *Coaching Orienteering*
Donna and Steve Fluegel and *Orienteering North America*
Greg Lennon, Technical Assistance and Advice, Quantico Orienteering Club

Special Thanks

Barbro Rönnberg, Secretary General, International Orienteering Federation
Orienteering USA
Orienteering Canada
Peter Goodwin, President, Orienteering USA
Patrick Ferguson, Drum Wizard, who saved my data when my motherboard failed at a critical deadline

Introduction to Orienteering

This chapter introduces a wonderful sport, orienteering, which is largely done outdoors. It explains the relevance of orienteering and how the sport is for anyone of any age or ability who has a desire to get off the roads and trails and experience nature up close or who wants to get from one place to another using navigational skills and techniques. Orienteering is both a skill and an art, as you will learn as you read this book. Although normally done individually, orienteering can also be a team sport, giving participants team-building experiences and fostering the full development of leadership and communication skills.

WHAT IS ORIENTEERING?

Orienteering consists of using a map, usually assisted by a compass, to move from one location or place on the map to others. The start is marked by a triangle. Other locations are marked by circles on the map and the finish is marked by a double circle. More details will be presented as you move deeper into the book, and you will see how the skills, techniques, and processes learned in orienteering can help you navigate almost anywhere under almost any conditions, whether you are in the woods, on urban streets, or in a classroom. However, the basics are that orienteering events are staged on a map using specific locations, are timed, and require you to navigate, whether you are walking, running, canoeing, mountain biking, riding a horse, or moving down a trail in a wheelchair.

Orienteering can be done recreationally for fun or competitively at local, national, and international levels. It requires decision making, which may have to be done under conditions of competitive stress and fatigue. Teachers love the way it stretches and challenges the mind and can complement almost any academic discipline. For business leaders, it hones mental agility and decision-making ability. Soldiers, Marines, and Navy Seals find it great training for combat skills. Coaches appreciate how it tones the body, improving fitness. Parents find it a wholesome, confidence-building activity for their kids. And green thinkers are enchanted by its gentle impact on the environment and its capacity to pull more of us into the great outdoors.

WHY LEARN TO ORIENTEER?

There are so many reasons to learn orienteering: As an individual, you may want to be a more fit, confident, and adventurous person who gets off the beaten path. As an orienteer, you may never have learned some of the basics or you may have forgotten them, slowing you down. For the teacher, orienteering is a fun sport that students can master at their own pace with little equipment and in almost any area. For the recreation or youth leader, orienteering is a sport that adds another dimension to the usual activities and is fun and continually teaches vital lessons in integrity and fairness in games and life. For adventure racers, expert navigation is the key to winning. For the Marine, the Navy Seal, the soldier, the park ranger, the smoke jumper, and the expert in search and rescue, orienteering hones the vital navigational skills of the profession. For the truck or car driver and helicopter or airplane pilot, the ability to run through the woods with a map and compass and do it well translates directly into finding one's way in the countryside, in the city, or in the air. For the hiker, trekker, hunter, bird-watcher, and fisher, the ability to use a map and a compass is an abiding need.

Having a Global Positioning System (GPS) unit can make navigation easy—until it doesn't! Recall the Rhodes family's reliance in 2009 on their GPS programmed to find the shortest route, which ultimately stranded them for three days in December in a snowy Oregon forest. That overreliance on GPS technology could have easily cost the couple their lives. The GPS unit cannot think, but you can, and your brain is always with you. You'll be far faster in the woods and better at route choice than any unthinking, GPS-dependent companion that relies, as one Marine colonel put it, "on two failing batteries and three wobbly satellites!"

Orienteering success builds confidence, parlaying fear of the outdoors into joyful appreciation. Success does not require winning against others, unless that is your motivation as you take part in competitive orienteering; it is more often determined by your mastery of the sport so that you can complete the course. Repeated success builds self-esteem, and perhaps the most important result is the lesson that failure is a temporary state, banished by analysis, smart training, and continued practice. In addition, orienteering is that rare discipline where studying your work (going over your maps and how you navigated through the woods and fields) is actually *fun*. Finally, as with few other sports, orienteering can be a lifelong, healthy obsession. The oldest competitive age groups in the United States and Canada are over 80 years old! Can 90 be far behind?

If you begin orienteering using the systematic instructions presented in this book, which have been developed, improved, and expanded over more than 20 years, you can become a competent orienteer and land navigator in mere months. If you already orienteer, this book will help you learn and prioritize new skills and techniques, recall forgotten ones, and train to overcome specific weaknesses.

Besides building navigation skills, orienteering gives the thrill of problem solving on your own and the excitement of off-trail running. It also provides many opportunities to participate in events (or even create them) and to meet new people.

BASICS OF ORIENTEERING

At its most basic level, orienteering is a sport with many variations that is centered on navigating on a map by translating the map symbols into what you see around you, or as orienteers say, *reading the ground*. Canadian and European orienteers might say *reading the terrain* or *interpreting the terrain*. Regardless, you are using the map to find your way. Chapter 3 explains the terms *ground* and *terrain* in depth.

In orienteering, not only do you follow your map, but you may also double-check your direction by occasionally glancing at your compass. Orienteers seek specific locations such as human-made or terrain features that are marked on their maps and easily identifiable upon arrival. These locations are called *controls* and are normally marked by control bags (or markers) of orange and white (see figure 1.1). Because there may be beginner, intermediate, and advanced courses at the same event, each control marker has a unique identifier, such as a three-digit number. You will know the identifier for each of your controls before you begin.

Figure 1.1 Control bags are orange and white, and they are designed to be seen from a distance. They signify locations marked on the map.

Competitors record their finding of each control by writing it on a scorecard, electronically recording it on a finger chip (called an *e-punch*), or using a variation such as writing down a specific fact, as in urban orienteering. Orienteering is most frequently done in parks and recreation areas, but it also works beautifully in buildings, classrooms, and streets and at playgrounds, rivers, and lakes. Following are various types of orienteering:

Automobile or ATV	Relay
Bicycle or motorcycle	Rogaine
Canoe or other watercraft	Running or walking
	Score
Cross-country	Skiing or snowshoeing
Geocaching	Snowmobile
Horseback	Trail
Line	Wheelchair

When first learning to orienteer, beginners move slowly and carefully. At the other end of the competitive spectrum, world-class competitors run faster than 6 minutes per kilometer (orienteering uses the metric system), or 10 minutes per mile. Running just under 10 minutes per mile will seem slow to road racers, but orienteering competitors are flying through the woods. And, despite their speed, world-class competitors are also moving carefully. They cannot afford the loss of time by even minimally going off in the wrong direction.

Orienteering Maps

Early orienteering in the United States relied primarily on the readily available 1:24,000 U.S. Geological Survey (USGS) maps, often simply photocopied in black and white. The USGS has mapped the entire United States, and its maps can be purchased in many outdoor stores or downloaded online. USGS maps are the maps most frequently used in search and rescue and are well suited for hiking, hunting, and fishing (see figure 1.2*a*). They can be used to start orienteering instruction if no better maps are available. Orienteering maps cover a much smaller area and are therefore easier to interpret, greatly helping the learning process (see figure 1.2*b*). As you see the larger orienteering map, outlined in black, fits easily within the smaller 1:24,000 USGS map of the same area. In general, orienteering maps will be newer and more up to date. See, for example, the road beside the water tanks to the north on each map. It has obviously been rerouted since the smaller map was created. Remember, because scales are fractions, a "larger" map shows a smaller area of the terrain and a "smaller" map includes more area. Later chapters will point you to

resources where you can learn to make your own maps, which has double value in that making maps improves your orienteering.

Orienteering Versus Land Navigation

Though similar, orienteering and land navigation are not the same. Orienteering builds on land navigation techniques to improve speed, skill, and confidence. Some basic skills and techniques are the same for both, but orienteering develops those skills and techniques well beyond land navigation. *Military land navigation*, as the U.S. Marines and Army call it, is useful to hikers, backpackers, bird-watchers, hunters, and fishers. Land navigation is obviously essential to members of the military and adventure racers, but it also finds a ready audience in college Reserve Officers' Training Corps (ROTC) units and high school Junior ROTC (JROTC) students. Park rangers and search-and-rescue personnel also use land navigation skills in their daily work and can hone those skills greatly through orienteering. Land navigation skills and techniques that have been further refined and practiced through orienteering benefit everyone described thus far, as illustrated in the sidebar.

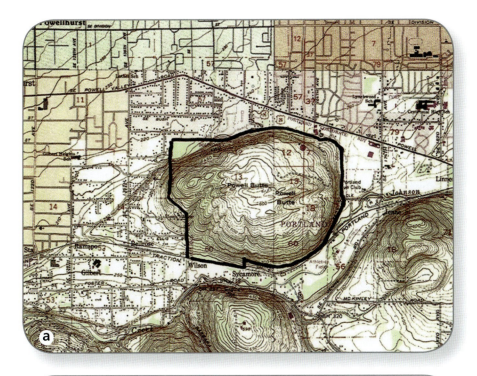

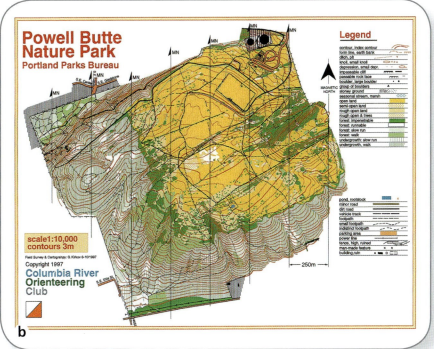

Figure 1.2 Maps of Powell Butte Nature Park in Portland, Oregon. Notice the difference between (*a*) the USGS map and (*b*) the orienteering map of the same terrain.

Courtesy of Les Stark of Columbia River Orienteering.

Scoring

As noted earlier, orienteering is a timed event. Participants compete against each other in categories based on gender, age, and experience (e.g., a beginner competes against other beginners). They score by visiting all of the orienteering controls in the correct sequence and crossing the finish line. In the cross-country or point-to-point format, each participant is assigned a start time. Start times are staggered so that orienteers are not often approaching the controls at the same time. This also helps prevent participants from following others (that is, following someone rather than navigating on your own), which is not allowed. To determine your score, your start time is subtracted from your finish time, and the fastest time on your course and in your category determines the winner. Everyone else scores in sequence based on each person's total time. In short, you score based on how quickly you complete the course against your peers. Most meets have a 3-hour time limit to complete a course, so it is possible to be disqualified for being overtime.

You keep track of the controls you visit in several ways, usually either manually (by punching a scorecard, sometimes called a *punch card*) or electronically (by inserting a data collection stick, called an *e-punch*, into a receptacle at each location). If using the manual system, each control has a plastic puncher (referred to as a *punch*) that resembles a small stapler. The competitor arrives at the control, places the scorecard into the open end of the punch, and presses the two sides together, just as you would press a stapler. Tiny pins on one side punch holes in a pattern on the scorecard in a box numbered for the appropriate control. The pattern differs at each control. At the finish, if the pattern on your scorecard is correct for each of the controls and if the punches are all in the correct boxes for the correct controls, then you have proof that you visited the controls. Take care not to lose your scorecard. If you fail to present your scorecard, you get no credit for finishing the course and the event never happened for you—true heartbreak!

In an electronic system, at each control the competitor inserts the data memory stick (the *e-punch* or more rarely called a *dibber*) into an electronic receptacle that records the time onto the data memory stick and usually beeps and flashes a small light to announce the successful recording of your arrival. At the finish line, there is a final receptacle, and then you proceed to the download area and insert your e-punch one more time in order to print your splits (how long you took between each control) as well as your total time. Be careful not to lose your e-punch or you will have the same sad result as if you had lost your scorecard, but worse—e-punches are a lot more expensive to lose!

Both of these scoring systems are explained thoroughly in later chapters. A third system often used in urban (or street) orienteering involves writing down something on your scorecard to prove that you visited the correct location, such as the name on a monument. You are more likely to encounter manual systems at smaller events and e-punching at larger events, especially events associated with orienteering clubs. E-punches can normally be rented at the latter.

The many variations of orienteering allow almost everyone to participate regardless of special interests or needs, including people who use wheelchairs, mountain bikers, skiers, horseback riders, people in automobiles or canoes, and, of course, in the largest numbers, walkers and runners. Probably the most unusual event in my experience was when armored personnel carriers at Fort Benning, Georgia, tore around pine-tree-lined

Off to the next control! Before moving to the beginner course, kids learn basic skills and have fun with string orienteering.

tracts and roads, madly searching their maps for controls at road junctions, nearby fields, and small hills. The soldiers had so much fun that they hardly realized they were training!

Older adults who like to jog or walk claim that orienteering keeps the mind fit as well as the body. The mental challenge of answering the question, "Where is that control and how do I get there?", backs up the claim that orienteering is the thinking sport. Simply getting to each control enhances fitness and challenges the intellect. Not only do mature adults benefit from orienteering, but much younger people do as well. For example, string orienteering includes children as young as four or five.

BENEFITS OF ORIENTEERING

Orienteering offers many benefits, but its real attraction is that it is fun! It is a joy to walk and run through forests and fields. If you like competing, there are many age and skill-level groups to fulfill that wish. The ultimate quest for the orienteer is to find the balance between mental and physical exertion, to know how fast you can go and still be able to interpret the terrain around you and execute your route choice successfully.

Orienteering is a lifetime fitness sport that challenges the mind. It offers the obvious development of individual skills in navigating while problem solving to locate each control. Decision making is paramount: Should I go left or right? Should I climb that hill or go the long way around it? These decisions that constantly arise require thinking more than quick reactions or instinct; again, that is why orienteering is called the thinking sport. And remember, these decisions are being made under competitive stress and increasing fatigue, helping you to become mentally tougher in other stressful situations. Orienteers learn to be self-reliant since most orienteering is individual, and even in the team and mass-start versions, teammates usually practice individually to improve.

Orienteering builds self-esteem; it takes courage to forge ahead by oneself through unknown areas, particularly in the forests that are not familiar to those who live in cities. So many easily reachable, beautiful outdoor areas exist in the United States, Canada, and the rest of the world that feeling comfortable in the outdoors triples the pleasure of being there. Every time you locate a control or relocate yourself from being temporarily misdirected, your confidence grows. Spatial relationships become more meaningful as the orienteer has to plan how to get from one place to another and figure out whether the chosen route goes uphill or downhill and when and how far. Good orienteers learn to stay aware of their surroundings as they plan what they will see along the route to the control, a talent that is useful whether you are driving to your grandmother's or trying to find your way back from a classroom on your first day of college. How can you plan what you will see? The map symbols and contours will describe it for your imagination. Orienteers learn to recognize and use new resources, whether they are the map and compass, the park or playground, or the more personal resources of fitness and mental agility.

Not only is it thoroughly enjoyable to get out into parks and forests and off the paths to experience nature while orienteering, but also being a trained and experienced navigator can be plainly useful or even lifesaving. On a simple level, you need never be lost again. A complete definition of *lost* has two parts. First, you do not know where you are located. Second, you do not know how to get to a known location. Even if they are temporarily mislocated, orienteers have the skills and techniques to relocate themselves and to continue on to their destination. Orienteers fully understand the L.L. Bean T-shirt that quotes its founder: "If you get lost, come straight back to camp." Even if you do not know where you are, if you know how to get back to camp, then you are not lost. You can toss the word *lost* right out of your vocabulary, because as an orienteer you won't ever need it again!

Another important outcome of orienteering is increased confidence. You may be timid but would like to build your confidence and become better at a sport than anyone around you, or perhaps you simply wish to be more comfortable in the outdoors. Gaining the skills and techniques to be able always to find your way out of the woods builds confidence in all aspects of your life.

Athletes who are tired of running circles on a track or slogging along paved roads find running cross country to be refreshing while at the same time good for building endurance and muscle. Outside of Florida and parts of Texas, most orienteering areas tend to be hilly, not flat. Undulations in the terrain provide the right environment for athletes and nonathletes alike to develop strong hearts, legs, and lungs.

Teachers have found that orienteering relates to every academic discipline, from math to history to environmental awareness to public policy, and it does so in new and interesting ways. Orienteering at Valley

One international orienteering competition in Norway ended in the building that housed the 1994 Winter Olympics hockey competition. After running a long course that included a steep climb up a ski slope, orienteers navigated with a map of the interior through a dark cave using weak flashlights, entered a lower floor, and had to find their way through dimly lit rooms and corridors until they suddenly burst into the brightly lit hockey arena with the finish line directly across the ice—the long way! Despite their fatigue, every orienteer found it highly satisfying to throw themselves down and slide headlong, backward, or spinning across the ice to the finish.

Orienteering is a lifetime sport. Technically difficult but physically less challenging courses are designed for mature competitors.

Forge, Pennsylvania, brings American history right to your own footprints. Counting paces and measuring on maps teach the metric system through action without obviously doing so. Keeping personal records to improve while training implements data collection, logical thinking, and demonstrable self-improvement. Writing about your experiences improves word discipline and grammar while teaching audience focus. Playing by the rules imparts ethics training and standards of fairness.

Finally, people who enjoy orienteering become enthusiastic about environmental stewardship. Orienteers believe in the motto, "Take nothing away; leave nothing behind," another way of saying that orienteers clean up their trash and don't pick the flowers. Because orienteering is gentle on the environment, orienteers do not damage the areas they cross, nor do they cross over areas that are fragile. Orienteering mappers are careful to mark as off-limits areas that are inhabited by endangered plants and animals or that are private land on the maps they develop for competition and training. Event directors and coaches work closely with park rangers and wildlife managers to protect local environments and fragile habitats.

PLACES TO ORIENTEER

You can orienteer anywhere you can make or obtain a map. Orienteers navigate in classrooms, schoolyards, city parks, urban areas, residential areas, streets, state and national parks, and wilderness areas. Even better, you can orienteer in your community, throughout the United States, and all over the world. Orienteering map symbols and appropriate colors are approved by the International Orienteering Federation (IOF) and are followed around the globe (for example, blue stands for water). Therefore, if you pick up an orienteering map in China or Russia, you do not have to read Chinese or Russian to understand the map well enough to orienteer on that map. Symbols are further discussed in chapter 3.

HISTORY OF ORIENTEERING

Orienteering began in Scandinavia in the late 1900s as a form of military training. *Orienteering* was initially a military term that referred to crossing unknown

In March of 2008, a group of American friends and colleagues were severely injured when a terrorist bomb exploded in a restaurant in Pakistan. The least injured person, a long-time orienteer, took charge despite a concussion, two burst eardrums, shrapnel wounds, and a back injury. She organized the evacuation, moving the entire party, including one person carried in a chair, to the street. There, she commandeered a police truck with bench seats in the back. She wanted to get everyone to the American embassy, but the driver, who spoke little English, drove instead to an Islamabad hospital that the orienteer had never visited. While the hospital was giving the injured the best care they could, she called for help from the American embassy on her cell phone. Although she had never been in that area, she had kept up with her surroundings and knew her cardinal directions (the mountains were to the north). She was able to give excellent directions to her location so that help arrived within minutes versus hours. Later, she told this author that many years of orienteering made keeping up with her location second nature to her.

areas with the use of a map and compass. Major Ernst Killander in Sweden played a major role in developing the rules and principles of orienteering as we know them today. He organized the first large orienteering competition in Stockholm on March 25, 1919, and 220 competitors took part.

The development in the 1930s of a more reliable compass with a liquid-damped needle further increased the growth and popularity of orienteering. Björn Kjellström, coinventor of this protractor-type magnetic compass, moved to the United States in 1946 and held a competition at the Indiana Dunes State Park in 1947. He contributed to the development of orienteering in North America for decades.

International Orienteering Federation (IOF)

Orienteering development in Europe surged after 10 countries formed the IOF in May 1961 in Copenhagen.

With both the Federal Republic of Germany (West Germany) and the German Democratic Republic (East Germany) as members, German was initially the official language of the IOF. The first IOF Congress established a commission to work on the international competition rules for orienteering. The first European championship was held in 1962 and the first world championship in 1966. By 1969 the IOF had published international specifications for map symbols, and it has continued to update and publish the rules and specifications for map symbols since then. Although orienteering is not an Olympic sport, the IOF is recognized by the International Olympic Committee (IOC) and has supreme authority over international orienteering. The IOF, now housed in Helsinki, Finland, recognizes four orienteering disciplines: foot orienteering, ski orienteering, trail orienteering, and mountain-bike orienteering. English is now the official language.

Compared with Europe and Canada, orienteering development in the United States was slower. Early in the summer of 1967, the United States Marine Corps (USMC) Physical Fitness Academy at Base Quantico in Virginia adopted orienteering as a better way to train for military land navigation. Then in the fall of 1967, Harald Wibye of Norway helped the Delaware Valley Orienteering Association (DVOA) stage a public orienteering event at Valley Forge, Pennsylvania.

Growing Popularity in the United States

An early orienteering enthusiast was Marine Corps Major Jim "Yogi" Hardin, a fit reconnaissance Marine recently returned from Vietnam. In the military, *reconnaissance* is often shortened to *recce* and refers to scouting out unknown areas for paths, roads, water crossings, and enemy locations. Recce Marines receive special training in moving across unknown terrain with map and compass, so when Yogi attended his first orienteering meet in Guelph, Ontario, he thought he'd show the civilian orienteers how to move quickly through the woods. Five hours later when the tired major stumbled out of the woods, Canadian professor Alex "Sass" Peepre, the meet organizer, had taken down the start and finish area, passed out the awards, and sent the competitors home. As Peepre stood there, arms folded, foot tapping the ground, Major Hardin walked up with a sheepish grin and said, "There is more to orienteering than meets the eye. What do orienteers know that I don't?"

Major Hardin's curiosity and immediate recognition of the value of orienteering helped drive the Marines to form teams and develop doctrine that spread throughout the Marine Corps under the auspices of the USMC Physical Fitness Academy. Later, Marines took the lead in founding the United States Orienteering Federation (USOF) in Virginia in 1971, and the United States joined the IOF in 1971 as the 21st member. Today *USOF* is rarely used and *Orienteering USA* is the way we refer to our national organization. *Orienteering USA* sounds as if it is for everyone, and it is!

Army teams formed at Fort Belvoir, Virginia, and Fort Benning, Georgia, developed additional expertise and helped spread orienteering into Army ROTC units in many colleges and universities. Unfortunately, in the aftermath of the Vietnam War, the federal defense department and the individual services were operating on curtailed budgets and began to cut programs. One of the earliest eliminated was the USMC Physical Fitness Academy, followed by a de-emphasis on orienteering in Army ROTC. The latter occurred more from the loss of expertise than funding. Fortunately, Orienteering USA, while struggling, did survive. Many of the

early orienteers who came to the United States from Scandinavia as well as those from the Army and Marine Corps continue to contribute to U.S. and Canadian orienteering to this day.

Most orienteering activity in the United States today is nonmilitary and in the hands of competent civilian volunteers, whether they are hosting events, forming clubs, publishing the national magazine (*Orienteering North America*, or *ONA*, as it is better known), or running the national organization, Orienteering USA. Orienteering does owe a great debt to its military origins, which clubs and Orienteering USA are happy to pay back whenever they can assist ROTC, JROTC, the military academies, and the occasional training course for current members of the military.

As orienteering in the civilian community moved forward, military orienteering suffered from the frequent transfers of its members from post to post. As a result, the expertise to coach and train college ROTC students rapidly degraded. With the absence of competing teams, skilled new military orienteers rarely developed. Military orienteering remained barely alive, chiefly at the USMA at West Point. Today, West Point orienteering has experienced a resurgence, and the military academy is the perennial collegiate powerhouse and national champion in orienteering.

Though orienteering at the collegiate level has nearly disappeared, orienteering in the civilian community has thrived with the exciting expansion of orienteering into U.S. high schools through JROTC. Despite the title and uniforms, cadets are civilians and high school students with the advantage of having a formal structure and its resources to learn orienteering. School leagues exist in several states, including California, Washington, and Ohio. JROTC competitions can be fierce, especially among Navy units in the South. All come together to compete for some beautiful trophies in the annual interscholastic national championships staged by various orienteering clubs around the nation and sanctioned by Orienteering USA.

Unlike many European countries (and Canada for a time), orienteering in the United States received no government funding. Orienteering USA (then called *USOF*) struggled along as an all-volunteer, educational, nonprofit organization. Perhaps the paucity of government funding as well as our distance from the birthplace of orienteering partially explain why orienteering events in Canada or the United States may draw from 50 to 800 competitors, but such events in Scandinavia

Orienteering in Canada

Orienteering Canada (formerly the Canadian Orienteering Federation) was formed in 1967. The founding orienteering associations were Ontario, Quebec, and Nova Scotia. Orienteering Canada joined the IOF in 1969. Canada and Japan were the first two non-European federations to join the IOF.

Björn Kjellström, the Swedish co-inventor of the protractor-type, liquid-damped magnetic compass in the early 1930s, was instrumental in introducing North America to orienteering. He organized events in Canada and the United States in the 1940s and 1950s. As mentioned earlier, Alex Peepre, a physical education professor at Guelph University in Ontario, organized many events in the 1960s and 1970s to help develop the sport, and through his influence on the Marines, he helped establish the sport in a more formal way in the United States.

may have more than 20,000 participants! During this time, European, Canadian, and occasionally American orienteers wrote several excellent texts on orienteering and mapping, such as *Orienteering for Sport and Pleasure* by Hans Bengtsson and George Atkinson (Stephen Greene Press, 1977), *Mapmaking for Orienteers* by Robin Harvey (British Orienteering Federation, 1st edition 1975, 4th edition 1991), and *A Basic Manual for Orienteering* by Jack Dyess (Colonial Press of Belpre, 1975), to mention just a few. Meanwhile, U.S. orienteers developed local instruction of varying quality. The national organization helped where it could, mainly through clinics at summer conventions and year-round through articles in its excellent publication, *Orienteering North America*. Today, excellent training in a systematic format is offered by OUSA through its excellent courses for orienteers, coaches, and teachers. This book is the latest initiative to bring orienteering skills to everyone.

Advances in Mapmaking

As the sport progressed in the United States, European advances in orienteering mapmaking were imported, along with European mappers. The civilian orienteering world moved into five-color, detailed, 1:15,000 scale maps for major competitions. (Orienteering competition uses the term *meets*.) Such detailed maps rapidly improved training effectiveness so that orienteering expertise spread in civilian orienteering as it receded in the military community. Today, Orienteering Computer Assisted Drawing (OCAD) software has made detailed orienteering maps available to every orienteering club. OCAD is already linking into widely available public databases created by LiDAR (light detecting and ranging) capability for even easier mapmaking. LiDAR uses a laser pulse from an airplane to the ground, integrated with GPS and inertial measurement unit (IMU) technology, to make high-resolution topographic maps. It looks down through even moderate tree cover to accurately map objects and the contours on the ground below and can even detect objects as small as individual boulders and fallen trees!

Good map and compass skills highly complement the use of technological advancements such as GPS units, and those skills are essential for route planning or when either the batteries or the satellites fail or are jammed. Orienteering using GPS units occasionally happens for fun, but it is incredibly slower than running on a good map.

WHAT ORIENTEERING IS NOT

In addition to understanding what orienteering is, it is important to understand what it is not. Orienteering is not simply following a magnetic bearing (an azimuth) and counting your paces, although both are useful to the orienteer. Pace counting and azimuth following are often mislabeled as *land navigation* or *orienteering*. *Dead reckoning* is the term the military uses to describe pace and azimuth. If pace and azimuth are all you know, woe unto you when you encounter a high mountain, uncrossable water, or a tall brick wall or enter a competitive meet! Orienteering will teach you to handle those and many other challenges with ease.

Orienteering is not following another person. The vast majority of orienteering disciplines are done by the individual. Following others can lead to disqualification, as mentioned previously. Orienteering is not a race where speed always wins. Like the tortoise and the hare, the competent orienteer will beat the merely fast runner every time. Mastery of the skills and techniques in this book will make you a competent orienteer, a good teacher, and a better trainer and navigator.

Orienteering is not just something soldiers do. Adventure racers, hunters, backpackers, bird-watchers, hikers, and many others practice and enjoy orienteering. Orienteering also is not geocaching, although that can be more fun for the orienteer than the inexperienced would-be enthusiast. Orienteering is not for cheaters. Cheating in an orienteering event can lead to a lifetime ban! Orienteering is a sport based on individual integrity and honesty.

COACHING CERTIFICATIONS

Recently, Orienteering USA has vigorously addressed the requirements to train, teach, and certify to help the growth of orienteering. For example, Orienteering USA supports Zero to Orange in Three Days, a beginning orienteering course developed by former North American and three-time U.S. orienteering champion, co-author Bob Turbyfill. Over three days, the Zero to Orange Course takes the student from knowing zero about orienteering to completing an intermediate (or orange) course in two hours or less. Additionally, it is a great review for those who already orienteer. This book is based on the Zero to Orange course. With the assistance of the U.S. Olympic Committee, Orienteering USA members developed a coaching manual, three levels of coaching, and courses to support both. Olympic Level 1 coaches are certified to teach and coach orienteering at the local level. Olympic Level 2 coaches work at the national level, and Olympic Level 3 certification indicates qualification to serve the federation at the international level.

What makes a good orienteering coach? Interestingly, the same characteristics that make a good teacher make a good coach. First, you do *not* have to be an orienteer! But you do have to do your homework—you need to know your subject. Find out about the sport: Master this book, get a copy of the coaching manual from a vendor, go to an orienteering meet, download the *Orienteering Training Manual* at http://orienteeringusa.org/sites/default/files/pheifferOTM.pdf, and so on. Once you have a basic understanding of the skills and techniques and a nearby map, work with your competitors and have them chart their progress (see chapter 10 for more information). Just as a good teacher gives tests to determine what has been learned, a good coach tests the team with meets. Each individual's meet time compares against a test score and must be further broken down to find what areas to teach and coach. To quote the general who formerly commanded the Marine Corps' training command, "Training without testing is playing." Good coaches have their competitors analyze their own runs to determine strengths and weaknesses. A coach without data is a coach who is guessing. A coach with data knows exactly what needs work.

Additionally, OUSA sponsors orienteering certification at three levels of competence—Navigator, Pathfinder, and Expert—and anticipates adding a fourth level, Distinguished Expert. Most beginning orienteers are highly motivated to move forward in their competence and to have it recognized by an official certificate. For more information about the navigation certification program, go to http://orienteeringusa.org/youthleaders/certification/navigation. Adventure racers have found it highly useful to orienteer until they can be certified at the Navigator level.

Orienteering coaching in Canada is offered through a partnership between Orienteering Canada and the Coaching Association of Canada (CAC). You can find information about coaching in Canada at www.wgacarto.ca/NCCP/Coaching.htm.

LEARNING TO ORIENTEER SYSTEMATICALLY

Do you have to learn how to orienteer systematically? Can't you just go out and do it? Actually, you can do just that. You can figure out the skills and reinvent some of the techniques on your own over several years if you're good—and, by the way, most people will get faster with experience. Or you can pick up the skills, techniques, and processes from this book, from your teachers and coaches, and from practicing and competing. If you go about it systematically, you can become a competent orienteer and land navigator in mere months. If you already orienteer, you can learn and prioritize new skills and techniques, recall forgotten ones, and train to overcome specific weaknesses. Or, you can just muddle through. Either way, you're in the woods, doing something healthy. Coach Turbyfill developed the course leading to this book after observing that many orienteers were learning in haphazard fashion, because despite excellent instruction in some phases of the sport, there was no overall systematic approach taking participants to a high level of competence.

SUMMARY

This chapter has described orienteering. It has listed the many benefits of the so-called cunning running from this healthy and mainly outdoor activity. It has briefly traced the history of the sport and hopefully motivated you to give orienteering a try, whether it just sounds new and exciting or whether you want to be able to find your hunting spot every time you go into the woods with your map. Perhaps you wisely plan to acquire the skills that could save your life or someone else's rather than dangerously following unthinking technology. You may like the idea that you can orienteer in many foreign countries, or you may simply appreciate that everyone can orienteer in some fashion. The main purpose of chapter 1 was to convince you that orienteering is doable and fun. If any of these reasons appeal to you, read on—orienteering is for you!

Fitness, Nutrition, Equipment, and Safety

Buy a pace counter (or pedometer) at a fitness store and it will usually contain a brochure advising that walking or running 10,000 steps a day will maintain good fitness and help maintain a healthy body weight. What better way to cover several thousand of those steps than hiking in the country, jogging along paths, or running through meadows and trees? Not only do you get to enjoy the many pleasures of nature, but you can also set, obtain, and enjoy the goals of finding your controls in the shortest time, by the shortest route, or with the least outlay of energy. You can choose how competitive you wish to be and it is all good exercise!

This chapter is aimed at both competitors and everyone else involved in orienteering, from coaches to teachers to competition organizers. It covers fitness gained from orienteering as well as how to train, eat, and drink. In addition, it discusses the gear and clothes needed for orienteering. Last but not least, safety in orienteering is examined and emphasized.

FITNESS

Being physically fit is a must for success in all orienteering events except for trail orienteering, which leans more heavily on mental acuity. Fortunately, orienteering contributes to fitness, agility, and stamina. It would be nice to say that orienteering also improves one's balance, but I was born clumsy and haven't seen much improvement despite years of running in the forests. As with any other sport, before you begin to train, get a thorough physical from your doctor to ensure you are able to perform hard physical workouts without detrimental effects to your health. Whatever your doctor's advice and regardless of whether you intend to stroll or run like the wind, follow your doctor's orders.

Orienteering specifically contributes to fitness in three ways. These are the distance covered, climb, and interval running.

Distance

First, start with simply the amount of walking or running required to complete a course. Beginning courses may seem short to the experienced road racer—that is, until you have tried them! After you progress from the most basic course, you will find orienteering has more in common with cross country running or steeplechasing in the many ways it works the whole body. The white or beginning course is 2 to 3 kilometers long (orienteering is a metric sport), which is less than 2 miles. The longest and most expert course, the blue course, can be 10K (over 6 miles) or more. In the United States, there are seven levels of difficulty and length for national meets, although local meets often shorten that number. National meets are called *A-meets*, and local meets may be called *B-meets* if they offer the full range of courses or *C-meets* if they offer less. Lengths and the technical difficulty of courses are presented in chapter 8.

Tons of articles and books have been written on how to train to improve your distance running (also known as endurance fitness). Most advice and coaching boil down to increasing your stamina. To increase your stamina, simply walk or run farther as you gain fitness. It sounds simple, but most of us overdo that aspect. No matter at what level you start training for distance, ease into those increases. A standard rule of thumb is to increase your weekly mileage by no more than 10 percent. Therefore if all you can run or walk when you start training to orienteer is 100 yards (91 m) per day for six days (always take a rest day each week), then move up to 110 yards (101 m) the second week. Likewise, if you are already doing 5 miles (8 km) a day, six days a week, for a total of 30 miles per week (48 km), then add no more than a half mile (.8 km) per day the next week so that your total is now 33 miles (53 km). By the way, if you listen to your body, you do not have to run the same distance every single time. As you read further, you will find that we encourage you to vary your workouts so that you run hills on some workouts and do intervals on others. Regardless, do not increase your total weekly distance by more than 10 percent in any one week.

Climb

A second contributor to fitness comes from climb, which is officially measured on an orienteering course by following an optimal route between each control and counting every contour line that goes up, or climbs (hence the name). An optimal route is one that would likely be followed by an experienced orienteer. (Route selection is well covered in chapter 6.) Going downhill does not subtract from climb. Course designers carefully consider climb for each course and seek to comply with a generally accepted international standard of no more than 4 percent climb over any course. In a flat area such as around Houston, Texas, there may be little or no climb at all. In the steeper regions around Lake Tahoe, California, climb sometimes exceeds 4 percent

Training for course climb is a must for success in orienteering events. Here, Carol Ross competes at the World Orienteering Championship in Trondheim, Norway.

because there is so little flat running or walking that can be included in the course. The beauty of the Lake Tahoe venue more than compensates for the exertion of the additional climb. Once you have seen the area, you will want to orienteer there as often as possible.

If you have never paid much attention to climb on your walks or runs, be assured that 4 percent climb is an excellent workout! As mentioned, climb is measured in optimal lines of travel between controls. Very few orienteers, whether brand new or experienced, follow exactly the same route, so your own climb will differ from the officially measured climb. Your climb may be much more than the official climb, particularly if you have what the Army calls the *airborne mentality*. This outlook of doing things the hardest way to show that you are tough causes you to run joyfully up and over every hill you come to, greatly increasing your climb. On the other hand, your climb may be less if you save energy by going around some hills on your course (i.e., selecting an optimal course). A rule of thumb is to use the same energy going up as you do in staying flat but going twice as far. In other words, if you have a choice

of going over a hill on a line that will cover 200 meters or running around the side of the hill for 400 meters, the two routes will use about the same amount of energy unless the hill is very steep, in which case running around it saves far more energy. How you choose which way to go (route selection) is discussed in chapter 6. Suffice it to say that climb is a major consideration and that the best orienteers train for it, as you will see in the discussion of hill repetitions.

Intervals

A third contributor to fitness occurs because orienteering is an interval sport. You begin from a complete halt at the start line—unless, of course, you run up breathlessly just as you are supposed to start, shouting, "I'm here! I'm here!" This is not the recommended procedure. From the start, you run or walk briskly to the first control, where all must again stop to mark their scorecard, either manually or electronically. This stop–start process is followed until you charge (or amble) across the finish line after visiting every control.

Interval training occurs when you move from a slower speed (or a halt) to a faster speed and repeat the sequence over and over. Interval workouts build speed and endurance much faster than single-speed running or walking do; however, the well-trained athlete will do more same-speed running simply because interval training is more physically demanding and takes more recovery time. Almost anyone who attempted consecutive interval training day after day would soon find her muscular and cardiorespiratory systems fatigued, making the body more prone to injury.

Two excellent exercises for orienteering are interval workouts and hill repetitions (or hill reps), especially if combined with distance running or walking. Both exercises improve your fitness for climb, stamina for distance, and speed.

Interval Workouts

A common interval workout on the track is to run one lap of the track at or near your fastest race pace, followed by a slow jogging or walking lap. Interval training in street running can be as easy as speeding up from the telephone pole nearest you to the next one you can see down the street or by replacing telephone poles with city blocks.

Hill Reps

Hill reps are exactly that. Find a hill where you do your running or walking and go up it at about 80 percent of your race pace. Turn around at the top and jog or walk comfortably to your starting point. At the starting point, turn around and run or power walk back to the top at the previous 80 percent pace.

When you first begin interval and hill-rep training, don't overdo it. If you can do three repetitions and approximately maintain your speed, you have made a good start.

Training With a Partner

The key to fitness is the discipline to work out whether you want to or not. Although I played football, basketball, and baseball in high school and soccer in college, my fitness was specific to those sports. In other words, I could sprint up and down the basketball court or the soccer field, but running 5 miles (8 km) was beyond me in high school and something I never did even when fit for soccer. Later when I sought to try out for a military competition that included orienteering, one requirement was to run 5 miles (8 km) in 35 minutes

Once while working out with the Columbus State University (in Columbus, Georgia) cross country team, my running mate and I were left far behind on the first hill rep because the many inexperienced runners ran much too fast the first time. On the second repetition we moved up to second place (we ran side by side) and stayed there behind the best runner for the remaining nine hill reps. Few of the new runners completed even four reps, and all exhausted themselves on the very first one. The lesson is to run at only 80 percent of your best pace to start, and if you cannot keep that up for three times in a row, run slower. Hill reps build stamina so that you can stay close to your distance running speed on hills. Particularly as you begin, do not sprint. Sprinting is running as fast as you can for a relatively short distance. It burns up too much energy, eviscerating stamina. Save the sprints for your short-distance interval workouts.

just to try out. While struggling around a large recreation complex one day, I ran into a mathematics professor from my college, Dr. Albert Van Cleave. Albert immediately suggested we train together even though he was far fitter than I was. He was also much more knowledgeable and a super coach and friend. From this experience I learned the great value of having a training partner. When I was lazy or the weather was wet or cold and I thought about skipping my workout, Albert would call and off we would go. When he felt that way and I called, off we would go.

Having a running partner (or partners) whose workout schedule fits your own is the best impetus to keep you working out—in other words, if you do not have the discipline yourself, forge a partnership to keep you at it. By the way, it took me nearly five years to outrun Albert in a race, and from then on we were neck and neck most years as we alternated beating each other. Also as we pushed each other in our workouts, our racing times dramatically improved to the point that we both ran 5 miles (8 km) in less than 30 minutes in numerous races. There is no doubt in my mind that I improved that much because I had a training partner.

Overtraining

In just a few weeks, you should begin to notice a real improvement in your fitness. However, do not overtrain! Once a week on the track and once a week on the hills is plenty for the average orienteer. If you're just starting, do one or the other once a week, but not both.

Pay attention to your running times, too. If your interval times degrade to slower and slower times per interval, lay off for a week before doing them again. If that does not work, do the intervals at a slower pace and add more slow laps in between the fast running or the hill reps.

Make sure you listen to your body. If you are sore to the point that you don't recover within two days, make the workout easier until your body and mind can handle the harder work. If you are too frequently sore, you may be more likely to quit, so be smart about your training. Increase your workout by no more than 10 percent in any one week and listen to your body's fitness indicators—both pain and the absence of pain can tell you how hard to train. This is worth repeating: Before you begin to train, get a thorough physical from your doctor to ensure that you are able to perform hard physical workouts without detrimental effects to your health.

NUTRITION

What you eat is extremely important for fitness, growing in importance as you improve your orienteering ability. Americans eat way too much junk food, which contributes to the current epidemic of obesity in the United States. Most of us would be better off losing a few pounds, especially if we orienteer. Remember climb? The fatigue of carrying excess weight up a hill brings home just what obesity is doing to us on a daily basis, not to mention the increased wear and tear on the knees and back. Interestingly, a skilled but overweight orienteer can triumph over a physically fit but poorly skilled orienteer. It is in our best interests to maintain a healthy body weight, but sometimes it is

nice to see people who have worked hard on skill and technique enjoy success from their efforts. There are many books and articles on nutrition, but the bottom line to losing weight is to expend more calories each day than you eat.

Liquids

Liquids are an important part of your overall diet. Sugary drinks such as colas and some sports drinks will add weight even if you otherwise eat sensibly, so you should avoid them. Frequent consumption of diet soft drinks is also not recommended, because they bring almost nothing healthy to help meet your body's needs—especially your body in training. Studies have shown that diet drinks stimulate the appetite and fail to send a "full" message from the stomach to the brain, leading to the overconsumption of calories. Look around at mealtime and you will note that diet drinks often accompany overeating. If you truly want a healthy body, consider the nutritional value of every bit of food and drink that you consume. Of course it is okay to have the occasional cookie, piece of cake, or soft drink, but if these foods and nonfoods are a regular part of what you eat, make some changes!

Orienteering thrives with strong bones, so unless you are lactose intolerant, milk should start your day, whether in a glass or poured over a bowl of healthy cereal. If you can't drink milk, orange juice fortified with calcium provides natural energy and vitamin C while also starting your day off well.

Proper hydration during training and competition helps keep your mind working despite fatigue and helps ward off heat-related problems. Standards for placing fluids on orienteering courses recommend having water available at least every 2.5 kilometers, with more frequent placement if it is extremely warm. Advanced course designers often forget that the beginners on the shorter, easier courses still may be out for hours as they learn to orienteer. Therefore, if you are a slow orienteer, carry your own water or recovery fluid. (Hydration packs such as Camelbaks are readily available and do not interfere with your movements.) Likewise, be sure to hydrate when you train.

Orienteering and training for orienteering are both great ways to burn calories. However, be careful not to use your increased activity as an excuse to eat far more calories than you need.

If you are an event organizer, put enough water on the beginning courses! Never shortchange your training or competitive events when it comes to hydration. It is better to have too much water on a course than too little.

Replenishing After a Workout or Meet

At the end of an exercise or competition, a well-chosen, low-sugar sports drink that replenishes electrolytes speeds recovery. If available, you may wish to imbibe small amounts of sports drinks as you work out or compete. Try drinking them slowly during training to see if they upset your stomach. Because most national competitions run for two days, an electrolyte-replacement drink in each day's finish area enhances recovery of energy, mental agility, and sense of well-being. Electrolyte replacement is most effective soon after the expenditure of effort. In other words, the quicker you can drink after exercising, the more beneficial it is to a quick recovery. Waiting several hours to drink, although better than not drinking, is a sure recipe for a slow, delayed, and inefficient recovery. Because some people do not like or cannot tolerate electrolyte-replacement drinks, water is usually the only drink provided on the course, and it should always be available at the finish. If there is a choice, go for the electrolyte-replacement or nutritious drinks first. Even fruit juices (without added sugar) are generally better for you than water. Studies on the sports nutrition scene extol low-fat milk as the best recovery fluid. Regardless of your choice, start drinking immediately. By the way, not all electrolyte drinks are equal, so do your research on the Internet—you will find some that are much better than others. Caffeinated drinks and alcohol absolutely should not be used for fluid replacement, especially immediately after a hard workout.

EQUIPMENT

Orienteering is not gear intensive for the individual, but a number of items are needed. These include a compass, a whistle, a watch, an e-punch (possibly), clothes, and shoes.

Compass

A good beginning compass has a movable bezel (the importance of which will be explained later) and various scales on the front edge and the sides of the baseplate. Because most orienteering maps are metric, your compass should have a millimeter scale. The millimeter scale works perfectly on the 1:10,000-meter scales of most orienteering maps until you are good enough to run the top levels that have a 1:15,000 scale. If you already have a baseplate compass and it has no scale or the wrong scale, simply tape a piece of athletic tape across the front edge and use a nonsmearing red pen to make your own scale. One way to obtain the correct scale is to copy it from someone else's compass, and a second way is to copy it from the map. If you do not have a compass or you leave yours at home, you can rent one at most meets. Compasses are discussed in depth in chapter 3.

Whistle

A good plastic whistle is an important safety device. Buy a pealess whistle, which is a whistle that works when wet (figure 2.1). At the end of this chapter, the section on safety explains how to summon help by repeatedly blowing three short blasts. It also explains why you must stay in one place if you do send such a signal. Three short blasts mean, "Come to me." Many orienteering clubs sell safety whistles emblazoned with the club name and logo. Finally, most meets require participants to carry a whistle, and all meets should!

Figure 2.1   It is vital to carry a pealess whistle in case of emergency.

Watch

An inexpensive wristwatch that will help keep you within the time limits is an essential piece of equipment.

As will be discussed in the section on safety later in this chapter, you should *not* rely on carrying your cell phone on a competitive orienteering course, although carrying a cell phone is encouraged in training. Regardless, never carry your cell phone to keep up with the time, but always wear a wristwatch and consider it an essential part of your equipment.

E-Punch

Another piece of gear that orienteers generally acquire when they are able to attend meets that use electronic punching is their personal electronic probe. The e-probe (more commonly called the *e-punch*) is a small, elongated piece of plastic containing an electronic chip (see figure 2.2). It attaches to a finger (usually the index finger) by an elastic band. The e-punch costs about the same as a good compass. Later chapters go into more detail about e-punches, which are not only fun to use but also have great training potential.

Clothing

A good beginning approach to clothing is to think about what orienteering clothes should specifically do

Figure 2.2 The e-punch is worn on the finger.

for you. First, they should be lightweight, not weigh you down (see figure 2.3). Second, they should not hold water but shed it easily. Wet clothes are uncomfortable and heavy and will slow you down. Third, they should resist long rips so that when you get the occasional snag, you aren't left with large areas of your anatomy either showing or vulnerable to Mother Nature. Fourth, they should protect you to some degree from

Figure 2.3 Orienteering suit (also called an *O-suit*).

odious plants such as poison oak and poison ivy, which you may not recognize or notice. Fifth, they should have at least one closable pocket for carrying your emergency whistle and, hopefully, a spare compass. Sixth, it is rewarding to wear something that cushions your shins from any banging. No one is quite sure why, but orienteering leads to banged shins almost as much as soccer does. Therefore, it is a good idea to wear some type of shin guards, such as the gaiters that you often see on experienced orienteers. Gaiters are padded over the shins and slide on over the socks and pant legs right up to the bottom of the knee (see figure 2.4). To stay in place, most have a Velcro fastener to slip through the front shoestring of your shoe and a tie string looped around the top of the gaiter just below the knee.

In the earliest days of orienteering, before gaiters were available, orienteering socks were used. These long socks had a rubber or plastic shield molded to the front in order to turn thorns aside, but they provided no cushioning when you hit your shin on the occasional downed tree or rock formation. Gaiters have largely replaced these socks, but orienteering socks with improved shields have come back strongly. Using the new orienteering socks eliminates gaiters from your orienteering gear. The new socks are lighter as well, but they provide little padding if you bump your shins going over a log or a fence.

Orienteering attire can be wildly colorful for the frequent orienteer. However, to get started, any old pair of long pants will do, but the lighter in weight, the better. For a top, an old long-sleeved shirt works. Your feet will be fine in an old pair of running shoes or light hiking boots. Why does the word *old* precede every item of clothing? Because once you depart from the open trails of the beginning course, you will be traveling cross country, dodging briars and fallen trees, and sometimes moving through thick brush. All of these snares have heard the long-ago AT&T "Reach Out and Touch Someone" commercial, and you are liable to get rips and tears in your orienteering pants, shirt, and even shoes right off the bat. A nice reason to wear a long-sleeved shirt is to keep those rips and tears on your clothes and not your skin. Be aware that male orienteers, through some macho genetic input, may feel it manly to return with bleeding forearms and a scratched face. Some even go so far as to run in shorts, supposedly for speed, but more likely for postrace "I've got more scratches than you!" appeal.

Ripstop Fabric

Orienteering clothing is generally made from ripstop material for the reasons just described. It is lightweight, cool, and dries quickly when wet. Most O-suits do little to keep the wearer warm, but being in motion takes care of that. They are also easy to wash out in the sink for back-to-back events and can be hung over the shower rod to dry. Today's modern military clothes are both lightweight and resistant to tearing as well (ripstop), and they have lots of pockets if you are the type who wants to be prepared for any eventuality. (Hint: Don't fill up all those pockets—they get heavy!) Therefore, surplus military pants and shirts make excellent starter orienteering clothes.

Underclothes

Running shorts are usually comfortable, and on hot days, you can strip out of your long pants at the finish and be acceptably attired in your running shorts. Women should strongly consider wearing a sports bra. There are many good brands at any sports store or outlet. Avoid 100 percent cotton socks. Cotton socks hold water and sweat, so once they get wet, they stay that way—not healthy for your feet. Any of the modern running or hiking socks will generally work

Figure 2.4   Gaiters.

well, especially the various wool blends. Orienteering is a cool-weather sport in most venues, so cold feet from wet socks can be miserable. A spare set of dry socks can be a real friend at the finish line.

Shoes

There are many kinds of shoes designed specifically for orienteering. Unfortunately, most of these shoes are designed for use on one or two types of terrain. The popular spiked shoes are great until you cross a large, sloping rock surface, at which point they may slip right out from under you. Additionally, many orienteering shoes provide little cushioning and support for the entire foot. Because they are fairly expensive, our advice is to avoid shoes designed specifically for orienteering until you become quite good. In the interim, most running shoes, and especially trail-running shoes, will suffice, although the uppers are easily torn. Some soccer shoes provide good traction on slippery terrain and are inexpensive and widely available. Should you happen to have weak ankles, there are high-top orienteering shoes designed just for this condition, but high-top, light hiking boots can do the same.

Running cross country on uneven ground is a sure recipe for spraining an ankle if yours are already weak. Any orienteer with weak ankles should immediately obtain a resistance exercise band and use it to strengthen the ankles. They really work. Most bands come with instructions, but a quick exercise is to sit on the floor with back straight and legs stretched forward, feet together. Place the band across both arches and provide resistance by pulling the ends of the band toward you. Then turn the left foot out to the left using only the ankle, fighting the resistance of the band. After 10 reps, repeat using the right foot. Then cross your ankles and repeat the exercises to work the inside of each ankle. Over time work up to 50 repetitions.

SAFETY

Orienteering is a very safe sport, and we keep it that way by stressing safety. Safety planning is directly proportional to the number of participants (and number of organizers); the type, location, and duration of the event; and the weather. A simple training event at school with a few students may well be covered by the school's safety plan (it is up to you to find out!) and

the resources and people at hand. However, if you are the organizer of an event in a large national park or forest with hundreds of participants, you will obviously need to make more extensive preparations, as further discussed in this chapter. Regardless of the size of your event, always insist that participants carry a whistle and wear a watch (see chapter 8), and always have water available on the course and at the finish.

Time is such an important safety consideration that it deserves further discussion. Most events have a three-hour time limit that begins when the competitor starts. Thus, as mentioned earlier, a watch is essential equipment. Although beginners are encouraged to carry a cell phone in training, cell phones are not allowed in major competitions. One reason is that a cell phone can disable an e-punch receiver, and another is that many cell phones have GPS navigational aids, which are against the rules. Beginners (and sometimes more experienced orienteers) often do not understand the implications of being overtime and causing a search effort, so they pay little attention to the three-hour rule. Initiating a search-and-rescue effort carries serious consequences, from notification of law enforcement and possibly family members to the major disruption to completing the meet so that a search effort can be organized to look for you. Meet officials initiate a search because they assume you are mislocated or injured. On the other hand, law enforcement officials must assume that a crime has occurred! So the rule is clear: *Report in!* It is the competitor's responsibility to reach the finish line within the time limit whether you have found all but one of the controls or none at all. And the absolute worst safety misbehavior is to sneak off the course and go home without reporting to a meet official, resulting in a needless search effort. Teachers, coaches, and team captains must be certain that all of their competitors have reported to the finish line before leaving the venue. However, that does not remove the full responsibility from the competitor to report to the finish line.

Safety planning is based on Murphy's Law, which states, "What can go wrong, will go wrong (and at the worst possible time)." As the Scouts say, "Be prepared," because Murphy will strike! Murphy's Law sounds humorous, but it has been proven true over and over. Another name for safety planning is *operational readiness planning* (and other variations), in which the planners try to consider every possibility of what might go wrong and plan remedies in preparation for those situations.

Some actions are so fraught with danger that they are simply prohibited. For instance, if there is a pond,

A Good Plan Worked

One hot and humid day in Texas, 35 military reserve officers spilled out of buses at Bastrop State Park for the final orienteering test in their quest to earn a position on the United States CIOR team. (The acronym *CIOR* comes from the French initials for Interallied Confederation of Reserve Officers.) CIOR hosts a three-day military event for male and female reservists from many countries who assemble in three-person teams to shoot the host nation's pistol and rifle, run a 500-meter obstacle course, swim a 50-meter obstacle course in uniform (fortunately without having to wear boots), and pass a battlefield first aid test that is simulated very realistically! Finally, back to the theme of this book, competitors run a 15-kilometer orienteering course with several tests of military skills, such as navigating while running on an aerial photograph, reading maps, estimating distance, and throwing dummy grenades for accuracy, among others.

The organizers of the Bastrop meet were staging a CIOR orienteering course. As every meet should, they began with a written safety plan. Two Army Reserve medics and an ambulance were staged in the center of the more or less circular route that the competitors would run counterclockwise in an attempt to locate all of the orienteering controls in the fastest time. The medics carried radios, as did observers stationed at various controls along the course. Everyone understood that it was a hot and humid day, but the competitors had had several weeks to acclimate to the heat and humidity, so the conditions were not unusual. Water and sports drinks were placed at most controls (IOF rules specify every 2.5 km, but good sense said more frequently in this case).

One part of the course, about three-fourths of the way through, was blocked by a hill. Therefore, a second vehicle, a truck, was located on this hill so its radio could reach both the medics in the center and the observers around the periphery of the course. The winning time was expected to be about 90 minutes, and all the participants had a three-hour time limit from their individual starts. At their level of training, everyone was expected to complete the course in approximately two hours. A friend and I were waiting in the truck, and just under two hours into the event, the call came through to us: "Runner down at control 13! Suspected heat casualty!" We immediately called the medics with specific instructions to stop when they saw our parked truck at a small pull-off on a road near control 13. Then we zoomed down the hill, parked the truck, and grabbed a towel and a container of ice and water.

My partner, an Army Reserve chemical officer who had trained with Special Forces for two years in one of his assignments, meaning he had excellent first aid training, handed me the map and said, "Take us to control 13. I'll carry the gear." I do not think I have ever felt more pressure in any competitive orienteering event of the hundreds I've run. This might well have been someone's life on the line. Fortunately, I remembered to slow down to speed up (meaning, don't rush off in haste until you are sure where to go). I took a brief time to study the map, starting with the location of control 13 and working back to our parked truck. After I decided on a route, I took a compass bearing for a safety backup and we headed into the woods at a trot. There was no good attack point on our side of the control, but I did note a linear catching feature should we run past 13. (Attack points and catching features are presented in chapter 5).

Good fortune was with us as we hit the target right on the nose. We found the competitor, a U.S. Navy Reserve deep sea diver, sitting groggily on the ground under the shade of nearby trees. She responded briefly to my partner's questions and then passed out. I had never studied the symptoms of heat exhaustion or heatstroke (I should have, and you should too!), and I was terrified that she was dying! My Army buddy matter-of-factly took charge of the patient, and we loosened her clothing to facilitate breathing, doused her liberally with ice and cold water, and picked her up in a two-man sling carry. The observer passed on a radio report that the medics had topped the hill and would arrive shortly at our truck. Although I was fit and strong, I found carrying someone for 400 meters to be quite fatiguing, especially since we were walking in a somewhat sideways configuration to make a two-man sling of our arms.

When you have orienteered a number of times, you begin to notice the traces people leave when they move through the woods, such as leaves that are turned over, showing a darker or lighter side than other leaves nearby. These traces may be nearly invisible to the untrained eye, but we had no trouble following our own trail back to the truck. Developing a keen observational skill for such tracking is highly useful in search and rescue.

We yelled out to the medics periodically, and what a relief it was to hear them answer as we came closer. They met us about 50 meters into the woods and immediately assessed the pilot's condition. Within seconds, they reported that her vital signs were good. While they were checking her vital signs, my job was to keep cold water on her head and neck to begin cooling her body temperature. Our helicopter pilot had had a minor case of food poisoning the night before, but being fit and tough, she had decided to compete anyway, not realizing that the food poisoning symptoms left her dehydrated before she even started. Despite drinking sports drinks and water, she could not overcome her initial dehydration, which simply worsened as she ran in the heat. Fortunately, she acceded to the wise suggestion to stop at control 13 while the observer called for help.

This story ended well. After a cold shower and an IV from the medics, she was able to dance that night at the party celebrating the end of team tryouts. There are many safety lessons from this incident.

Safety Lessons

First, the organizers had a written and well-considered safety plan with proper equipment and trained people. In other words, the staff had thought about what might happen and had written a plan (writing can clarify your thoughts immensely) in advance to deal with whatever might occur. Second, competitors should listen to their bodies. The helicopter pilot had been sick the night before and unwisely tried to compete anyway, not realizing that recovery from severe dehydration takes time (usually days). Third, although the medical personnel understood the symptoms and treatment of heat-related injuries, I should have been better prepared. All of the competitors and staff had full instruction because it is always hot in Texas in the summer. However, I had arrived only for that day's event so I had missed the class on heat injuries. Fourth, because of the heat danger, radios, an ambulance, and medical supplies were placed strategically around the course in order to reach any victims quickly. To put it another way, the organizers planned the event based on the premise that what could go wrong, would go wrong (even though no heat incidents had occurred during the previous three weeks of training in the high temperatures). Sorry, Murphy, you lost this time.

stream, swamp, or lake marked on your orienteering map as uncrossable, do *not* try to cross it even if you are on the swim team or have webbed feet. Why? Because there are no lifeguards on orienteering courses, so if you get into trouble, chances are good that no one will be there to help you. It just makes sense to obey the rules and go around those features.

Safety Plans

Meet organizers should always have a written safety plan. Writing a safety plan helps your mental preparation for emergencies and clarifies your thinking. An excellent sample safety plan including potential search-and-rescue procedures can be found online at www.orienteeringusa.org/sites/default/files/safetyplan_0.pdf.

Weather

Weather is an important consideration when writing your safety plan. Safety plans should consider weather conditions from temperature (too hot or too cold) to

wetness to thunderstorms with lightning and even tornadoes. If a recent storm has dropped lots of trees, the meet area may no longer be useable, so check it out. Orienteering in snow may be fun if you're dressed for it but dangerous if you slip or become incapacitated. Also, it is too easy to follow other competitors' tracks after a snowfall. When it snows, it is time to switch from foot orienteering to ski orienteering.

Phone Numbers

The published safety plan should include phone numbers for the nearest medical responders and hospitals. At the Bastrop meet (see sidebar), each staff member had copies of the appropriate phone numbers. Additionally, a list of possible dangers was read to every participant, ranging from the rare danger of snakes, to irritant plants such as poison oak and poison ivy, to the occasional strand of barbed wire still existing in a park that had once been grazing and farmland. All competitors and staff were reminded to carry a whistle and were told the international orienteering distress signal (see next section).

Blasts on a Whistle

A thorough safety plan should detail the various whistle blasts used to communicate in orienteering. Three short blasts on the whistle mean, "I need help. Please come to me." That also implies that *you will stay in one spot* after blowing the whistle. Two short answering blasts mean, "I hear you and I am coming to you." If you are completely lost or significantly injured, stay where you are and blow your whistle periodically until we find you! Under universally accepted standards, any orienteer who hears three blasts of a whistle must stop competing immediately, find the person, and assist as needed. Therefore, as a competitor, do not use the three-blast signal unless you are injured or hopelessly lost and have given up competing. On the other hand, if you hear the three blasts, go to that person's aid immediately. You will be given a sporting withdrawal from the event and you will deserve a commendation!

Critters

Finally, before the Bastrop competition began, all competitors were directed to carefully examine themselves for ticks after finishing and to watch out for wasps. All of us liberally sprayed our legs with insect repellant to ward off chiggers, ticks, and other free riders we might encounter. Although I personally hate running into spiderwebs, spiders want nothing to do with you either (like most other critters in the woods) and will get out of your way or off your body if given half a chance. That may be true, but I have been seen doing the slap-that-spider-off-me-while-wildly-gyrating-my-body dance by many of my so-called friends, who then have to tell on me to everyone who missed the show.

Poisonous Plants

High school orienteering coach Matt Pheiffer initiated a smart move at his orienteering meets in South Carolina. Coach Pheiffer simply posted a photograph of any dangers, such as poison ivy, that might be encountered in the meet area. Until I saw his photo, which he downloaded from the Internet, I did not realize that poison ivy comes in three forms. It can be a bush, ground cover, or a vine. You don't want contact with any of them! Downloading those photos was a great idea. Copy it.

Leave the Wildlife Alone

Although they are not generally a safety hazard, we should leave the birds and animals alone in order to be responsible visitors into wildlife habitats. Nesting birds are particularly vulnerable to errant footsteps, so watch where you put your feet. Most of us don't want to step on the occasional dozing snake, either! Just remember that if the snake senses you coming, it will usually head away from you as fast as possible. Likewise I have come within a foot of a fawn blending perfectly with the dappled sunlight coming through the overhead canopy. I was trailing six orienteers who, like me, had completed their courses and were heading back to the parking lot along a path. Though it was tempting to shout, "Wow, a fawn!", that would probably have ensured that the baby deer would leap away, separating it from where its mom had told it to hole up until she came back. And surely no one has to tell you to never approach bear cubs because bear mothers are very protective.

Safety Azimuth

Event directors are responsible for advising all participants of the safety azimuth or safety bearing associated with the event. An azimuth or bearing is simply

At one meet in Georgia in January, unexpected springlike temperatures encouraged most competitors at a high school meet to orienteer in minimal clothing. Immediately after the last starts, when many of the coaches and teachers had just gone out, a cold front arrived, drenching everyone in rain and dropping the temperature 20 degrees. Shivering competitors crossed the finish line only to find their coaches and teachers had locked the buses and vans, so they could not dry off or get warm clothes. Quick thinking by the organizers prevented any hypothermia. One simple solution was to have as many people as possible huddle close together under a small roof. Students on the outside moved in toward the center as they chilled and students in the center moved to the outside as they got warmer. Everyone cooperated and it worked.

a direction on your compass (such as west or 270 degrees). Normally the safety azimuth will take you to an easily recognizable linear feature such as a paved or gravel road, a large start area, a subdivision, or a shopping center—in other words, something that you cannot miss if you walk in the direction of the azimuth from the competition area. Often the instructions will advise that when you reach a paved road, for example, you wait there until someone comes to pick you up. When a competitor has not returned within the announced time limit, one of the first actions is often to drive the perimeter of the competition area to see if that competitor has made his way to the nearest road. More information about azimuths and bearings is given in chapter 3. Be aware that the words *azimuth*, *bearing*, and *heading* are often used interchangeably to mean a direction and are often given in degrees—as in, follow an azimuth (or bearing or heading) of 79 degrees.

Second Compass

The safety azimuth is another good reason to carry a second compass when you orienteer. (Azimuths and using your compass are fully discussed in chapter 3.) Should you fall and break your compass, you will have a backup to finish the course or to head for safety. By the way, few orienteers get lost to the point of being unable to finish their course within the time limit, so the safety azimuth is rarely used—but remember that Murphy's Law always lurks. As you become more proficient, you will eventually reach a level of skill that allows you to always relocate and continue; being mislocated then becomes a temporary situation.

Hopefully this portion on safety has not frightened you from the great sport of orienteering. There are occasional scratches, bumps, and turned ankles from orienteering; however, more serious injuries are quite rare. Also remember, one good trait of most creatures you might encounter in the woods is that it is their nature to avoid humans. Therefore, if given time and opportunity, they will seek to move away. There are a few exceptions, such as grizzly bears and animal mothers with young, but those are rare and should certainly be mentioned by event organizers if they might be near. I have orienteered on grizzly bear migration routes in Western Canada, and all competitors were told exactly where those migration routes were and to avoid those areas. I never saw a grizzly, though—just brown bears that went the other way, thank goodness!

NEVER GET LOST AGAIN

Not only is orienteering thoroughly enjoyable as you get out into the parks and forests and off the paths to see and experience nature, but being a trained navigator can also be plainly useful or even better, lifesaving. On a simple level, you need never be lost again. Even if you do not know where you are, if you know how to get back to camp, then you are not lost, just temporarily mislocated.

A few other thoughts about orienteering as lifesaving: Orienteering is a safe sport and even beginners rarely get mislocated. When you are out in parks and forests, you are generally surrounded by people, roads, and buildings outside the park and you are near other orienteers inside the park. On the other hand, on those rare occasions when you realize you are thoroughly mislocated and cannot find your way back to camp, orienteering teaches that you should stop immediately. We have already told you to blow your whistle three times to summon help. If you are on a road or trail, just sit down until someone comes and finds you. Search-and-rescue professionals teach the same lifesaving lesson. In other words, stopping is what you should do if you lose your way while you are hiking, hunting, or in any other outdoor setting, not just orienteering. If you keep moving, search-and-rescue professionals just have a larger area to search, which means that they will likely be slower to find you than if you had stayed in one place. Studies show, however, that most healthy people over the age of six keep moving, so orienteering teaches you an important lesson that most people do not know: Stop moving and make yourself as comfortable and as visible as possible. Search-and-rescue professionals also teach that the person who has the utmost responsibility of saving your life when you are missing is you—so wouldn't you rather be at home in the woods and able to find your way back to camp in almost any situation? Orienteering can do that for you.

SUMMARY

Chapter 2 has introduced the kinds of fitness to be gained from orienteering and has laid out some simple training activities to improve your ability to climb hills, go longer distances, and become a faster runner or walker. You now know how to dress for orienteering and what to bring to a meet, such as your own watch, whistle, and compass (you can also rent a compass at most meets). The chapter ends by reassuring you that not only is orienteering a safe sport, but it can also teach safety lessons that can protect you in many navigational situations. Chapter 3 will now introduce the two most common tools for navigating—the map and the compass.

Map and Compass

Orienteering is a skill sport that is based on land navigation and requires the use of tools to navigate. Although there are five skills based on the tools for navigation, there are only two tools required for *land navigation*—the map and the compass. As you will learn in this chapter, one of these tools is more important than the other. Let's start with the two tools, map and compass, and progress in chapter 4 to the five skills associated with the map and compass. Later you will see that *orienteering* adds three additional tools: the clue sheet, a scoring device (scorecard or electronic punch), and a watch. These additional tools will be discussed in depth in later chapters.

MAPS

There are many kinds of maps for many uses. For navigational purposes, a map is a two-dimensional depiction, or representation, of a three-dimensional surface. A major positive for the map is simply that it provides so much information. Only the map can tell you what land and water features lie between you and your target. The map can show you roads and trails that go in or near the direction you want to go. (Moving along roads and trails is almost always faster than pushing through the woods.) Maps can show features along the way that will keep you located and let you know that you are going in the correct direction. Even better, maps describe the features around your target so that you will know when you get close. Of course, in orienteering, when you actually arrive at the correct location, you should find a nice control marker hanging there, shouting your success!

A map is a communication (think of it as a letter to you using symbols). By using map symbols, the geographic mapmaker (usually shortened to *mapper*) communicates to the map user a representation of the features of an area that he or she has mapped.

Distance on a Map

Maps are made to a scale. Orienteering maps are often at a scale of 1:10,000 or 1:15,000. A scale is simply a statement of a relationship. It is a fraction: A scale of 1:10,000 (which is usually written somewhere on the map) means that any measurement on the map represents 10,000 times that distance on the ground. Fortunately, we do not have to make conversions as we orienteer. The metric system makes translation of the map scale easy. The 1:10,000 scale means 1 centimeter

on the map equals 10,000 centimeters on the ground, and 10,000 centimeters on the ground equal 100 meters, which is just short of the length of a football field and one of the end zones. Therefore, 1 centimeter on the map is slightly shorter than the playing surface of a football field and one of its end zones. Even better, your compass (see later in this chapter) has one or more scales to translate distances on the map into meters on the ground. When you use the centimeter scale on a compass to measure the distance between two locations, you simply translate the number of centimeters on the scale into hundreds of meters on the ground. For example, 3.5 centimeters on the scale is 350 meters on the ground. You will learn more about measurement when you learn about the skill of distance estimation by measure and pace, but the key is that all you have to do is use the appropriate scale on the compass and measure correctly on the map. Then you will know how far to go—no conversions required!

Airplanes and satellites, using various tools from cameras to lasers, depict the features below them to provide data to make accurate maps for navigation. Maps, then, are depicted as a bird would view them when flying high above but with symbols added. The maps we use for orienteering can be printed on a variety of materials (paper is usually the least expensive) and are often sealed in a plastic bag to avoid water damage. There are many other kinds of maps, from the electronic maps displayed on your GPS, to those on your computer, to the diagrams in your favorite mall. Navigation using any of these maps requires many of the same skills as orienteering. Certainly, you will find yourself a better map user as your own skills grow.

Orienteering Maps

In the early days of orienteering, many of the maps used were the USGS maps at a scale of 1:24,000—still used in most adventure races and by search-and-rescue teams. Quite often, orienteers simply made a black-and-white copy of the USGS map and took off through the woods. It was not a great tool for navigation, but it was all that was available at the time.

Colors

Today, orienteering maps are much more accurate and detailed. These maps are usually in one of three scales, and they use five colors. Colors used for orienteering maps include blue for water, brown for contours and landforms, shades of green for the thickness of vegetation (you can jog through light-green vegetation, but you might have to crawl under vegetation drawn in dark green), black for human-made features, rock features, and special objects, and yellow for fields and other open areas. White is not considered a color for orienteering maps. It indicates open, or runnable, forest—a major difference from the USGS maps, where green indicates forest. Landforms and contours are further explained in this chapter.

Magnetic North Lines

Orienteering maps have lines representing magnetic north. These north arrow lines may have an arrow point on the north or top end of the line and are 500 meters apart or 250 meters apart on the 1:5,000 map. The magnetic north lines run parallel to the sides of the map. They play an important role in using the compass.

There are three norths: true north, magnetic north, and grid north. True north is the direction of the geographic North Pole, directly under the North Star. Magnetic north is where your compass normally points, and grid north is the top of the map you will use. Magnetic north is extremely important

in orienteering because the magnetic compass needle points to magnetic north, and you must orient the map and line up your route relative to magnetic north. If there is a variation between magnetic north and grid north, the map legend on U.S. government maps may show that in the form of a magnetic variation diagram (see figure 3.1). However, having magnetic north lines already drawn on the map allows the orienteer to use the compass without having to convert (by adding or subtracting) from grid north to find magnetic north. Other information may include the name of the map, the name of the mapper or mappers, the names of the field checkers, the name of the orienteering club that paid for the map, and the date or dates of the work. (Note: A field checker takes a rough map, aerial photo, or old map out into the area to check it in the field and determine what should be changed and what is correct. Most field checkers are volunteers. It's a great way to improve your map-reading skills.)

Three Common Orienteering Map Scales

Map scales, as explained earlier, are simply fractions that show the ratio of distance on the map to distance on the ground. For a 1:15,000 scale, this would mean that 1 of any unit on the map would be equal to 15,000 of that same unit on the ground. If we wanted to use inches, a 1:15,000 map scale would mean that 1 inch on the map would be equal to 15,000 inches on the ground. It is difficult to relate to 15,000 inches, so orienteers use the metric system instead. In this instance, 1 centimeter on the map would be equal to 15,000 centimeters, or 150 meters, on the ground.

One way to understand map scale is by realizing that the bigger the number on the right side of the ratio (in other words, the smaller the fraction), the more land is shown on the map. A map with a 1:15,000 scale has more land squeezed on it than a map with a scale of 1:10,000. However, a map with a scale of 1:10,000 is easier to read and use for fine navigation. Also, with a 1:10,000 scale, 1 centimeter on the map is equal to 100 meters on the ground. This is approximately the length of a football field plus one end zone (which is 110 yards—close enough). Later, when we teach you how to pace count, you will learn how to pace off 100 meters on the ground. You can measure the distance on the map that you want to go by using your compass scale. Most compasses have one or more scales to translate distances on the map into meters on the ground. When you use the centimeter scale on a compass to

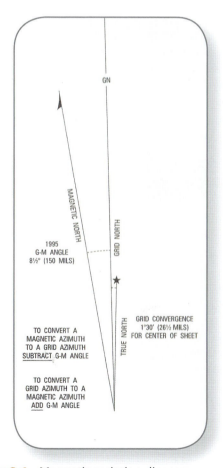

Figure 3.1 Magnetic variation diagram.
Quantico Military Installation Map V8345, Edition, 2-NIMA, 1:50,000

measure between two locations, you simply translate the number of centimeters on the scale into hundreds of meters on the ground; for example, 3.5 centimeters on the scale is 350 meters on the ground on a 1:10,000 map. You will learn more about measurement when you learn about the skill of distance estimation by measure and pace, but the key is that all you have to do is use the appropriate scale on the compass and measure correctly on the map. Then you will know how far to go.

The scale for the longest and hardest orienteering courses (the blue and red courses) uses a ratio of 1:15,000. Elite orienteers must be able to read this on the run. Their compasses will have a 1:15,000 scale to facilitate quick measurements. Most other course maps now use a scale of 1:10,000, which makes them easier to read by older eyes and by orienteers who are still learning.

Finally, the third map scale is for special maps for fun events such as sprint and trail orienteering. Orienteering maps for these specialty events are drawn at a scale of 1:5,000 and 1:4,000, so the features are even larger and even easier to read. These two scales give such a blown-up view of the area mapped that they are used interchangeably here. In other words, if you attend a sprint or trail orienteering event, the area portrayed by either scale is so large that the difference is negligible. There is not likely to be a 1:4,000 or 1:5,000 scale on your compass because the area portrayed is so large you can see where you need to go. However, you can use the centimeter scale as long as you remember that 1 centimeter is 200 meters on the 1:5,000 map and close to that on the 1:4,000.

To recap, maps come in all sizes, shapes, and scales, but the standards used in orienteering competitions include the 1:15,000 orienteering map for the top men's and women's course, the 1:10,000 map for most courses (those below the top two elite courses), and the 1:5,000 or 1:4,000 for specialty events such as the sprint and trail orienteering courses. Remember also that map scales are fractions, so a 1:5,000 map is considered a larger scale map than a 1:15,000 map (which can be a little confusing).

These orienteering map standards do not rule out using other types of maps for specific events. A hand-drawn map of a schoolyard or even a classroom lends itself to orienteering in a small space. Some military navigation training and tests, which may involve orienteering, are done on 1:50,000 maps, and hikers also occasionally use maps of this scale. Even an aerial photograph downloaded from the Internet can serve for a small or special event. Finally, some clubs may try to use up old maps and give you a 1:15,000 map for courses other than the elite two.

Although orienteering maps for competitions are of high precision, mapmaking itself is an excellent classroom or individual activity that can be used to teach practically any subject. Mapmaking improves your map-reading ability even faster than field checking. (Mapmaking instructions are found in the orienteering training manual at http://orienteeringusa.org/sites/default/files/pheifferOTM.pdf).

Legend

Once you have glanced at a map to be sure it is the right one for whatever you are doing, your eyes should go immediately to the map legend. Occasionally orienteering maps will not have a legend on the actual map in a plastic bag that you use for the competition. However, there should be a legend keyed to that map that is readily available to all. It may be at the event registration or at the start, so be sure to ask! Why is the legend worth reading so thoroughly? Once you have mastered the information in an orienteering legend, you can orienteer anywhere in the world because all orienteering maps are drafted using the same international standards as published by the IOF.

The legend contains valuable information about the map, including the symbols for roads, buildings, streams, and so on. Other valuable information that may be printed on the map includes the scale, contour interval, title or name of the map, and credits (e.g., mapmaker). The IOF maintains a published record of all acceptable symbols for use on orienteering maps, including those for boulders, rocky fields, cliffs, or anything else shown on the map. (See the IOF symbols at http://backwoodsok.org/control-descriptions-and-map-symbols-explained.) Figure 3.2 shows two sample standard legends.

Any nonstandard Orienteering USA symbol that is used on an orienteering map must be shown and clearly explained in the legend. Any special symbols that are not IOF approved must be clearly spelled out and available to all competitors. This is often done in the course setter's notes, but it must be given to each competitor or placed in a location accessible and frequented by the competitors.

When looking at the map legend for a particular orienteering event, always pay attention to the *x*s and *o*s because they do not always represent the same features on every orienteering map. *X*s and *o*s are the handymen or wild cards of legends, used to depict local features not well represented by standard legend designations. A green *x* could be a tree stump on one map and an evergreen tree in a deciduous forest on another map. You want to know what the *x*s and *o*s represent *before* you start.

The legend of the map is particularly important for special features, which are features that are peculiar to a certain map and that may not be widely found elsewhere. For example, in one area of the Northeastern United States, DVOA has mapped a ground feature peculiar to their map. Early tradesmen, called *colliers*, built level platforms in the forest in order to cook wood down into charcoal. Today all that remains of their work are small, flat areas in the woods. DVOA mappers use a small brown triangle on the French Creek orienteering map to show where these charcoal platforms existed.

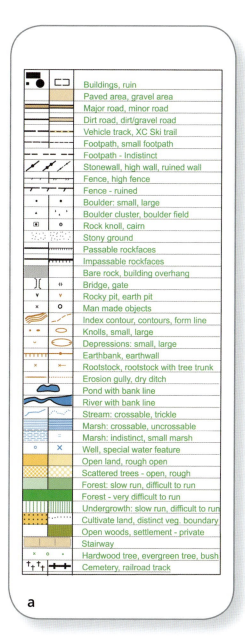

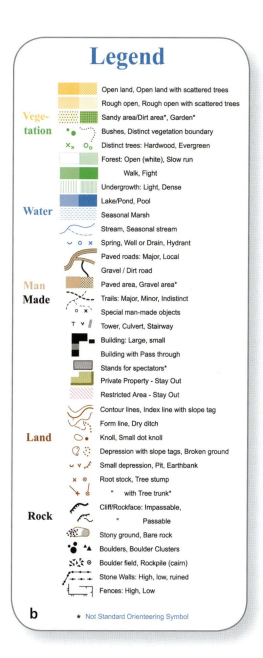

Figure 3.2 Sample standard legends.

When Coach Turbyfill was orienteering in Europe, his map had an unusual symbol, a brown star, used to designate anthills. When he came across his first anthill, it was 6 feet (1.8 m) high—definitely a special feature not found on most maps! As you move along your route to the control, various features visible on the map and along your route confirm that you are where you think you are. The orienteering technique of noting features along your route is referred to as *collecting features,* and it is explained in chapter 5.

Landforms

Five basic landforms are described in this chapter. All are important to orienteering, and using the correct terminology is equally important. Since water only flows one way—downhill—we define all landforms in relationship to water flow, assuming you are either *in* the landform or *on* the landform (e.g., *in* a creek bed, *on* a hilltop). Likewise, when we describe the slope of the ground and use terms such as *up* and *down*, we refer to high locations as *hilltops,* the tops of ridges as being *up,* and lower places such as streams as being *down.* As an example, if you were on a hilltop, you would expect to go *down* to a stream. If you were standing beside a stream, you would expect to go *up* to a ridgeline. The technical name for the flow of water across the terrain is *hydrography* (see chapter 9).

When a map is drawn, how does the mapper show which way the water flows—in other words, which way is up and which is down? How does the mapper show steepness or relatively flat ground? And how does the mapper show the shape of land features such as hills?

Up and *down* can be found using the brown contour lines on the map. A contour line traces points that are at equal height or elevation. They show the height and shape of landforms. When contour lines are drawn close together, the terrain is steep. When they are farther apart, the terrain is flatter. Although not officially part of the legend, most maps list the contour interval under the map scale. Contour interval indicates how much vertical elevation is shown by each contour line. An example of a contour interval is 5 meters, or about 16 feet. When you move from one contour line to another, you change your height by 5 meters either up or down.

A good way to visualize contours is to think of a hill rising out of a lake. Just as the lake would touch the hill at exactly the same height all the way around the hill, the contour line will touch the hill at the same height all the way around the hill. Raise or lower the level of the lake by 16 feet and you can draw another contour line above or below the first. Now, draw the contour lines up and down the hill in your mind (without the lake) and you see the function of contour lines. As you visualize contours, remember that the hill is not perfectly round. It may have dips, outcrops, and streams that alter it. Consequently, the contour lines can twist and turn so that they follow the imperfections of the land. Once you get to the top of the hill, the contour line meets all the way around and there are no more contour lines above it. Remember, since your map is limited to the width of the page, some contour lines simply stop at the edge of the map. Matching the brown contour lines on an orienteering map to the actual flow of the terrain is a must for the orienteer who wants to succeed.

The five landforms are reentrants, spurs, depressions, hills, and saddles. Each will be described in further detail next.

Reentrant

In military terms, a reentrant is an angle that is pointing inward (such as across the end of a salient) and therefore is commonly used to refer to something as simply pointing inward. In orienteering terms, a reentrant is often explained as a terrain feature on the ground where rainwater would flow down to reenter the circulating water system via a stream. Reentrants can be quite small or as large as a valley. If you stand in a reentrant, you will see that three sides are all higher than the one side where the water can flow out. In other words, a *reentrant* is defined as three sides up and one side down (see figure 3.3). Reentrants are visible on a map where the brown contour line(s) have a dent, shaped something like a U. Turned around, those same u-shaped contour lines could look like a nose, indicating a spur. How can you tell the difference? Check which way the water flows. In the map segment shown in figure 3.3, water would not likely be flowing down a spur, so you can tell that the water flows down the

Figure 3.3 Reentrants.

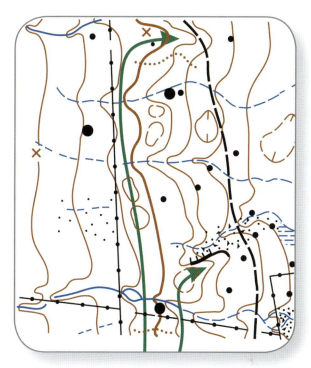

Figure 3.4 Spurs.

several reentrants from left to right, or since this map is oriented correctly, from west to east. Water does not normally run through small reentrants unless it is raining or has rained recently. Larger reentrants may have a stream. A valley-sized feature is not referred to as a reentrant for orienteering purposes because most valleys would be larger than an orienteering map. Other terms outside of orienteering are *valley* and *draw*.

Spur

A spur is a land feature in which the land drops away noticeably on two sides and then slopes more gently downhill on one end and uphill on the other. If you were standing on a spur and looking down the spur, you would clearly notice that the terrain goes downhill away from you in three directions. Thus, a *spur* is defined as three sides down and one up (see figure 3.4). In this map segment the spur to the west is gently sloping downhill as the brown contour lines are further apart than for the middle spur, which would be a bit steeper since the contour lines are closer together. The spur to the east is fairly broad so that if you went in the center of the spur you might not see the reentrants to the north and south that define the spur. Other names for a spur are *finger*, *ridge*, and *nose* (rarely). *Finger* is also used in orienteering. Although *ridge* is not an orienteering term and usually refers to a much larger feature, you may hear it used simply because it fits the larger feature. However, all three terms (*finger*, *spur*, and *ridge*) generally mean the same type of land feature, although *spur* is the preferred orienteering term.

Depression and Pit

Most people know what a depression is. You might define it as a hole in the ground that has a bottom. At the bottom, the only way to go down is to start digging. Thus, the definition of a *depression* is all sides up (see figure 3.5). Note that the brown contour lines that mark the two depressions have at least two tic marks inside the circle so that they are not confused with a hill, which can be similar in appearance. Another form of depression often found in orienteering is called a *pit*. Think of a pit as smaller and steeper and a depression as larger and often shallower.

Hill or Knoll

Orienteering uses two terms, *hill* and *knoll*, for what is essentially a hill, as well as occasionally the term *mound* for a small bump in the land. The three differ by size, with the hill being the largest, the knoll usually much smaller than a hill, and the mound a feature that you can often see over when standing by it. A knoll or a mound can be on a hill but not the reverse. By definition, if you are standing on a hill, all sides slope down away from you (see figure 3.6). The hills pictured on this map segment would be called knolls by most orienteers. Because they are each only one contour line high and the contour line for this map is 5 meters,

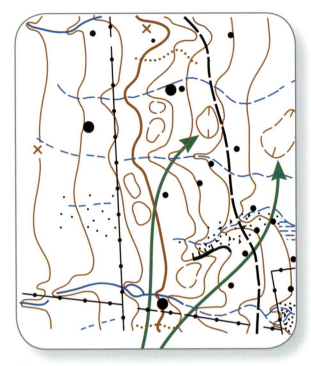

Figure 3.5 Depression and pit.

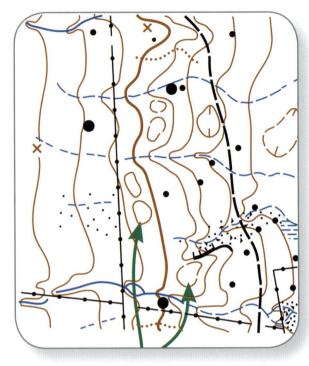

Figure 3.6 Hill or knoll.

they are small enough to call *knolls*, but they are too tall to see over, so they are not mounds. Small hills are knolls, and if really small, they are mounds. Mounds are obvious because they are small and hills because they are large, but knolls are a judgment call. Each has a definable top where everything is down and you can only go up with a ladder or a tree.

Saddle

A saddle landform occurs between two hills and connects them. If you stand in a saddle, the land slopes up on two sides toward the two hills and down on the other two sides. The definition of a *saddle* is thus two sides up and two down (see figure 3.7). Note that a saddle always requires higher ground on two sides, so saddles typically occur between hills.

The five landforms are easy to recall if you know that you are personally equipped with a digital landform designator—simply use your hand and you can make all five landforms. First, make a fist with your palm facing down; now any one of your knuckles can be a mound or hill since all sides slope downward. The skin between any two knuckles makes a nice saddle (the skin slopes up on two sides and down on two sides). Any one of your four fingers represents a spur. If your fingers are tight, a reentrant is formed between two fingers (mentally pour some water in at the top and imagine it running between the fingers and out

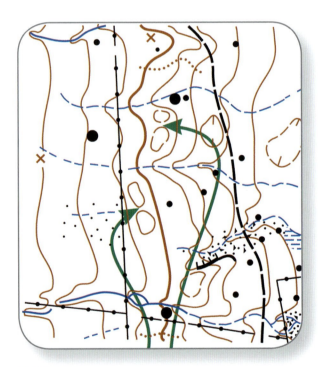

Figure 3.7 Saddles.

the bottom). Finally, turn your fist over and open your hand in a cupped position. The cup of your palm is now a depression with all sides higher than the bottom. If you could make the depression in your palm smaller and with steeper sides, it could be called a pit.

Linear Features

Linear features run more or less in a line (not necessarily a straight line) and have connectedness. Examples can be a road, trail, fence, or stream (now there's a rarely straight line!), or even a spur, finger, reentrant, valley, or ridge. Connectedness does not have to be perfect, either. Think of a stone fence that has a gap in it but you can see where it picks up again. Should the gap be wide or the foliage thick, you might not be able to see where the stone fence starts again, but it should be on your orienteering map. If a road or path stops and does not continue, it ceases to be a linear feature, but if a path happens to be running along the top of a ridge and ends but the ridge continues, you could hop right off the end of the path and continue in the same direction along the landform, exactly as you had been following the road or path.

Why is it important for you to know about linear features? Linear features that you can readily identify are the best aids to moving to your orienteering destination *quickly* and, providing you learn to estimate distance well, *accurately*. Speed and, above all, accuracy in navigation are the keys to success in orienteering. A good quote to remember is, "In orienteering (and in life), it is better to be accurate than fast." In the map segment shown in figure 3.8, you could take a compass bearing and go straight to the control through the woods. However, by simply moving a little to the east, you could orienteer beside the stream paralleling your direction and perhaps run faster than through the woods. Additionally, you will know exactly where you are when the stream intersects the path and you can quickly move to the control from that attack point. (Using attack points as an orienteering technique is presented in chapter 5.)

Also in figure 3.8, there are a number of linear features. The trails are obvious as is the long (blue) stream flowing north to south. In addition, there is a small stream coming into the larger stream from the east. Not quite so obvious is the long spur running northwest to southeast. It is the one with the six brown knolls clustered near together on its nose. There are others that run shorter distances but which could be useful for nearby controls. One such is the reentrant and intermittent stream flowing into the larger stream from the west. Note that an intermittent stream is one that may flow year-round but which likely has water in it during wet portions of the year.

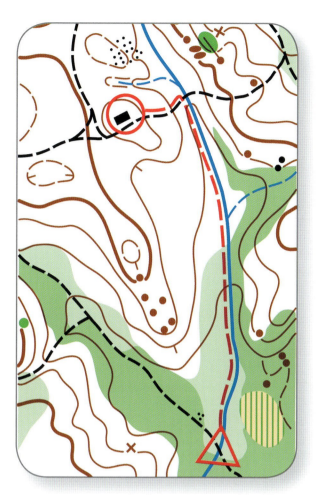

Figure 3.8 Linear features.

COMPASS

A compass, like a map, is a tool for navigation and orienteering. Compasses work because the earth acts as a huge magnet with two ends: the north magnetic pole and the south magnetic pole. There are three norths in most locations on the earth—true north, grid north, and magnetic north. Magnetic north is the north we use in orienteering. Around 4,000 or 5,000 years ago, the Chinese are thought to have been the first to discover that a certain rock, called a *lodestone*, would always point to the north if allowed to float freely (probably on a small sliver of wood)—the first use of magnetic north. Compasses today are built around this centuries-old discovery. They house a magnetic needle that always attempts to point to magnetic north, although it can be misdirected by a magnet, another strong compass, some metallic objects, and occasionally power lines. In better compasses, the magnetic needle is immersed in a lightweight oil to dampen its movement.

Orienteering is based on the principle that if the magnetic needle of your compass points to magnetic north, and your map shows you where you are, and you know where you wish to go, then you can combine the compass and the map to successfully navigate to your objective. Chapter 4 goes into detail about navigating with the compass.

Baseplate Compass

Several companies provide excellent compasses, and it is worth spending the money to get a good one—remember that for many, this is a lifetime activity, and a good compass can last for years. On the other hand, if you are not sure that you will enjoy orienteering, an inexpensive beginning compass works just fine. Since orienteering is a moving sport, you want a baseplate compass, sometimes called a *platform compass*.

The baseplate compass has three main parts: the baseplate, which is a plastic platform that you can hold in your palm; a round dial, called a *bezel*, filled with light oil and divided into a 360-degree circle; and a magnetic needle floating in the light oil in the bezel (see figure 3.9*a*). The magnetic needle is often red on the north-pointing end and white on the south-pointing end. The magnetic needle may also have a small glow-in-the-dark application on the north end for night use. So the three parts are the baseplate, the bezel, and the magnetic needle (sometimes called the *north magnetic needle*). Baseplate compasses for orienteering also have one or more scales on the front or side of the baseplate. One model even allows the orienteer to slide various scales on and off the front of the platform, making it easy to match up correctly with the scale of the map.

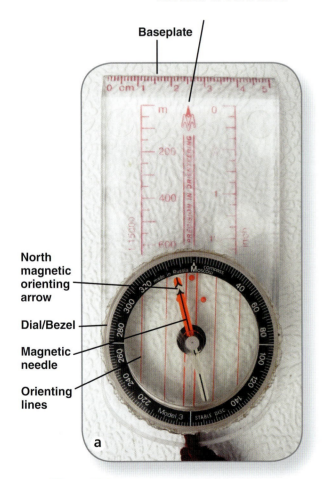

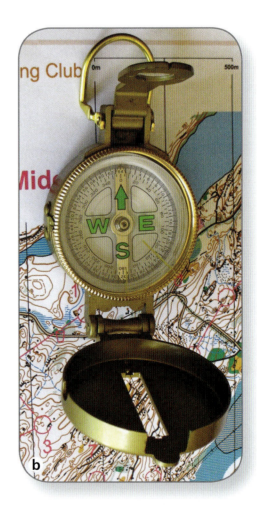

Figure 3.9 (*a*) Baseplate compass; (*b*) lensatic compass.

Since we like to teach in fives, for orienteering purposes we consider the scale as a fourth part of the compass and the lanyard, which you should always use to fasten the compass to your wrist, as the fifth part. Of course, your compass works just fine without the scale and the lanyard, so for navigation, they are not considered main parts of a compass.

The military uses a fine compass, the lensatic compass, which perhaps served well to adjust artillery fire (in the old days) and for very slow land navigation today. However, the lensatic is not very suitable for orienteering (see figure 3.9*b*). Among other deficiencies for orienteering, the lensatic compass requires the user to stop moving and sight through it. No orienteer is going to waste that much time when you can actually read a baseplate compass on the move.

Thumb Compass

The thumb compass used by some advanced orienteers has the same three parts as the baseplate compass and usually a millimeter scale as well, but instead of a lanyard, it has a stretching band to go over the thumb, so its fifth part is the thumb band (figure 3.10). On most compasses, the bezel can be turned or rotated. On others, the bezel does not rotate. Some baseplate compasses have small magnifiers and other add-ons. A thumb compass is worn on the thumb and unlike the most common use of the baseplate compass, it is kept in constant contact with the map, which is held in the same hand. You have to keep the magnetic needle

Figure 3.10 Thumb compass.

aligned with the north magnetic lines on the map and keep the map oriented to the ground to provide the directional control you need for any compass work. Should you decide to purchase a thumb compass, be sure you know which bezel you want: rotating or fixed. Despite the fact that a compass is a cool navigational tool, remember that it is a 3-degree instrument (meaning it can be off 3 degrees to the left or to the right and still be considered accurate enough for most purposes) and that it is secondary to the map.

Precision Compass Reading

Looking at the compass shown in figure 3.11, you can see that orienteering compasses have a direction-of-travel arrow centered in the front part of the compass. Note also the north magnetic orienting lines inside the bezel (the dial in the middle). These lines are fully red in figure 3.11 but can be red on the north side of the north magnetic orienting arrow (the double red line in the center is usually arrow-shaped) and black on the south side of the north magnetic orienting arrow, relative to the center of the bezel where the magnetic needle is attached. These colors help prevent the orienteer from reversing the compass and going in exactly the opposite direction (a mistake commonly referred to as a *180*, because you are heading exactly 180 degrees from the direction you should be going).

The following five steps detail the procedure for precision compass reading:

1. Place the compass on the line of travel with the *direction-of-travel arrow* pointing in the direction you intend to travel.

2. Rotate the *bezel* until the *north magnetic orienting lines* inside the bezel are parallel to or right on top of the north magnetic lines on the map and the *north magnetic orienting arrow* is pointing north on the map.

3. Measure any appropriate distances from where you are to the control or from where you are to any point or feature that you are trying to find, such as a road, stream, and so on.

4. Place the compass in the palm of your hand with the *direction-of-travel arrow* pointing away from you and the back of the *baseplate compass* against your stomach. Then rotate *your entire body* until the red end of the magnetic needle comes to rest inside the *north magnetic orienting arrow*.

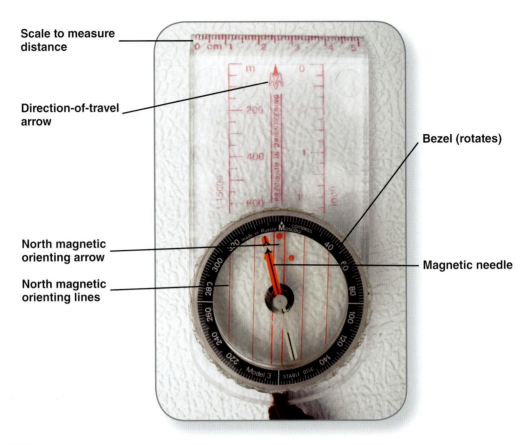

Scale to measure distance

Direction-of-travel arrow

Bezel (rotates)

North magnetic orienting arrow

Magnetic needle

North magnetic orienting lines

Figure 3.11 Example for precision compass reading.

5. Follow the *direction-of-travel arrow*. The best way to follow the direction-of-travel arrow is to find an object such as a tree or rock that is directly in line with the arrow and move quickly to that object. Then find another such object and repeat the process. Because the dial is segmented into equal markings representing the degrees of a circle, you could actually follow a specific numbered direction, called a *bearing* or an *azimuth* (thus the term *safety azimuth* in chapter 2), but since you are trying to go fast, there is no need to peer so closely at the numbers on the bezel—just run to the object directly in line with your direction-of-travel arrow. For training or playing a game, following a specific numbered bearing or azimuth can be fun. (Always remember that people do not walk in straight lines, so your bearing game should keep the distances short.)

Examples of Azimuths

If you travel directly west, your bearing or azimuth is 270 degrees, representing the 270-degree angle between magnetic north (which is 360 degrees on your compass) and west. Go south and your azimuth is 180 degrees. For travel between south and west, your azimuth will be between 180 and 270 degrees, such as 225 degrees (southwest). *The azimuth in degrees will line up with the direction-of-travel arrow.* You may also hear a bearing or azimuth called a *heading*. A heading is simply the direction you are pointed, so for orienteering, it is a useful term because it describes which way you are headed. However, remember you are using an instrument with a 3-degree error, so while following a bearing of 89 degrees sounds quite accurate, it is hard to do, and it almost impossible for any distance over 450 meters.

Back Azimuth: The Intentional 180

A back azimuth is the same maneuver as the dreaded 180 except that you do it on purpose because you want to go back to your last known location. The quick and easy way to set up a back azimuth is to stop, turn around, and face the direction that you came from and let the white end of the north magnetic needle settle in the red north magnetic orienting arrow so that you are going in the exact opposite direction from your previous route. As soon as you return to a known or recognizable location, decide which way you wish to go and proceed more cautiously in the correct direction to your next destination, with the red end of the north magnetic needle where it is supposed to be.

MAP OR COMPASS?

Time for a question: Which is more important to successful navigation, a map or a compass? Or to put it another way, which would you rather have to find your way?

Most of us (myself included, before I knew better) are likely to answer that we'd prefer to have a compass. Gadgets are fun and more attractive than a piece of paper with symbols on it. However, this is the wrong answer! For several reasons, maps are far more important for getting successfully from one location to another over any appreciable distance.

First, all the compass can give you is a vector or direction. It cannot give you any details of what you will encounter along the way. Second, the typical compass is a 3-degree instrument, which means it can be off 3 degrees to the left or to the right. There are compasses that offer 1 degree of accuracy, but they are more expensive and require slower movement for accurate reading, which makes them less useful for orienteering, where speed is part of the sport. So, if you have a typical compass and you walk or run 1,000 meters, you may be 52 meters to the left or right of the place you wish to find, even if you walked a perfectly straight line. If you are in the woods, you probably would not see a control that is more than 52 meters (just over 170 ft) to your right or your left, so you must read the map. By the way, if you still are not used to thinking in meters, just remember that a meter is just a little longer than a yard (about 10 percent: 36 in. = 1 yd versus 39.37 in. = 1 m). Therefore, in our example, 52 meters would be about 57 yards, which is close enough for measurement in the woods.

DRIFT

Now let's think about walking a perfectly straight line. There are almost no situations in orienteering where you can walk a straight line for very far, and worse, most of us do not walk straight. We drift left or right! A compass or a GPS is the most useful in places that are flat and without many features, such as a desert or a snow-covered flat area with few trees—in other words, where you can see a long way. If you can see a long way and your compass points you toward a nice feature such as a big rock, a building, or an unusual tree, then you can walk a reasonably straight line by heading directly toward that object. What if, however, there is a deep ravine or a raging river between you and the object you can see? Obviously you cannot walk straight to it, and once you lose sight of the object, you will probably drift left or right.

Why do we drift? No one knows for sure, but sometimes the ground is responsible. If you are walking around the side of a hill, gravity is working against you and you are likely to drift gradually downhill without even noticing. Other times, you may drift because of your habits. When you go around trees, rocks, ditches, or other obstacles in the same direction, you tend to drift in that direction. If you always go around to the left, you will probably drift left. Perhaps some of us have one leg that is slightly shorter than the other, and that can make us drift to the side of the shorter leg.

Navigation skills are based on two tools, the map and the compass. If you are still unconvinced that the map is the more important tool, think of it this way: Suppose you are running an orienteering competition and you trip and fall beside a deep well. Would you be more likely to find your way if your compass fell into the well and disappeared into the cold water far below or if your map did? Regardless of what your parents or the supply sergeant would say about the loss of your compass, the map is the more important of the two and is quite sufficient to complete the course. If you salvaged only the compass, you would have to use the safety azimuth (see chapter 2) and accept defeat.

Despite these drawbacks to the compass, it can be extremely useful as an aid to the map. It can start you off in the correct direction, give you a vector when there are no good features to guide you, and point the way with sufficient accuracy when the distance is short.

Here's one other thought about the compass. There are two kinds of orienteers: those who have broken a compass during a race and those who will. So as a precaution, carry two compasses.

As will be seen in later chapters, the map provides much more information and assistance in navigation than does the compass. Sufficient at this stage is the observation that you could find your way over some distance to a location with only a map, but you'd be hard pressed to do the same with just a compass. Likewise, you would not know what to expect along the way with a compass, but you would with the map.

TERRAIN AND GROUND

Let's look at two terms that have similar meanings. The terms *terrain* and *ground* appear often in orienteering, so it is time to define them. *Terrain* includes all features encountered as you proceed along on the orienteering map. It is represented by symbols, and though it generally refers to natural features such as landforms, water features, and vegetation, it also is often used interchangeably with *ground* to include what you are actually walking upon. *Terrain* is usually broadened to include human-made features such as buildings and roads in that they are located on or in the terrain and can be used to navigate. Human-made features are also represented by symbols on the map. *Ground*, on the other hand, is a more specific term and usually means the earth that you are walking or running over to get to the next location. Coach Turbyfill adds that *ground* equals *dirt* (he is a former Marine and Marines tell it like it is). Ground can be dry dirt or wet dirt, but it is just dirt. Rock is a form of tightly packed dirt of varying composition. It could be iron or diamond or marble, but to the orienteer it is just something to walk or run across and therefore dirt.

It is useful to use correct terms in orienteering, yet *terrain* and *ground* are often used interchangeably when they should not be. Hopefully, you now know which is which and won't have to muddle through either the reading of this book or the conversations of other orienteers now that you have the concepts clear in your mind.

Know your drift. Coach Turbyfill drifts predominantly in one direction when he uses a baseplate compass and in another direction when he uses a thumb compass. He has no explanation for why he drifts in different directions with the different compasses, but it probably comes from how he holds them (see the next chapter).

He may not know why he drifts, but he knows that it happens and he knows which way he is prone to drift with each compass. Knowing this information is important to his overall navigation strategy. As he often says, "Do you want to know which way you drift before the race starts or find out after the race starts?" One of the exercises presented in appendix A shows how to determine your drift so that it can help you navigate instead of hurt you. Should you have a GPS device (such as a Garmin watch), you can use that during training to track your drift. Prohibition of GPS devices in orienteering events is discussed in chapter 7, but they have great value for training.

The admonition to "keep the map oriented to the ground" is an example of orienteers slipping up and using *ground* to refer to both terrain and ground. Keeping the map oriented to the ground means matching the symbols you see on the map (the terrain) with the actual features represented by those symbols that you see as you move across the ground. Correctly, the admonition should be, "Keep the map oriented to the terrain (as you move)." Keeping the map oriented to the terrain is presented in detail in chapter 6.

SUMMARY

This chapter explained the importance and use of maps, the significance of map scales, and a little information about map symbols. If you are math challenged, do not be put off by the use of scales. You will quickly adjust to using map scales and probably will never be asked to explain them! The types of terrain over which we orienteer and which are represented on maps were likewise discussed. That fascinating tool, the compass, got a little history, and its essential parts were presented as well as both the baseplate compass and the thumb compass. Even a little terminology, such as *terrain* and *ground*, was included. Chapter 4 presents the five skills of using the map and the compass and how to navigate using those five skills.

Navigational Skills

Chapter 4 segues from the introduction of the two tools for navigation, the map and the compass, to the actual use of those tools in the five skills of orienteering. The five skills are:

1. Precision map reading

2. Rough map reading

3. Precision compass reading

4. Rough compass reading

5. Distance estimation by measure and pace

All five skills are associated with the map and the compass. The four obvious ones are precision map reading, rough map reading, precision compass reading, and rough compass reading. The fifth, distance estimation by measure and pace, has two components: the first, measurement, is associated with using the scale on the compass to measure a distance on the map, and the second, pacing, lets you know approximately how far you have traveled while walking or running. Precision map reading and precision compass reading are often used either together or in sequence, as are rough map reading and rough compass reading. However, none of the skills stands alone because you should always use distance estimation, and that skill requires at least one of the others. On the other hand, you may occasionally use all five skills when orienteering from one control to another.

ESTIMATING DISTANCE BY MEASURE AND PACE

Although we listed it fifth, distance estimation by measure and pace is the one skill that a good orienteer always uses, so we'll start with it here. Distance estimation by measure and pace has two components. One component requires measuring the distance on the map that must be traveled to reach the control. You simply use the correct scale on the compass to measure the distance between any two locations on the map. The second component is the distance on the ground that you are traveling as you move toward the control. Distance estimation by measure and pace is estimation because it is difficult, if not impossible, to measure the exact distance on a flat map when that same distance on the ground may go uphill or go downhill—nature's way of reminding us that the map is two-dimensional and the actual ground is three-dimensional. Remember

how a map is similar to what a flying bird observes looking down at the ground? Well, the bird does not have to walk, so the distance it flies between any two points on the ground could be measured as a straight line. However, if you have to walk between those same two points, you may find that the land goes up a hill or down to a stream, making the distance longer for you than for the bird. Remember also that almost no one walks in a straight line for very far. Thus, the distance you measure on the map is an approximation of the distance you cover orienteering. Still, it is accurate enough that it can be your best friend in finding the control.

The second part of distance estimation by measure and pace is up to you. You must have a good estimate of how far (in meters, because orienteering maps are metric) you have walked or run toward your goal. To do so, you must determine how many steps you take to travel 100 meters. Remember that 100 meters is just a little shorter than the length of a football field plus one end zone. To be exact, 100 meters equals 109 yards, 1 foot, and 1 inch (or for you math experts, 96/100th of an inch).

Determining Your Pace Count for 100 Meters

The easiest way to determine how many paces it takes you to travel 100 meters is to accurately measure 100 meters with a tape measure and then pace it off. Tape measures that are 100 feet (30 m) long are common, but many athletic departments and hardware stores have longer ones for measuring athletic fields. Most tape measures also show meters as well as feet and inches. If not, convert from feet to meters.

Therefore, measure a distance that is 100 meters long and walk it using the double-step counting method. With the double-step counting method, you start with your left foot and count your steps every time your right foot hits the ground (that is, every other step). We use two-step counting because when you walk fast or run, it is hard to count every step. If you are up to 25 paces (a pace is two steps), you would say "twenty" when your left foot hits the ground and "five" when the right hits the ground. It makes the counting easier using two syllables with the two steps. With the single digits you might count "one and two and three and" to get the two syllables. Walk the distance at least twice and then average your count. Notice we use the term *pace count* instead of *step count*. The ancient Roman legions used the term *pace* to mean a measurement from heel to heel with a step in between—exactly what we are proposing. My own measurement comes out to 60 right-foot steps (each right foot step is a full pace) on a level surface such as a road, trail, or sidewalk. So every time I take 60 paces with my right foot on such surfaces, I know I have walked approximately 100 meters and I start counting my paces for the next 100 meters.

But wait, you're not done yet. You do not always walk when you orienteer; often you run. So, now run the same distance on the same surface at least twice and again average your pace count when running. My running pace comes out to about 41 on a smooth and fairly level surface.

Now you have a good way to measure how far you have traveled on a trail, a road, or even a football field. Are you done? No. Much orienteering takes place in the woods, so you also lay out a 100-meter course in the woods to see how much your pace count changes as you dodge trees and go around rocks. And, of course, sometimes you go up or down a hill; therefore, you must determine your pace count under these conditions as well. All of this sounds complicated and difficult. Don't give up. Start with the easy stuff, such as the path or sidewalk, and use that as you begin. Move up to the woods later as you try more difficult orienteering courses.

Learning to count your paces simply takes practice and then it becomes second nature. And, it is extremely useful for informing you that you should be close to the control you seek or perhaps that you have charged by it and need to turn around. Remember, your pace count is an estimate. As with all orienteering skills, the more you practice counting your paces, the more proficient you become at this half of the skill of distance estimation by measure and pace. After many years of estimating distance, some advanced orienteers rely more on how the terrain feels than on their pace count, but that takes lots of practice and it almost never fails except when it does! If you were that orienteer, you

might have won if your estimation had not failed you. So, measure and count! If you don't master distance estimation by measure and pace, you will experience a lot of frustration overrunning and stopping short of controls. Distance estimation by measure and pace is easy to teach and to learn, leading to success and eliminating frustration from going an incorrect distance.

Using the Map to Estimate the Distance You Expect to Travel

Now that you know your pace count for 100 meters, you also need to know the distance that you expect to travel. Every baseplate compass has one or more scales (see figure 4.1), so you simply place one end of the compass scale at your starting point and lay that scale along the line you will travel to the control (see figure 4.2). Don't forget that you must use the scale on the compass that is the same as the scale of the map. If your route is a straight line, you can immediately get a good approximation of how many meters you must travel to get there. If your route is not a straight line, measure shorter distances. For example, if you are curving around a hillside, you can measure and run a series of shorter straight lines to get a good approximation of the distance—but remember, there is a good reason we call this orienteering skill *distance estimation*. It is not exact.

Look at the *compass scale* in figure 4.2. It is a millimeter scale. To convert to centimeters, simply divide by 10 (because 10 mm equal 1 cm). For convenience, orienteering converts millimeters to centimeters.

In figure 4.2, the distance from the control circle on the left front of the compass scale to the control circle in the middle is 30 millimeters (3 cm) and therefore 300 meters. If you are walking, count your 100-meter walking pace three times. You should be close to the control. In other words, if your pace-count of

Use peer instruction. Teachers and coaches, if you have a group for the pacing activity, be sure to pair students off and have them explain to each other what they are doing, why they are doing it, and what the pace counts are. It took us more years than we'd like to admit to figure out that the instructor in front is often unaware that some students are not learning; however, peers know right away. To our delight, we have found that peers are often surprisingly good at teaching each other. If they get it, they can usually explain it to each other. This tip applies in many, many situations.

Figure 4.1 Centimeter scale on a baseplate compass, which is the same as a 1:10,000 scale.

Figure 4.2 The circle on the left is used to draw control locations; the triangle on the right is used to draw start locations. Ten millimeters above (on the mm scale) is 1 centimeter, which is 100 meters on a 1:10,000 scale map.

your right foot hitting the ground is 60 paces per 100 meters, you count to 60 three times to cover the distance. If you have navigated and counted correctly, you should see the control marker. Because sometimes you can see a control marker from 50 meters away or more, glance ahead occasionally to look for it. *Remember in most meets there are other courses in the woods;* therefore, do not be fooled by a control that you can see but which is obviously too close or too far away—seeing another control can pull you off course like a magnet if you are not careful.

How do you keep track of how many times you have paced out 100 meters? It is your choice, but for me, I count any distance over 300 meters on my fingers. I extend my thumb as my pace hits 100 meters, curl my index finger under my thumb for 200, and continue until my little finger signals 500 meters traveled. Then I start on the other hand if necessary, but that is rare. Should you have ranger beads on a string, you simply move one bead down from the top (or up from the bottom) every time you go 100 meters—just be sure to reset back to one end or the other before you start your next count. Don't expect to be exactly at the marker, but you should be close.

One other thought—start your pace over frequently when you know exactly where you are on the map so that you rarely go more than 300 meters before starting again. Why? Because your pace count is an estimate and the more distance covered, the greater the compounding of any errors. Note that if you are constantly coming up short or long, this is useful information for your event that day and you may wish to modify your 100-meter pace count. If your pace count is way off, check the map scale again to be sure the map scale and your compass scale match.

Remember to learn to estimate your pace count under varying conditions: walking on relatively flat ground such as on a trail, running on the same, walking in wooded terrain, and running in the same.

As mentioned, some experienced orienteers can look at the distance between controls and make an accurate guesstimate of the actual distance. How do they do this? Well, an orienteering friend from Colorado who has won numerous orienteering championships trains by using old orienteering maps, picking out a point to leave from and a point to go to and estimating the distance. Then, she checks it with the scale on her compass. In other words, she practices this component of the skill. After years of orienteering, I am fairly good at this, but I always measure unless I can see my destination (such as the finish line). I can measure quickly and I am reassured to have good distance estimations, not guesses. Be aware that guesstimates work until they don't.

Beware of compounding the error. Suppose that your 100-meter pace count is short 5 meters because you are moving over rolling terrain. When you travel 100 meters, you are 5 meters from the control and should see it. After 200 meters, you are 10 meters short and it is more difficult to see. At 300 meters, you are now off a full 15 meters and may not see it at all. So, start your pace count over when you come to a place on the map where you know your location. Being off on your pace count is another reason we teach you to read the terrain and follow along on the map to augment the skill of distance estimation by measure and pace (figure 4.3). You do not rely on a single skill in orienteering.

Finally, repeat all four conditions, but do them going uphill and downhill. Again, pacing sounds difficult and there's a lot to remember, but keep in mind that it is an estimate—it does not have to be perfect, just close. Practice will make pace counting nearly automatic.

Because the recommended pacing calibration is an estimate for 100 meters, when you get beyond several hundred meters, the error factor becomes greater. Therefore, you should restart your pace count when you come to an easily recognizable feature on the ground or on the map, such as a stream, fence, or large boulder. Dividing your route into shorter segments (or legs) provides the excellent benefit of keeping you in contact with the map and the terrain on a more frequent basis, and it will improve the accuracy of your distance estimations.

In the example shown in figure 4.4, I first measure the distance on my map from control number 4 to control number 5 (about 540 meters). (Remember, controls are those orange and white markers that you want to find, and they are marked on the map by a red circle.) Then I measure the distance from where I'm standing at control number 4 to the stream about 240 meters away. I count my paces for the first 200 meters and then expect to come to the stream by the time I am halfway through the third 100 meters of pacing (this is an estimate and I may not run as straight as I'd like). As soon as I have the stream in sight, I measure the distance to the ditch across my line of travel and I start my pace all over again at the stream, knowing I have 300 meters to go to the ditch. This way I do not have to stop and think, "Did I just count 400 meters, or was

Figure 4.3 Procedures for Distance Estimation by Measure and Pace

On the Map

1. Measure the distance on the map using the correct scale.
2. Measure everything, everywhere you intend to go on the map.

On the Ground

1. Use the double-step counting method from a known place. Starting with the left foot, count every time the right foot strikes the ground until you arrive at the destination to which you have measured. Each double step is counted as one pace.
2. Count only when you are moving forward in your direction of travel. If you have to go around an obstacle, do not count the paces that are off course unless there is a chance you may need to retrace your steps (such as coming to an impassable barrier before getting around the obstacle). Then you will want to return to your route and perhaps go around the obstacle in the opposite direction. As soon as you have paced off 100 meters, say "One" to yourself and start pacing the next 100 meters; then softly say "Two." Keep repeating the pacing cycle until you arrive.
3. Having practiced your pace count over a 100-meter course, you should have a 100-meter pace estimate. If you have measured correctly, you will have an idea of how far you need to travel and therefore you should know when to stop moving forward.

the map relationships to know precisely where you are when you get to a certain place. Therefore rough map reading should allow you to move ahead faster than precision map reading.

Precision Map Reading

The compass plays an initial role in precision map reading in that it ensures you are facing in the correct direction with the top of the map pointing north. Once you know your position on the ground and have located that same area on the map, you are ready to move toward your objective, rarely referring to your compass again (if at all). Your task now is to observe features visible both on the ground and on the map in the direction you wish to travel and to use them to guide you.

A map is a sketch frozen in time. Terrain changes through storms, erosion, and the actions of people and machines. Should you come upon some feature in the terrain that is not on your map, your first thought should be "Am I where I think I am?" If there is enough evidence that you are located, then you next consider if the feature might have been changed by natural or manmade events. If the latter, a good map will still take you by or around the change if you navigate carefully because no competent meet director is going to send you into an area on a map with major changes from what is shown. Good maps survive well over time and terrain only changes slightly, so your first thought should be of your own possible error and not that of the map.

In figure 4.6, you are again located in the start triangle and heading to the path junction marked by the circle. Paying close attention to your map, the first ground feature you should notice is the large boulder on your left (the black circle), which, according to the line of travel, you will pass closely. Next you should notice the two dirt (brown) mounds in front of you. Your line of travel will take you directly between them. Each of the features is at a precise location on the map and on the ground; therefore, this is precision map reading. The third feature that is easy to find is the pond, which you will skirt on the right. Finally, if you curve a bit toward the smaller boulder on your right, you should arrive at the path, slightly to the right of the junction. Once at the path you turn left. This route will take you to the path junction. Figure 4.6 illustrates collecting features, a technique that will be presented in chapter 5. The purpose of this map segment is to demonstrate precision map reading. The path junction is not a control but another precise location on the map. As noted

In the 2005 World Trail Orienteering Championships in Japan, American David Irving finished in a tie for the first-place gold medal with Evaldas Butrimas of Lithuania. Both men scored 16 points. However, Evaldas protested a tiny map error on one control that he had scored incorrectly and that David Irving had scored correctly. Meet officials upheld his protest and threw out that control, leaving Evaldas with 16 points and dropping David to 15 and the silver medal (still the highest finish for a U.S. competitor in a world championship). Mr. Butrimas' skill in precision map reading brought him and his country a gold medal that did not have to be shared.

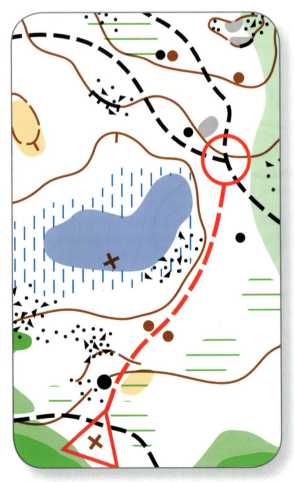

Figure 4.6 Precision map reading involves closely tracking small map details.

you would be wise to approach it slightly to the east and south so that if you came to the trail but could not see the junction, you would only have to turn left or north on the trail to come to it. This technique, aiming off, will be presented in chapter 5.

Rough Map Reading

Rough map reading, like rough compass reading (which is described later), allows you to move quickly because there will be an easily noticeable feature on your line of travel to guide you, stop you, or locate you. Rough compass reading is often used with rough map reading because with both skills, you are navigating without knowing precisely where you are until you reach some definite feature. Of course, you should also be using the skill of distance estimation by measure and pace. Combining these three skills at the correct time can produce amazingly fast movement through the woods. So, check your compass to be sure your map is facing north and you are on the correct side of the map (more on being on the correct side of the map in chapter 6). Now move out in the correct direction.

In the map shown in figure 4.7, you can charge uphill through the woods quickly because you know a large field is not too far ahead in your path. Likewise, so long as you are climbing the hill and not going around it, you will come to the field. Since running a straight line is shorter than drifting too far left or right, rough compass reading complements rough map reading very well. The orienteer in this case veered slightly to go around the small green patch (known as *fight*), which would have been slower running than the white area on the map that is open woods. Regardless, use your compass to be sure you are running approximately north. A quick glance at the map tells you that the field has several features (the two near corners and the small patch of forest growing on the far side) that will help you locate yourself more precisely as soon as you arrive at the field, which should be about 200 meters away (always measure on your map and count your paces). You know it is 200 meters away because you would have been able to measure it on the full map from which this segment was taken. When you reach the field, you will be somewhere in the field or on its edge, so you are using rough map reading until you determine precisely where you are by using either locations one, two, or three, which are precise locations on the map (and which now shifts you to precision map reading). Thus, on this leg you have used four of the five skills: rough map reading, rough compass reading, precision map reading, and distance estimation by measurement and pace.

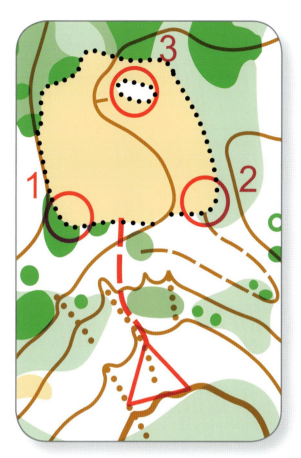

Figure 4.7 Rough map reading involves navigating by larger features, in this case a large field.

Linear Features

Rough map reading is most often used when you have a linear feature that will guide or stop (catch) you when you reach it. When you have a linear feature to catch you, you can run or walk as fast as you can without regard to precisely where you are. Why? Because when you reach the linear feature (e.g., a stream, a trail, or the edge of a field), you can easily locate your position. In figure 4.5 when you were following the stream or running down the path, you did not know precisely where you were, but you knew where you were in relation to the linear feature. For instance, when you had left the stream and not gotten to the hill, you were somewhere on the path, but precisely where you were was not important until you got to the base of the hill and had to leave the path and climb the hill. From the base of the hill to the building on top, it didn't matter where you were on the hill—just that you were on the right hill! And because you knew your pace count for 100 meters, you always knew roughly where you were as you ran along the stream, along the path, and up the hill.

Recall from chapter 3 that a linear feature is any feature that runs in a line, more or less, and only rarely in a straight line. It sounds obvious, but it can take some thought to realize how many features do run in a line. If the line crosses in front of you or if it runs the same way you are going, it can help your rough map reading. Linear features are so useful that they are one of the first features you should look for on maps. A road or path is a linear feature because it starts somewhere, goes somewhere, ends somewhere, and is generally connected together the entire way. Likewise, a stream can be a linear feature, as can a ridge or ravine. Other linear features might include power lines, the edge of a large open field, the edge of a lake, a stone wall, or a fence. When you are using rough map reading and moving fast, these features provide a reference (here we go with relationships again) to a certain or known feature that you can find on the map and on the terrain. They either stop you or guide you in the correct direction, and they help you determine quickly where you are in relation to other features on the terrain. Therefore, you can go fast, checking off those other features as you pass them.

During rough map reading, distance estimation is important, as you might guess. From the example shown in figure 4.8, you would expect to see the path crossing your line of travel in 300 meters. You know this distance because you would have been able to measure it on the map from which this segment was taken. If, in counting your paces, you find that you have gone 350 to 400 meters without crossing the path, then something is wrong. For instance, the path may have been hidden by leaves and you missed it, or you may have made a 180 (see sidebar) and gone in the opposite direction. (Chapter 6 tells you what processes to use when your navigation is not working out.) To avoid the compounding errors introduced earlier in this chapter, use linear features as appropriate to start your pace count all over again. Extending any pace count beyond 400 meters lessens the accuracy because your count is only an estimate. Small errors that won't greatly affect your accuracy over a course of 200 to 300 meters can

turn into large errors that will mislead you at longer distances.

This is a good time to remind you that you normally navigate using several of the five skills at the same time. For instance, in the previous example, you found that rough map reading is often combined with rough compass reading since both rough skills emphasize speed over knowing precisely where you are. Also remember that one of the combined skills will always be distance estimation. Now let's cover precision compass reading.

Figure 4.8 Distance estimation is important for rough map reading.

 If the features you pass are not matching the features you expected to see from the map, you may have gotten turned around and made the dreaded 180 mistake, named for running 180 degrees off from the direction you planned to go (in other words, in exactly the opposite direction). Everyone makes a 180 sooner or later, and it is just a matter of recognizing it and recovering from it. Recovering from a 180 is covered in the skill of precision compass reading, which follows shortly.

PRECISION COMPASS READING

Precision compass reading uses the direction-of-travel arrow on the compass (see chapter 3) to travel as precisely in a straight line as you can. The standard method for following a direct compass heading is to use your direction-of-travel arrow to show you precisely where you should go. Then pick out an object, such as a tree or big rock, that is directly in line with the direction and walk or run to that object. At that point, you pick a second object, line it up, and go to it. Theoretically, if you execute the method perfectly, you will follow a straight line to your end objective (the control marker), and by measuring on the map and counting your paces, you will know almost exactly when the control should appear. However, recall that your compass is a 3-degree instrument, meaning it could be pointing up to 3 degrees left or right. This 3-degree error puts a definite limitation on the distance for which you can use the skill of precision compass reading. For orienteering purposes, you should never try to go more than 450 meters using precision compass reading. The exception to this rule is if you are in a flat area with nearly unlimited visibility, but that rarely occurs in orienteering.

Your orienteering compass will point in the right direction if it is set up correctly, so you won't need to read the actual degrees—just follow the direction-of-travel arrow. On the other hand, the lensatic compass, described in chapter 3, gives an exact degree heading when you look through it, but it also is only accurate to within 3 degrees. Regardless, anyone who finds the desired control over those distances of 2,200 meters (see sidebar) is either darned lucky or is using skills in addition to precision compass reading and distance estimation.

ROUGH COMPASS READING

Rough compass reading generally follows the five steps described for precision compass reading except for what is in front of the direction-of-travel arrow. In rough compass reading, you do not precisely line up a tree or boulder but instead move in the general direction that the direction-of-travel arrow is pointing. By the way, trying to point the compass and go is a common mistake of beginners who think they are doing precision compass reading. It is also the reason dead reckoning is rarely precise. Instead, just pointing the compass and going (without lining up on an object in front of you) is using rough compass reading. Rough compass reading is used most often when you have a large or linear

---

Terrain Association

The military often teaches what it calls *land navigation*, or dead reckoning, using precision compass and distance estimation with insufficient emphasis on being able to associate the terrain you see as you cross the ground with the symbols you see printed on the map. Associating the terrain with the map symbols is logically called *terrain association*. This is an orienteering process described in chapter 6. I once witnessed soldiers at Fort Benning, Georgia, following azimuths and counting paces to find painted stakes during an eight-hour exercise. Some of the stakes were more than 1,000 meters apart, and even worse, the soldiers were not given a map as part of the exercise! As mentioned previously, this is a terrible way to navigate for distances in excess of 450 meters, yet I have seen instructions that tasked the student with following an azimuth of so many degrees for 2,200 meters!

Charles Ferguson and Coach Turbyfill are former military members who are strongly supportive of the military services. However, we would both love to see orienteering come back into military land navigation training, as it existed years ago. To paraphrase the quote from USMC Major James R. Hardin in chapter 1, which is still so true today: "What do civilian orienteers know that the military doesn't?" Major Hardin, Major Ray Velasquez, and Lieutenant Colonel Robert Thompson were instrumental in introducing orienteering into the Marine Corps. Because the Marines had a team, Army orienteering teams began at the Army Engineering School, then at Fort Belvoir, Virginia, and at the Home of the Infantry, Fort Benning, Georgia. So, at one time in orienteering history, the military was far ahead of the civilian community in orienteering. Today, the reverse is true.

One of my orienteering friends, a U.S. Marine, told me of her experiences in USMC's The Basic School (TBS), which all Marine officers must complete. To graduate from TBS, each student must pass the land navigation curriculum. My friend's instructions were to follow pace and azimuth to each control. I asked how that worked for her and she commented that she might have cheated! Knowing her high personal honor code, I asked how she cheated. (In actuality, other Marines have assured me that her technique was not cheating, but at the time she did not know that the training objective was to use your head, which she so ably did, versus blindly following a set of rules.) She told me that she figured out that the instructors, being human, might just drive as close to the control that they were setting as possible, park their Hummer, and walk in to place the control marker the students had to find. Therefore, she studied her map looking for any roads that ran within 200 meters of the control she sought. In every case there was a road nearby and an obvious parking location from which to walk in 200 meters and place the control marker. Therefore, she simply ran to the roads and then to the obvious location from which to walk in and set the controls. At that location, she then reverted to precision compass and distance estimation and followed her compass and her step count for 200 meters. She found all of the controls with ease.

To an orienteer, she was simply using rough map reading to find the correct road and precision map reading to locate the obvious attack point from which to use precision compass reading to hit the control dead on. The skill of precision compass reading is often used to get you from an easy-to-find feature, called an *attack point* (see chapter 5), to the control from a short distance away. Marines are taught both to obey orders and to think for themselves, so her instructors were pleased that she had built upon her prior training to figure out her procedure for herself. Self-learning tends to be permanent and repeatable whereas classroom instruction can be totally lost in 30 days or less if it is not used right away. Cheating would have been to use someone else's work to find those controls, but she found them all herself by using what she had been taught and what she could figure out. Know also that USMC land navigation today is far beyond just pace and azimuth.

feature in front of you that is going to locate you more precisely when you get there. In rough compass reading, it is less important to keep the magnetic needle exactly on top of the north magnetic orienting arrow. Why? The feature toward which you are running is so specific that it will not matter if you drift a little left or right. Since you are probably heading toward a certain target (e.g., a linear feature such as a river), you do not have to be exact because as long as you are moving in the correct direction, the river is going to get in your way whether you are a little left or right. However, the more you let the magnetic needle drift off the north magnetic orienting arrow, the more energy you will waste and the more time you will lose, so keep it close if not exactly superimposed.

In the map shown in figure 4.9, which is a continuation of figure 4.8, you know that you can run as fast as you can (remember, always keep up with your pace) until you run into the road that passes across your line of travel directly in front of you. Once you reach the road, you will be able to locate yourself based on the two curves, and you can navigate more carefully from there. Skillfully following a rough compass reading should put you somewhere near the middle of the road between the curves, but the red dots illustrate that if you arrive anywhere within the red dots from left to right, you will be able to locate where you are on the road. What is to stop you from drifting too far to the right? Although you are using rough compass reading to run fast, you never knowingly lose contact with the map (rough map reading), so you should notice the green on your right which is medium "fight" (underbrush that slows you down to at least a walk). Or, not long after you pass the trail, you will notice the ground going up several contours when you should contact the road before it gets that steep. Why aren't you worried about drifting too far left? Because the road swings down to your left and you will come to it eventually. If you have kept up with your pace you will know if you have gotten to the road somewhere between the two curves (also, you should be able to see one or both curves). So, you have lots of indicators from your skills to make sure you stay on course.

Figure 4.9 Rough compass reading is useful when you don't need to be precise to hit your target.

Rough compass reading is a useful backup check for three of the other skills. Which one is left out? Precision compass, of course! Most good orienteers will glance at their compasses on a regular basis to be sure they are not drifting too far left or right and to avoid the dreaded 180 described in chapter 3. They are practicing the skill of rough compass reading.

ORIENTING THE MAP

How, then, do we use the map? We have already mentioned the skills of rough and precision map reading, so how do you begin so that you can use them? Your first task is to orient the map. (Orienting the map is one of the five processes covered in chapter 6.) There are two steps to orienting the map. The first is to determine where north is on the map. It should be at the top.

Also, if north is at the top, all numbers and printing on the map should read left to right as in a book. The only maps this author has encountered where north was not at the top were locally made maps such as tourist maps, rarely used in orienteering. (On the other hand, my wife and I set up a simple military orienteering competition in Oberammergau, Germany, with the only map we could find on short notice—the local tourist map. It worked quite well.)

The second step is to hold the map with the top always pointed to the north (use your compass and apply rough compass reading to find north). Remember north is not up in the sky, so hold the map parallel to the ground. Then, keeping your north-oriented map absolutely still, move your body around the map until you are facing in the direction you want to go. Be aware that your natural tendency is to stand still and rotate the map. Doing so will get you in trouble. By rotating your body around the map and keeping the map oriented to north, the terrain features will appear in the correct positions as you move across the ground. Further help for orienting the map is in chapter 6.

In figure 4.10, suppose you wish to travel directly east to the next control on your map. Simply move your body around the map so that you are standing on the west side of the map. The map still points north and you now are facing east. As you move forward toward the control, you should see the same things on

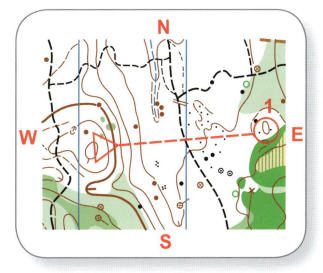

Figure 4.10 To orient the map properly for map navigation, turn this map 90° counterclockwise, so that you stand on the west side. The map demonstrates how the control number shows you north when the map is folded.

the ground in the same relationship that you see on the map. Imagine that you are standing on the east side of the hill (the triangle marks where you start) when you begin. You should notice that according to the map, you are to move downhill immediately. If you find yourself moving uphill instead, stop! You may have the map pointed south instead of north, or you may have positioned yourself on the east side of the map instead of the west, or you may not be in the start triangle. In this way, correctly orienting the map and your body will help you go in the correct direction every time.

PUTTING THE SKILLS TOGETHER

This section contains some examples showing how to use the five navigational skills. Remember that on most orienteering routes, several or all five of the orienteering skills will be used. Beware of overly depending on one or two of the skills simply because you do them well. Using all of the skills in the correct situations will increase your speed and accuracy.

Precision map reading is much like precision compass reading in that it is done more carefully and therefore is somewhat slower than rough map reading (although it can be done at speed). However, there is one big difference: You should not attempt precision compass reading for more than 450 meters (and that far only if there is no other choice), whereas you can use precision map reading (or rough map reading) for any distance on your map. Remember, however, that precision map reading is slower than rough map reading. The compass plays an initial role in all map reading in that it ensures you are facing in the correct direction with the top of the map pointed to the north. Once you know your position on the ground and have located that same area on the map, you are ready to move forward toward your objective, rarely referring to your compass again (if at all). Your task now is to observe features visible both on the ground and on the map in the direction you wish to travel and use them to guide you. Because precision map reading is generally slower, we use sprint orienteering to speed up and hone our precision map reading skills and for the much slower paced trail orienteering events.

SUMMARY

To help you navigate, chapter 4 adds the five orienteering skills to your understanding and use of the map and compass from chapter 3. Those five skills presented with examples of each are precision map reading, rough map reading, precision compass reading, rough compass reading, and distance estimation by measure and pace. This last skill should be used every time you orienteer, usually in concert with one or all of the other skills. Almost a third of the chapter spelled out the importance of determining, using, and knowing your pace count so that what you measure on the map will correspond closely to the distance you cover on the ground. To quote Coach Turbyfill, "Those who do not measure everything will count their lost time in minutes. Those who measure everything correctly and apply the information properly will count their lost time in seconds." "Lost time" here does not mean you do not know where you are; it means you waste valuable time going in the wrong direction or having to redetermine your position because you were careless about how far you needed to go to reach the control or some intermediate objective such as a road or stream. Chapter 5 will introduce the tried-and-true techniques to support the five skills.

Techniques

The first three chapters gave a short history of orienteering, discussed preparations to orienteer from gear to fitness, and introduced the orienteering map and compass. Chapter 4 described the skills of orienteering and their relationship to the map and compass. You might think of the skills as the performance proficiencies that you discipline your body to perfect: the tighter your skills, the better your performance. If so, chapter 5 presents the actual tactics of using the orienteering techniques that make your skills work for you.

By the way, even if you never intend to orienteer, you can use the skills as they apply to the techniques to find your way in a variety of tasks that you may never have thought of as navigation. For example, you and your family are driving down the interstate highway when traffic suddenly stops, then inches along, and lurches to a halt again. Unfortunately, you left your GPS unit at home. Luckily, you picked up a state highway map at the last rest stop, and up ahead you see an exit. Can you use precision map reading to find another linear feature (parallel highway) that will get you past the interstate stoppage and use distance estimation by measurement and pace (the speedometer) to make sure you don't miss your turns? Or, are you stuck like all the other sheep, too timid to leave the interstate for the unknown local highway system? Well, if you master the techniques given in this chapter and add them to the orienteering skills, you can take those other roads to bypass the trouble. You can sail home in comfort and confidence while the other sheep just complain and remain stuck in traffic.

Chapter 5 covers the five orienteering techniques that you should master in order to do well at orienteering and other navigation. These techniques are the foundation of good navigation with map and compass.

The five orienteering techniques are as follows:

1. Finding attack points

2. Aiming off

3. Collecting features by thumbing along

4. Catching features

5. Following handrails

The five techniques are associated with specific orienteering skills. As you recall, the five orienteering skills are precision map reading, rough map reading, precision compass reading, rough compass reading, and distance estimation by measure and pace. These orienteering techniques evolved over long years of practicing, teaching, and coaching orienteering and learning from others. The techniques are thought processes (or plans) to use the terrain as you see it on the map while using your orienteering skills appropriately. They are listed in no particular order of priority except for the first, which should always be used on every leg of every course, just as you should use the skill of distance estimation by measure and pace on every leg of every course.

FINDING ATTACK POINTS

An attack point is the closest feature to the control that you know you can find and from which you can then find the harder-to-locate control. Using attack points is the most important technique that you will ever use in any form of land navigation. You must be able to clearly identify the attack point on the map and on the terrain. Because the attack point is something you know without any doubt that you personally can find, it may not be the same for everyone. It is the last thing you expect to locate before your final approach to your destination. Every leg of the course has an attack point. On a short leg, it may be that you will make your final approach from your current control, in which case the control you are leaving has become your attack point. On a longer leg, you may aim for an intermediate destination such as the edge of a pond. That location becomes your attack point for the control.

In an earlier example from the land navigation training at the Marine Corps TBS, the student guessed where the instructors would logically park their Hummer to walk into the woods to the control location. Noting that there were drivable roads and a close location from which the instructors would know exactly where to start for the control, she would run to that easy-to-find location, not knowing that such a location is called an *attack point*.

As noted, it is difficult to follow a straight line in precision compass reading for very far. Remember also that for any distance over 450 meters, precision compass reading is practically impossible unless you are crossing an open field and can steer to a visible object that far away. Therefore, it makes sense to locate an attack point, preferably within 200 meters of the control, and then move, using the fastest possible approach (usually the appropriate rough skills) to arrive at that attack point, where you switch to one of the two precision

Clearly marked on the map, the opening in the wall is used as an attack point.

skills. Using distance estimation by measure and pace the whole way will also keep you from making errors.

What are some attributes of good attack points? First, they have to be easier to find than the control itself. Second, they should not take you too far out of the way. Third, they should be quicker to locate than the control. Fourth, they must be readily identifiable. And fifth, when you reach the attack point, you must know you are there.

Attack points are often much larger features than the control. In the TBS example, the student used either a crossroads or an intersection of one road into another. These are large and generally easy to see on the map and on the ground. The corner of a lake or a pond often shows well on the ground and the map, as does a readily identifiable field, making all three good attack points. Again, be alert if there are a number of ponds or fields close by so that you do not assume you are at one field or pond when you are at another. The dreaded parallel error (see the sidebar) probably torments orienteers more than the dreaded 180-degree error (see chapter 4). Keeping the map oriented to the terrain and perfecting the skill of distance estimation are key to avoiding a parallel error.

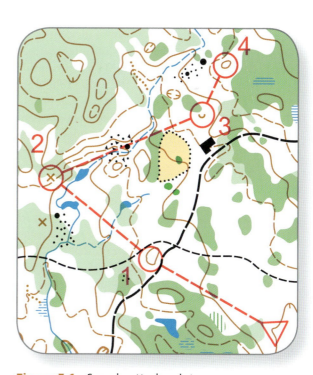

Figure 5.1 Sample attack points.

Parallel Errors

The term *parallel error* refers to mistaking one landform or object for another, usually with one that is nearby. A common parallel error is to look for the control by going up or down one spur that parallels a nearby spur when the control is actually on the other feature. In other words you are searching the wrong spur. You should be on the one beside it. Making a parallel error because I hurried too much has knocked me out of first place more than once. Parallel errors can occur with almost any nearby linear features or with nonlinear features that are similar (from cliffs to boulders to human-made features such as cabins at a park). The features simply need to be close enough and similar enough so that you are at one but think you are at the other.

It is worth repeating that the best way to avoid a parallel error is to be sure the map is oriented to the north and that your body is on the far side of the map from your direction of travel. In this manner, the terrain or human-made features will appear in the proper sequence as you move forward, and something as simple as counting each similar feature will help avoid a parallel error. Whenever possible, approach parallel linear features, such as ditches, from the side so that you may easily count them as well. At one event I came straight down a hill from my attack point trying to dead reckon my route to hit the middle ditch of three ditches. Because all the ditches flowed in the same direction as I was running, I did not see the first ditch. As soon as I saw the second ditch, I assumed it was the first and immediately turned left to the third ditch thinking it was the middle ditch. I lost a lot of time when it would have been easy to use the skill of rough compass reading to aim a little right, measure my distance by pacing, and cut across the ditches, counting them successfully by approaching from the side.

In going from the start triangle in figure 5.1 to the first control, an obvious, fast, and easy-to-find attack point is the path junction to the east of the control. In this map the dashed red line simply connects the controls; it does not show your route. My preferred route would be to run at an angle to the path on my right and then move as fast as I could to the path junction, which would be my attack point. Experienced orienteers might use the small hill upon whose edge the control is located as their attack point. Going from control 1 to control 2, the northeast corner of the westernmost pond is an excellent attack point. On the other hand, note the possibility of a parallel error if you are actually at the other pond to the north while thinking you are at the southern pond. Proper distance estimation helps to prevent any parallel error with the third pond, which is much too close to control 1. Navigating from control 2 to 3, you have a choice of attack points, either the edge of the field, the pronounced bend in the stream, or if you wish to get closer, the building beside the trail. None is particularly better than the others; they simply illustrate that you may have several choices for an attack point—just pick one and go.

What is the attack point from control 3 to control 4? If you used the skill of distance estimation and you learn that control 4 is only 135 meters from control 3,

you can use control 3 as your attack point and follow a compass heading to control 4. Remember, control 3 is easy to find (you are already there!), and it is a short enough distance to use precision compass reading. If you thought you had to have another attack point such as the large boulder to the east of point 4, at least you have the process down cold. Just don't forget that your attack point should not take you too far away from the control you are trying to find, and in this case the small hilltop may be easier to locate than the large boulder.

To sum up, the technique of finding an attack point requires the orienteer to find a more easily locatable place (or point) from which to attack the control. It must be easier to find than the control, not too far out of the way, and readily identifiable on the map and on the ground. Remember also that the best attack point may be behind the control, forcing you to run a little farther but insuring that you find the control quickly. You should always select an attack point. Some orienteers eschew using an attack point for each control, but as with distance estimation and other skills, techniques, and processes, we can say, "That works for those orienteers—until it doesn't!" In other words, orienteer correctly and it will serve you well. Get sloppy and you may get away with it for a while, but bad practices will eventually betray you.

AIMING OFF

The technique of aiming off is exactly as it sounds. It is useful if there is a linear feature crossing your path, and it is even more useful if the control is located in or on the linear feature. While using the skill of rough compass reading, you deliberately travel to one side or the other of the control toward a linear feature. If you deliberately head to the right of the control, when you hit the linear feature you know that you need to turn left to find the control. You can aim off by setting your compass direction arrow slightly to the right or left of your control and go in that direction. Aiming off is helpful because if you go straight at the control and don't see it when you hit the linear feature, you don't know which way to turn. If you deliberately head to the right of your control, you know that you have to turn left when you get there.

In figure 5.2, you know that the control is located in the bend in the stream. If you try to run directly toward the control location and don't see it upon arriving at the stream, you do not know if you are to the left or to the right of the control, and you may lose valuable time searching in the incorrect direction. However, if

you aim off to the right, you can immediately turn left upon arriving at the stream and move quickly to the control. In this example you could also aim off to the left—just remember to turn right at the stream.

Why can't you run straight to the control? If you like to gamble, you can, but remember that luck is not a strategy. First of all, if you are using your compass, it is a 3-degree instrument, meaning that it has a built-in error that may put you left or right. Second, and probably more important, most people drift either left or right, as discussed earlier. Unfortunately, although most orienteers have a predominant drift, they do not have a perfectly consistent drift. So although you may drift to the left most of the time, you will drift to the right at least occasionally. Consequently, drifting is not an acceptable strategy for knowing where you are when you get to the stream; you must aim off to be certain.

Are there guidelines on whether to aim off to one side or the other? Yes. Look at figure 5.3, and let's get a bit technical. If the axis of the feature is nearly perpendicular to your line of travel (so that your path and the linear feature meet in a perfect *T* with your path being the shaft of the *T*), you should play to your predominant drift and aim in that direction. Otherwise your drift may overcompensate for your aiming off enough

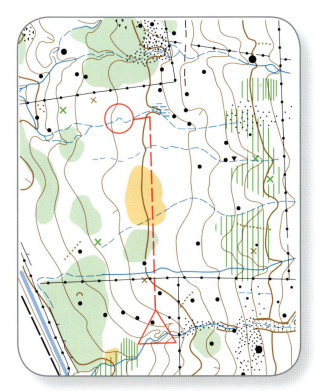

Figure 5.2 Example of aiming off.

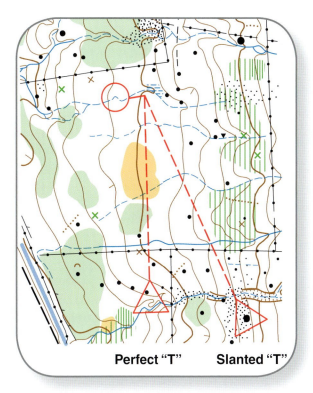

Perfect "T"   **Slanted "T"**

Figure 5.3 Example of the perfect *T* and the slanted *T*.

Before I learned the technique of aiming off, I tried to use precision compass reading to go to every control. I had never heard of precision compass reading, so I called my method *dead reckoning*. I had been assured by any number of land navigation instructors that dead reckoning would work over any distance—even well beyond 450 meters.

In England in my first international competition as the orienteer for my three-person team, the third control was located just beyond a power line and in the edge of the woods. What is nice about having a control on a power line is that the power company usually cuts the underbrush under the lines, making an obvious linear feature that can be used as a handrail or a catching feature, and the poles and angle corners in the line can be used as attack points. Such a trimmed or mowed linear open area is called a *ride*. The power-line ride ran across our route at a 90-degree angle as we ran from control 2 to control 3. It would have been so easy to aim off to the left (which was slightly uphill) and then to look for the control while running downhill in the ride. The open area made for easy running and clear visibility into the woods, but I had never heard of aiming off, so I was using dead reckoning. As I came out of the woods on the west side of the ride and saw the open area and then the woods on the east side of the ride, my heart fell, as did any confidence. I had no idea if the third control was directly ahead of me or to my left or right. I immediately envisioned a frustrating search on one side or the other of the control, probably in the wrong direction (I did know about Murphy's Law) and costing my team a great deal of lost time. In this case we experienced a happy ending, which is a violation of Murphy's Law. Just before I admitted my mistake to my teammates, the British soldier who sat hidden by the control stood up to light a cigarette, clearly marking the control. Yes, unbelievably, it was directly in front of me. This rarely successful orienteering method is called *dumb luck*.

to place you on the wrong side of the control anyway. You will then go in the wrong direction to look for the control on the linear feature. If the linear feature is not perpendicular to your axis of advance (your path is the shaft of the *T*, which now has a slanted top), you should aim off in the direction that takes you to the linear feature the fastest so that you can use that linear feature as a handrail (again see figure 5.3, slanted "T"). Using handrails is the last technique in this chapter. The technique for the slanted *T* if your drift is right is the same as the perfect *T*. A recommended course of action for the slanted *T* may not be to go to the side of your drift but to overcompensate by aiming off further to the right to ensure you travel the shortest distance. However, if your left drift is pronounced and you are uncomfortable aiming off to the right, go with it—hit the stream and come back to the right. Remember, it is acceptable to go past a control and come back to it if that is the faster route for you.

In all cases, the point is to use the linear feature to your advantage by setting yourself up to know where you are in relation both to the linear feature and to your destination. Remember, orienteering and other navigation are relationship activities. Where you are at

any given moment in relation to the features on the terrain is dependent upon how you associate those relationships as you maneuver in that terrain. Understanding the relationships is how you know where you are on the ground and on the map.

COLLECTING FEATURES BY THUMBING ALONG

The technique of collecting features as you move across the map (in your mind) and on the ground (with your eyes) is critical to the skills of rough and precision map reading. The features you collect are the significant features on the map and on the ground that are near enough to your route that you will observe (or collect) them as you approach and pass by them (see figure 5.4). There are at least eight possible features to collect, beginning with the rootstock (the brown "X") in the center of the triangle. A rootstock exists when a tree falls over and its roots are pulled out of the ground and protrude into the air. Rootstocks are not usually

Thumbing Along as You "Collect" Features

In actuality, this is only a 160m leg in open white woods. But what if these features were spread out over an 800m leg? Then you would be passing this series of features spread 100m apart. They could keep you on course, confirming that you are, in fact, exactly where you think you are, and alert you when you're nearing the control.

So keep moving your thumb on your folded map to your new location as you move through the terrain.

1. **Traveling in the correct direction you should immediately cross a trail (perpendicularly) with undergrowth on your right...**

2. **Then to a large boulder (is it on your left or right?) with a small patch of rough open with thicker growth on your right...**

3. **Then you're traveling down a small hillside with a broad spur on your left with a boulder field spilling downhill...**

4. **Passing between (or to the right or left?) of two dot knolls, you start approaching a broad shallow hollow to your left and in it is...**

5. **An indistinct pond with surrounding marsh, even a rootstock visible at the edge of the pond, and as you near the pond you see...**

6. **A field of boulders and stones just downhill on your left...**

7. **Then past a smaller boulder to your right...**

8. **And as you near the control, a trail comes up on a diagonal to your right, and you can see an uphill climb just past the trail junction where the flag is located. Congratulations!**

Figure 5.4 Sample for collecting features.

mapped unless the roots are at least a meter high. In figure 5.4, the boulder (2), the rock field (3), and the dirt mounds (4) are some of the eight features you may notice as you pass them. As soon as you positively identify a feature, you move your thumb up to that feature on the map. In other words, you are thumbing along, which is how to do the technique of collecting features.

How do you keep track of those features that you are collecting as you move through the terrain? Do you memorize them? Write them down? No, you simply place the leading edge of your thumb on the map symbol as you pass by the actual feature on the ground. Leave your thumb on that place on the map until you collect your next feature, at which point you move your thumb to the new feature. By the way, you should fold your map once or twice so that you can easily see your entire route. Proper map folding facilitates thumbing along. (More on folding your map is in chapter 9.)

Thumbing along is neither a skill nor a technique. It is the *how-to* associated with collecting features. It is a how-to because it has no value unless associated with collecting features. In other words, you don't thumb along just to hold onto the map (although that's good, too). The concept is simple but highly useful. To repeat: As you move along your route, move your thumb along with your progress every time you are absolutely sure

Distinct map features are used to thumb along the route to the control. Note the properly folded map.

of where you are (for example, when you come to a trail junction or a path and stream intersection that you clearly recognize). At the beginning of the race, put your thumb on the start triangle as you begin to move out along your course. The value of thumbing along is that it allows you to keep up with where you are on the map and the ground. More importantly, if you suddenly realize that you have gotten off your route and you do not quickly recognize where you are, looking down at your thumb on the map will reveal where you last knew where you were. At this point you generally are not far from that location. Do not move your thumb so that you can recover by going back to that known location.

How do you recover? If you were following a compass azimuth, you simply do a back azimuth (see chapter 3) or turn around and return to the last place that you definitely knew where you were, as carefully marked by your thumb. If you were following terrain features, you can apply the relocation process, fully explained later in the next chapter. Think of your thumb as it keeps your place in a book when you have to close it for a moment; likewise, your thumb keeps

your place on the map. The skill associated with collecting features by thumbing along is precision map reading, but you may well switch to another skill such as precision compass reading from the location indicated by your thumb (as, for example, if your thumb is at your attack point) or rough map reading if you are moving quickly using another technique such as a collecting feature. Regardless, your thumb at your last known location is your firm navigational foundation until you move it to the next known location.

Almost as soon as you leave the start in figure 5.4 (with your thumb at the edge of the start triangle) and cross the trail, you should notice the large boulder on your left. Why is this useful considering that you should know exactly where you are at the start? It reassures you that you are indeed heading in the correct direction and have not made a 180. If visibility through the terrain is good, you may choose to use rough compass reading, rough map reading, or both (I almost always use rough compass to be sure I start in the correct direction) to begin your route to control 1. Almost immediately you switch to precision map reading as you collect, or tick off by moving your thumb, the following features: the large boulder (were you to the left or right?) and the two dot knolls. Because these are distinct and you know precisely where you are when you pass each of them, you should move your thumb to each of them as you go by. Once you pass the dot knolls, you should see the pond to your left and the rootstock (the brown "X") on its edge. Then you pass a field of boulders and a smaller boulder to your right. Finally, just past the boulder you should see the path coming up on your right. With each distinct feature you move your thumb up to that feature on the map to indicate where you were last located.

How do you know that the collecting feature you see on the ground is the one on the map? This is an excellent question because similar collecting features can run in groups and be close together—perfect opportunities for the unwary to make parallel errors, as discussed earlier. The first step is to orient your map to the terrain and keep it oriented as you move across the ground so that you come to the terrain features in the order that they appear on the map. The second step is to maintain the accuracy of your distance estimation by frequently starting your count over as you pass a clearly identifiable feature (I try to restart my pace counting every 300 meters or less—see what works for you). The third step is to identify clearly what feature you are looking for (your clue sheet will tell you; see chapter 9), and be sure each feature you have selected appears in the correct sequence. If a feature appears to be out of sequence, check your compass. Have you done a 180? Are you going in the opposite direction from your intended route? Might you have mistaken one feature for another and made a parallel error?

Features that you can collect are useful as you traverse your route, but there is another useful technique to help keep you from running by the control: catching features. Unfortunately, not every control has such a feature, but when it exists, use it to speed up your approach.

CATCHING FEATURES

Catching features are any features that stop you from going too far past the control. They are like the arrestor cable on an aircraft carrier: They catch or stop you from continuing well past the control, just as the arrestor cable stops the aircraft from going too far and falling off the bow of the moving aircraft carrier. When you are using the technique of catching features, look for linear features and the slope of the ground as excellent signals that you have passed the control. In other words, if there is a stream or path (or any linear feature) directly behind the control and running across your route, and you come to that feature without having found the control, the linear feature will catch you, much like a safety net. You now know to turn around and search for the control behind you.

The slope of the land can also be a catching feature. If the control is on a hilltop and you find yourself crossing the top of the hill and starting down the far side, you have either gone too far or you are on the wrong hilltop (a parallel error). Likewise, if your map tells you that the land starts going up on the far side of the control and your pace count tells you that you are close to the control, when you start to climb up, that upward slope is your catching feature, telling you that you have gone too far. Another catching feature is obviously your distance estimation. Your 100-meter pace count may be off by 10 percent due to the rise and fall of the land, but if you have gone twice as far as you should, you have undoubtedly passed the control.

Finally, an unexpected catching feature for most of us is to reach another control that is after the control you are seeking (see figure 5.5). This is usually a surprise because of poor distance estimation, but at least you know where you are on the map (all controls are numbered or lettered as indicated on your clue sheet;

see chapter 9). You can now use this more distant control as both a catching feature and an attack point. Turn back toward the control you missed and navigate more carefully! In figure 5.5 there are a number of catching features. The red dots indicate possible routes of travel. On the far left, the first catching feature is the double stream junction where the stream splits into two streams. It is a catching feature because it is unique to this part of the map. It could now be turned into an attack point. This unique feature should have alerted the orienteer to his exact location, but unfortunately he went on northwest until bumping into the stone wall which is a perfect catching feature. Orienteers 2, 3, and 4 started out on a near identical route and then split along the way. Orienteer 2 went to the left, crossed the stream, and encountered the stone wall where she had the same predicament as orienteer 1. (Did orienteer 2 drift right or left of the control?) Orienteer 1 should know he is to the left based on the stream feature, but since he continued on to the wall versus turning right on the stream, his orienteering skills are somewhat suspect. Orienteer 3 wandered right into control 3 (a perfect catching feature), read the control identifier code,

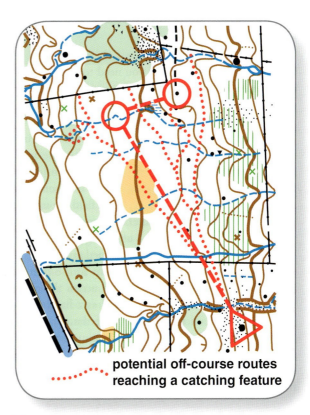

**potential off-course routes
reaching a catching feature**

Figure 5.5 Sample catching features, including a control past a control.

Many years after the experience in England, I taught orienteering to a number of Army land navigation instructors. Because of their strong reliance on pace and azimuth, I worked hard to get them to read the map, to use all the skills, and to use such techniques as linear features and aiming off. On the second day of training we gave them a course where the first control was a large rock and the second was a reentrant (small gully) intersecting a stream. The stream ran from left to right directly across any logical path to that second control. In between the two controls was a horrible mess of intersecting trails that ran in every direction except toward control 2. The obvious technique was to use the compass to aim off along with the skill of distance estimation by measurement and pacing.

Because the instructors all excelled in the Army's pace and azimuth technique, which combines precision compass reading and the pacing portion of distance estimation, I assumed they would aim off to the left (there were obvious terrain problems with aiming to the right), run quickly to the stream, turn right, run down the stream to the reentrant–stream intersection, and reach the control in record time. However, Murphy saw a chance to show up the teacher and jumped right in. Because I had so strongly urged them to read the map and use linear features, every single competitor tried to read and use the complex trail network between the two controls. Absolutely no one was able to find control 2 within any reasonable time. The lesson here for the teacher, coach, or instructor is to be careful what you ask for—you may get exactly that. My strong emphasis on using other methods of finding the control failed to communicate that you use the best technique or combination of techniques for any particular route—in this case aiming off and pacing. Instead, my students heard, "Do not use pace and azimuth (pacing and precision compass reading). Read the terrain." In other words, I failed to communicate a complete message.

reading, facilitating faster movement over the terrain. Whenever handrails are readily available, seriously consider using them if they are close to your route or if you have to cover a lot of distance between two controls.

USING THE TECHNIQUES WITH THE SKILLS

Throughout this chapter, the techniques have been associated with some or all of the five orienteering skills. Table 5.1 maps the full range of where they match up. Note that all of the five skills can be used with the attack point technique and that the skill of distance estimation by measure and pace is used with all five techniques. Let's think about the relationships in table 5.1. There is a reason why catching features are not normally used with precision map reading— if you are correctly using precision map reading, you should go directly to the control based on your accurate reading of the map and your distance estimation;

therefore, there will be no need to use the technique of catching features. The technique of collecting features is not normally used with precision or rough compass reading because collecting features uses the map whereas compass reading uses the compass (however, frequently glance at the map even when using the compass techniques—the compass tells where you are heading; the map tells where you are). Aiming off is associated with the skill of rough compass reading, and following handrails is associated with rough map reading (but remember to check the direction of the linear feature with your compass to avoid a parallel error or a 180).

TEACHING TIPS

To train or teach the attack point technique, use a large linear feature such as an open field, parking lot, or lake and place a control out of sight but within 100 meters of a corner. The objective is to run as fast as you can using rough map reading or rough compass reading to the attack point (remember to start with a distinct attack point) and then use its well-defined edge to go

Table 5.1   Techniques and Associated Skills

	Precision map reading	Rough map reading	Precision compass reading	Rough compass reading	Distance estimation by measure and pace
Finding attack points	X	X	X	X	X
Aiming off				X	X
Collecting features	X	X			X
Catching features		X			X
Following handrails		X			X

Reprinted from Coach Bob Turbyfill from the OUSA course: *Zero to Orange in Three Days.*

a short leg using precision compass or precision map reading to the control. By using that edge, you are also following a handrail. That same feature can be used to practice aiming off by placing the control on one end of the feature. Power lines, creeks, and paths are great props to practice handrails and aiming off (if aiming off will help you get to the linear feature faster). Using collecting features is best introduced during a map walk, where care is taken to keep the map oriented and note the features as they appear in the correct sequence. The features are observed and marked by thumbing along. Later this exercise can be done on the run. Revisit your handrails and place the control just before the handrail so that the handrail is now a catching or stopping feature. As you can see, you can practice the techniques in a fairly small area and often you can use the same feature to practice two or more techniques. Start slow and work up to running as fast as you can while still staying in control of where you are or where you are going.

techniques will make you a much better orienteer than anyone who simply blunders through the woods in an Easter egg hunt. Mastering these techniques and coupling them with the appropriate skills (plus being fit) will just about assure you a high finish in any orienteering event with your peers. The techniques of using attack points and handrails are of particular value as you first venture across unfamiliar terrain.

As with any other sport, merely knowing the techniques and when to use them is not good enough. You must practice using them in competitive conditions until they become second nature. Beware of overusing just one or two of the other techniques besides attack points, such as aiming off or collecting features. Becoming overly dependent on one or two techniques works just fine, until it doesn't. I have a friend who is a master at aiming off and uses it for every control. He eventually finds all of his controls, but he never wins. You want to win.

SUMMARY

Chapter 5 has emphasized that the five techniques are the methods used to apply the five skills. Likewise you have learned of the dreaded parallel error and three ways to avoid it—properly orienting the map, moving across parallel linear features where possible, and using good distance estimation by measure and pace. Additionally, this chapter introduced the how-to of thumbing along, which is how to use precision map reading. These five

Processes

Chapter 4 presented the skills of orienteering and their relationship to map and compass, laying the groundwork for chapter 5 to present the best techniques to use with those skills. Chapter 6 adds to your growing expertise by adding five processes to further enhance the skills and techniques:

1. Orienting the map

2. Simplifying

3. Selecting the route

4. Developing map memory

5. Relocating

ORIENTING THE MAP

As mentioned in chapters 4 and 5, it is important to orient your map correctly to the terrain at your feet. (Chapter 3 mentioned that orienteers often incorrectly say to orient it to the *ground* at your feet. They know what they mean, but you might as well be correct.) Remember to orient your map to magnetic north and to rotate your body around the map while holding the

After orienting the map, a decision must be made about which of several route choices to take.

map oriented to north so that you are on the far side of map from the direction of travel. (Refer back to chapter 3 if you've forgotten direction of travel.) If you are traveling north and you are on the south side of the map, you are ready to go! If your direction of travel is to the west, move your body around to the east side of the map. Beware—your natural tendency is to stand still and rotate the map, but doing so will get you in trouble. By rotating your body around the map and keeping the map oriented to north, the terrain features will appear in the correct order as you move across the ground.

Now that you have oriented the map, be sure you know where you are. When orienting the map at the start, look for the small triangle on the map that marks the start (as in figure 6.2). That should be where you are standing. Use the skill of precision map reading to locate other features on the map if you need further corroboration of your location. Now that you know how to orient the map when you are standing still, how do you do so when you are moving toward the next control?

There are four ways to orient the map (and to keep the map oriented) as you move along your route. Each one involves a specific skill.

1. Depending upon the terrain and your preference, you may use the skill of rough compass reading. Make sure the north magnetic needle in your compass and the top of the map are roughly lined up and the direction-of-travel arrow points toward the direction you want to go. Then, move out.

2. If you choose to use precision compass reading, place the compass on the map and align the direction-of-travel arrow in the direction you wish to go. Then, align the magnetic north lines on the map and the magnetic orienting lines inside the bezel with one another. Next, superimpose the north magnetic needle on top of the north orienting arrow and move out, following the direction-of-travel arrow. If you move toward a feature (e.g., distinct tree, boulder) aligned with your direction of travel, you can be precise. If you keep looking down at your compass needle while trying to move in a straight line, you will veer off.

3. To use the map by associating it with the terrain, you may orient the map with either rough map reading or precision map reading. This will force you to associate the terrain

We cannot overemphasize how important it is to get on the map, meaning that you know precisely where you are at the start. Trying to implement the techniques and apply the skills from an incorrect location is like banging your head against a brick wall. It feels better when you stop, but why did you start it in the first place?

with the map. Rough map reading (look at the big things and rotate your map to align with them) could be used if there is a large or linear feature that will let you know roughly where you are on the map and the ground upon arrival.

4.   Precision map reading (definite features such as a trail bend or various junctions or buildings) will help you orient the map and keep you oriented to the terrain while moving in the direction of the control.

All four skills will help you keep the map oriented correctly so that the features show up on the ground in the same sequence as you move that they appear on the map. As you progress in skill with reading the ground (or terrain) around you, you will find that rough map reading can be as fast as rough compass reading and precision map reading may move you with greater speed than precision compass reading (in most cases, precision compass reading is the slowest way to move across terrain). All of these orienteering skills can help keep your map oriented with the ground to keep you on course. We keep repeating ourselves, but by all means use the distance estimation skill no matter what other skills are assisting you.

One caveat: Do not bend the map. Bending the map is when you try to force the terrain to match the map or force the map to match the terrain. If you find your self-talk going something like, "Well, that hill on my right should be larger and the path to my left should run more northeast than north," you may be trying to force the map and the terrain to match when you are not where you think you are. Psychologists call this *confirmation bias*, when you confidently make the facts fit your expectations and ignore information that contradicts your expectations. All orienteers have done or will do this. Another indicator of forcing the two to match occurs when you start questioning the mapper's expertise. If you think the mapper did not draw the terrain exactly right, you may not be where you think you are. To avoid this mistake, take a little more time to be sure the two do match up. The match does not have to be perfect, but the relationships should be.

One of my own experiences in confirmation bias, or as I called it, *self-deceit*, occurred in my first meet using electronic punching. I left control 4 and inattentively laid out a route to control 6 without going to control 5. The whole way along my route, I kept carping to myself that the mapper, who had done such a good job of the map to control 4, had surely drawn poorly on my current route! It was not the mapper's fault; I was looking at the route to control 5 on the map but was moving to control 6 because of my momentary lapse. All I had to do was stop and question myself, but I was overconfident in my ability and execution, and it disqualified me as I got my electronic results at the finish for missing a control. I was in denial for about one second, and then I recalled that leg in which the map never matched up well and I knew what I had done. Argh!

SIMPLIFYING

Simplifying the finding of the control occurs when you use skills and techniques to make the navigation as simple as possible. Generally speaking, you do not want to note and observe every detail on the map or in the terrain. The goal is to simplify the process so that you can concentrate on fewer details. If your route takes you through an area with lots of little boulders but your control is at the base of a hill where there are a few big boulders, you can basically forget about the little boulders. It makes things much simpler by concentrating on the big boulders and the hill. This will also help you make the control as large as you can by noticing the feature it is attached to or the larger features nearby. Ask yourself, "How big is this control?" The answer is that it is as big as the feature it is on or near. Find that feature first and the control will be easier to find. When you select an easy-to-find attack point, you have begun to simplify. Likewise, chapter 5 gave the example of making the control as large as possible by aiming off to the side of the control and running to easy-to-find features. When you arrived at those features, you knew exactly where you were and where to go to find the control. Any time you can expand the control from the 50-meter radius of the circle drawn around it by adding another 50 meters or more with easy-to-find features, you have simplified your task by creating much larger targets to find than just the control. Rough map reading (particularly using the technique of catching features), following handrails, using attack points, aiming off, and collecting features all simplify navigation by allowing you to ignore map details that you do not need. When appropriate, precision map reading can also enlarge the target by providing features that point you right at the control. To quote the orienteer of the first-place female team from Canada after a CIOR competition in Italy: "It was like Colonel and Mrs. Ferguson drew a bright red line on the ground leading to every single control!" What we taught them is exactly what is in this book, and it certainly involved simplifying their navigation.

Basically, the map displays numerous features, as does the terrain. To select your best route, you must pare down the many to the important few that will best guide you to the control. Using the simplification process, the decision of which major features to use determines which skills and techniques will best help you stay on your route (and you may use them all). Orienteering maps show great detail, while other maps with smaller scales show fewer features. To hone your ability to see and select the important features, it may be to your advantage to train on a smaller-scale map, such as a 1:24,000. Using a map with less detail compared to the ground, which now has numerous features that you can easily see but are too small to be displayed on the 1:24,000 map, teaches you not to sweat the small stuff when you navigate—in other words, simplify!

Figures 6.1, 6.2, and 6.3 show how simplifying the map can make a dreadfully complicated map simple to use. Figure 6.1 presents a complex and detailed map, complicating the choice of a route by obfuscating it with overwhelming detail. Study it and think how you would travel to the circle.

In figure 6.2 the mapmaker has circled the three significant features that will take you straight to the control, ignoring all of the extraneous detail. First, go up the narrow reentrant, heading almost directly north and using the reentrant as a handrail. Crossing

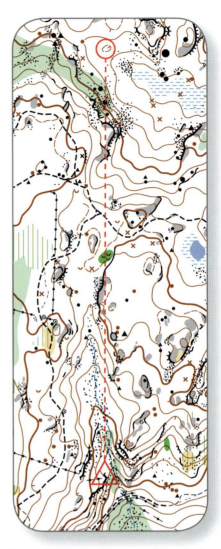

Figure 6.1 A complex and overly detailed map.

the small saddle at the top of the climb, drop down into the second broad reentrant which runs almost north northeast (or slightly to the right) and keep to the left of that reentrant. When you see the marsh and the boulder field just beyond the bottom of the reentrant, turn left past the marsh and boulder field and go straight to the little depression that is the control.

In figure 6.3, the mapmaker has removed all of the extraneous detail in order to portray the route clearly and simply. This third map is what you must strive to see first in your mind and then in the terrain as you simplify your navigational task. In this case there are two handrails (the reentrants), a collecting feature (the saddle, which is by far easier to see in figure 6.3, between the cliffs), and two other collecting features that redirect your route to the left. These features are

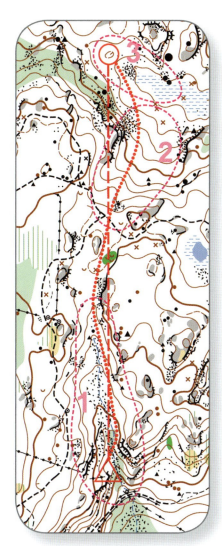

Figure 6.2 A map with significant features circled that ignores extraneous details: (1) Up narrow reentrant (across saddle); (2) down broad reentrant (keeping left); (3) turn left past marsh and boulder field.

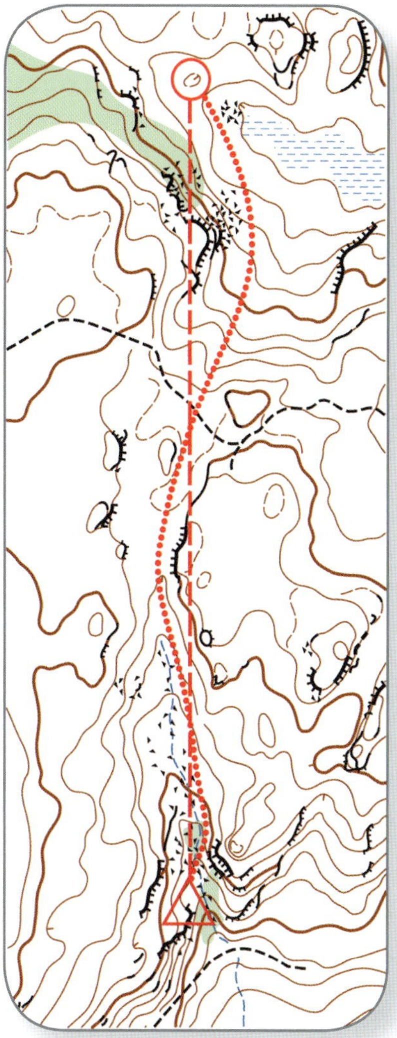

Figure 6.3 A map that shows a simple and clear route.

the marsh and the boulder field. There is even a trail that will cross your route with a small junction, which should be visible as you pass by it.

Now look back at the first map, figure 6.1. Is there a second route, which may be slower, but just as sure to get you there? Yes. Look for the trail to the west of the start triangle. I must admit that was my knee-jerk route choice until I observed the steep climb from the start triangle to the trail to the west. You will waste time and energy going for what appears to be easier navigation (i.e., you get to run on a trail about halfway to the control) and while it may appear to be a "safer" route, what

could be more secure than staying in the reentrant that you are already in at the start triangle and using it as a handrail? It is just as obvious as the trail.

SELECTING THE ROUTE

There is no doubt that good route selection and proper execution of the five techniques along your route are keys to success in orienteering. Considering that transit speed (how long it takes to get from one control to another and around the whole course) is the measure of your success, there are a number of factors to keep in mind. First, remember an old military axiom, "Better is the enemy of good." In other words, select a good route quickly. Don't lose time by attempting to select the absolute best route. Another bit of excellent advice from one of the highest-achieving North American orienteers in international orienteering competition, Canadian Ted de St. Croix, is to pick a route and stick to it. This does not mean that you cannot make small changes to improve your route as you progress toward the control, but it does mean that it is difficult to see the best route on your map for every control. Therefore, just pick a good route and move out. Over the span of a number of controls, you may pick a best route some of the time, a good route much of the time, and occasionally a poor route. However, so will the other orienteers against whom you are competing, so it evens out over courses, events, and time. On the other hand, if you waste precious minutes or even seconds by repeatedly trying to determine the best route for every control (with other things being equal, such as orienteering ability and race fitness), then you are going to lose to those orienteers who quickly pick a route and go with it.

Start With the End

How do you pick a route? Although we have briefly touched on it in previous chapters, the art of selecting a route from the start to the first control or from one control to the next control may still surprise you. To repeat one of the seven habits of highly successful people by acclaimed author Stephen Covey, start with the end in mind. In other words, start by looking at the target, which is the control you want to find. Our acronym for the process of route selection is *CAR*.

Control–Attack Point–Route (CAR)

CAR stands for **c**ontrol–**a**ttack point–**r**oute, the exact order in which you decide on your route. This concept was developed by Winnie Stott in *Armchair Orienteering II* (1987, Canadian Orienteering Federation).

To best explain it, let's start off with the opposite of CAR: Why not plan your route from where you are? After all, this is where you will start running. Don't do it! When you start route planning from where you are, you will often shortcut the route selection process by making a beeline for the control or by heading toward the nearest big thing you can find that is close to you and more or less on the way to the control. Then you will look for the next spot to jump to and you will progress toward the control in a series of jumps from one place or feature to another. What is so deceiving about this method is that it can work quite well for much of the time, particularly when you are just starting out and are not very fast anyway. When you begin any sport or meaningful activity, though, you should also begin building good habits immediately.

If you start route planning from where you are and work toward the control, you will tend to move in increments, often causing you to miss better routes in favor of going straight ahead or to overlook a good attack point near the control. Remember, your route should be simplified by going to the attack point, not the control. On the other hand, when starting from the control, you find the closest feature near the control that you know you can find to use as a good attack point, and then you work your route backward from the attack point to where you are. Note that the attack point does not have to be between you and the control. It may be to the left or right of the control and, in a few instances, on the far side of the control (think of a control just inside the woods with a field on the far side—you might choose to run to the field and come back to the control). Using CAR, the better routes should reveal themselves to you with little or no study. As a bonus, you will rarely be ambushed by an impassable feature that is close to the control

As you have read, Coach Turbyfill developed this course over almost two decades. I thought my most lasting contribution to the course came when I named the CAR process after selecting a poor route that cost me first place in a meet (story to follow). My pride in my acronym lasted for a few classes until one of our students asked, "Hey, isn't that concept in Winnie Stott's *Armchair Orienteering*?" I've checked and Winnie's superb training manual, *Armchair Orienteering II*, beat me to CAR by a long shot. This excellent Canadian orienteer and author put CAR in print long before I ever thought of it. As my high school math teacher used to say: "Pride goes before a fall and a haughty spirit before destruction." Thank goodness I did not have a haughty spirit!

and directly on your route but that you simply don't notice until you get there. If you did not use CAR, you now have to go around a swamp or a thicket or a logged area, losing time and energy.

CAR is particularly important in the orienteering events in which you must move and make decisions quickly and where any major error can put you out of contention. Some examples are in sprint orienteering, carelessly running into a cul de sac with no way out, or in ski or mountain bike orienteering, taking a ski trail or bike path that seems to start out well but takes you away from the control. All can be avoided if you work back from your destination.

Double Eye Sweep

For every leg of any course you should always say to yourself, "**C**ontrol" (telling yourself to look at the control first), then "**A**ttack point" (look for an attack point), and finally "**R**oute" (follow the route from your attack point back to your location). I simply say each letter of the acronym to myself as I go through my process. However, there is one more component to CAR—the double eye sweep. CAR is the first eye sweep over the map starting from the **c**ontrol to the **a**ttack point to the **r**oute. The first eye sweep ends at your location. On the second sweep you look forward from where you are toward the control. There are two reasons to do the double eye sweep. First, you can quickly check for a better route that you may have missed on the first sweep and, second, you can take a quick glance for a catching feature just beyond the control—since you started at the control with CAR, you may have missed a useful feature behind it. If there is a good catching feature behind the control, you may be able to move much faster on a different route using rough compass reading or rough map reading. With practice and experience you should be able to accomplish a thorough double eye

How Murphy Taught Me CAR

I had a great run going at an orienteering meet in New England, making no mistakes and wasting few seconds. Arriving at control 7, I quickly observed that the route to control 8 was straight ahead through 700 meters of complex terrain with lots of small features, including some small ditches, all beautifully drawn on the map. Being sure of my precision map reading and my precision compass reading skills, I set out immediately with great care over the complex and rolling ground (some so steep I had to crawl up the far side on hands and knees). With reasonable speed, I read the ground perfectly and hit the control like an expert marksman shooting a bull's-eye. None of the remaining controls gave me any problems and I surged to the finish, only to discover that an orienteer who usually finished behind me was 15 seconds ahead!

We sat down to compare maps and intervals. (Using electronic punching not only proves you have visited the control but allows the meet staff to print out your interval times between controls. With the printed intervals you can compare your times between controls with the interval times of other orienteers.) My friend was slightly slower than me on every single leg except from control 7 to 8, where he beat me by several minutes. While I was slogging up and down small but steep ditches, he had selected a huge field as an attack point, run a short way to the east where the ground was fairly level, and sped as fast as he could to the field. At the field, he simply turned left, ran to the corner, and used precision compass reading to go the last 50 meters to the large boulder that held our control. I had used a stream junction as an attack point, and although it was difficult to miss, it was also time consuming to get there.

In talking over my lack of success that day with Coach Turbyfill, he asked why I had not used the corner of the large field as an attack point. My answer was that I had looked from where I was on the map at control 7 to where I wanted to go on the map at control 8, and finding a good attack point directly between me and the control, I had not even noticed the field. He reminded me then that you must start from the control and work back to where you are. He was certainly correct. Had I started my route planning at control 8 by looking for an attack point, I would have seen the field well before I spotted the stream junction, and the correct route would have shown itself to me. Murphy laughed because he had lulled me into thinking I was doing well when I could have been much smarter and faster in my route selection if I had known to use CAR. Another way to look at this is that what works for you may not be what works *best* for you, so be open to change—there may be a better way.

sweep for most legs in less than a second. It is important to emphasize that the first eye sweep must be from the control to your locations. (Use CAR, it works!) Build the good habits first and they become instinctive.

Orienteering Techniques for Route Selection

The route you take to the control determines how many of the five techniques you will be using. Finding attack points, aiming off, following handrails, finding collecting features, and stopping at catching features could all be used depending on the route. Remember to see the control first and then look for a nearby attack point. Note that if the control is close to the start or close to the control that you have just found (usually less than 200 m), you may be able to use your present location as the attack point using the skills of precision map reading or precision compass reading. In other words, your location becomes the attack point from which you make your final approach to the control.

If the control is not nearby, select an attack point, determine your route, and decide how to get to that attack point. Is the attack point large enough so that you can simply aim off and be sure of hitting it and then turning right or left to find the control? Is there a nice handrail that will guide you in or close to the direction you wish to travel? If there is no good opportunity to aim off or use a handrail, does the terrain lend itself well to navigating by collecting features along the way to the attack point or the control? Or perhaps this will be one of those rare but welcomed locations where you can use the skills of rough map reading and distance estimation and either hit the attack point (or control) dead on or relocate yourself quickly at the catching feature so that you go to the control in minimum time.

These questions may be a lot to ask yourself en route to each attack point and then to the control, but keep two things in mind. First, sometimes you need to slow down to go faster (meaning haste without a clear plan generally costs you time), and second, the process of route selection becomes faster and better as you gain experience. In other words, the more you do it, the better and faster you become to the extent that you begin subconsciously to ask yourself these questions. When you have practiced enough, your eyes on the map will answer the questions before your brain can even ask them, and off you'll go at race speed.

DEVELOPING MAP MEMORY

The fourth process is developing map memory. Why is it called *map memory*? The first reason is that as you gain experience in orienteering, you will be able to glance at a map for seconds, rather than minutes, and remember what you see for longer periods of time. In other words, your ability to memorize parts of the map for short periods of time improves and you do not have to look at the map continually (which slows you down). The second reason is that once you measure a distance on the map, you commit it to memory until you have traveled that distance. There are a few orienteers whose map memory is so good that they look at the entire course and then put the map into a pocket and do the course from memory. (This is not fast, but it is another way to enjoy our sport.) For most of us, however, map memory is short-term memory that sticks with us only until we have traveled through the quickly memorized area and moved our thumbs to a new known location.

Depending on the terrain, you may decide to simplify and remember fewer but larger features. This often happens in rough map reading or rough compass reading. Or, you may need to remember more but smaller features if you transition to precision map reading. Map memory is accomplished either way. To change from precision to rough map reading, you may simply transition from picking up the small features on the map to remembering the larger features of which they are a part (recall the earlier tip to practice occasionally on a 1:24,000 map to improve your ability to ignore the small features in favor of the large). This will help you move faster by memorizing just a few large features. The reverse is to transition from the large features on the map to smaller features (which may be closer together), particularly as you get near to the control. Either way will work. And, your memory does not have to be perfect. You can glance back at the map whenever needed.

In figure 6.2, the map went from many small detailed features to a few large features, thus greatly simplifying the map and route choice. Suppose you had only been going from the top of the first reentrant through the saddle to the trail junction? Then you might well have simplified the map by focusing on the small features such as the cliffs to your left and right

Restarting your pace count can help your map memory of the distance you measured and memorized from the map. Because it is an estimate, the longer you continue a pace count without starting over, the less accurate your estimate is. Many orienteers start counting all over when they come to an easily recognizable feature along their route, particularly if the features are at least 200 meters apart. You'll drive yourself crazy if you restart, say, every 50 meters, but the objective of restarting your pace count is to keep the count small so that you do not wonder if you just paced 500 meters—or was it 600? If I see no good place to restart a pace count of over 300 meters, I say each additional 100 meters out loud to reinforce an accurate count. If I am really tired, I put my thumb on a new finger of the same hand every time I add 100 meters, switching back and forth between hands after every 500 meters. In other words, I am using my fingers on both hands somewhat like an abacus. Beginners should not encounter such long legs.

and perhaps picking up the trail between the two cliffs to the left to guide you right to the trail junction while ignoring other nearby details.

Another way to expand on map memory is to compare map memory to speaking a second language. Suppose you learn a foreign language well enough to translate from that language to your own—this is equivalent to learning to orienteer with the new language being the map and the translation being relating that new knowledge to the terrain around you. Now suppose you become proficient in that new language so that you no longer have to translate into your native tongue, but you can think in the new language. Well, very good orienteers eventually learn to think in map! They do not have to translate the map into the terrain around them, but they can visualize the terrain by simply reading the map. As you can imagine such a capability greatly speeds up and expands using map memory.

RELOCATING

Relocating? Wait a minute! Are we telling you that you are going to get *lost* out in the woods when you orienteer? Actually, we are telling you that, but we prefer to say that you are temporarily misoriented, not lost. *Lost* implies that you have no idea where you are and that you do not know how to find your way back, whereas *misoriented* implies that you can figure out either where you are or how to get to a known location. Additionally, Orienteering USA rules require all sanctioned meets

Giving back to the community, orienteers certify in search and rescue (SAR) from the National Park Service.

to have a search-and-rescue plan for participants who are truly lost (so we will come look for you), and they strongly recommend that all meets have such a plan.

OK, you are not really lost, so what are some circumstances where you may need to relocate? One is if you have actually made an error, such as a 180 or a parallel error, and gotten off course. A second occurs if you are using precision map reading and your next collecting feature does not show up on the ground as it appears on the map. (Do not assume the mapmaker made an error! You probably made the error.) A third may happen if your pace count is supposed to bring you to an easily recognizable point and that target (the linear feature, the catching feature, and so on) does not appear. These are just a few possibilities, but you should think of it this way: Everyone gets temporarily misoriented at one time or another, but whoever recovers quickest, wins!

Recovering

You are temporarily misplaced. How do you recover? *SOFA* is an acronym contributed by Andrew Comb, as a West Point Cadet. Andrew knew that an easily remembered acronym would help him recall the steps in the correct sequence.

> **S**top moving.
> **O**rient your map.
> **F**ind a feature in the terrain (on the ground).
> **A**cquire that feature on the map.

These steps are in the order you should do them, and by far the most important is the simplest: **S**top moving! If you have drifted off course, made a 180 or a parallel error, or run by your catching feature, you will only exacerbate the damage by continuing to move. Even experienced orienteers who don't use SOFA often have an interesting thought process that goes something like this: "I think I know about where I am, so if I go just a little farther or if I simply run in a circle, I will find what I'm looking for." Don't do it! Only occasionally, when you have miscounted your pace, is this weak process going to work. Running in a perfect circle is difficult in the woods, so you are likely to drift even farther away from your route. If you've already run too far, running farther just makes it worse.

As soon as you stop moving, **o**rient the map (using your compass) to north. Hopefully, it was already oriented to north, but if not, you now have a clue as to a possible error. Put your body on the correct side of the map facing the direction you thought you were going. Were you? If not, which way did you drift off? This may help, but if not, go back to SOFA. Now that you know which way is north on the map and which way is north on the ground, turn your body in a circle and **f**ind a feature in the terrain that you can see clearly on the ground and that is large enough or distinct enough that it should be on the map as well. If you cannot see

an acceptable feature on the ground because of reduced visibility (such as being surrounded by trees), move carefully with your map oriented until you do find one (see the next section on thumbing along for a good way to do this). Now, **a**cquire that feature on the map that you located on the ground and you know where you are again.

Using figure 6.4, assume you intended to go from control 2 to control 3, but being excited, your route out of control 2 was 180 degrees off and you traveled northwest instead of southeast. In 150 meters you realized that you were going downhill instead of across several reentrants, and you stopped. You have completed the first step of SOFA successfully. Now, knowing for sure that you made a 180-degree error, you use your compass to orient the map to north (step 2), and you luck out. While you are looking north, a large truck drives east on Bull Pond Road, and your hearing, if not your eyesight, tells you the paved road is to the north and not far away. Now you have completed the third step of acquiring a feature (the paved road) although you may not actually see it through the trees. You turn in a circle and realize there is no other major feature that you can acquire on this portion of the map and there is no other large road. Thus, you have acquired what is probably the most useful nearby feature, and you run to the paved road. Once there you can precisely locate your position from the curve in the road, the marsh on the north side, or the obvious hilltop rising on the north side of the road. Once you know your location, you start back up the hill and orienteer to control 3. Yes, it cost you time to go to the paved road, but most orienteers would lose far more time trying to acquire tiny (and parallel) features such as the small marshes and cliffs. A second option if you were fairly sure you had made a 180 would be to reverse the compass and head back to control 2. Regardless, take decisive action. Do not wander or attempt to muddle through.

Thumbing Along

In relocating, particularly when acquiring a feature, thumbing along can be very useful. Remember, thumbing along is how you keep up with where you are on the ground by marking your location on the map. It is simple. Whenever you pass a clearly recognizable location on the ground that is also distinct on your map, simply move the thumb of the hand that is holding the map so that the leading edge of the thumb is right on, but not over, the feature. If you are at the start waiting to go to control 1, where do you place your thumb? You put it on the start triangle on the map as soon as you move away from the start and no longer need to see the map of the start (because you are now moving to the next distinctive feature on the map and on the ground and the start is behind you).

Why is thumbing along important here? Because if you do not see any feature on the ground that you can locate on the map, then you can go back along your route (remembering your pace count) with some certainty to the last point at which you knew your location, as marked by your thumb. If you are standing on a relatively flat area with no obvious terrain or human-made features to the front or either side, then your best bet may be to bite the bullet and return quickly to your last known point—it will save you time versus wandering aimlessly hoping to find something.

Using Attack Points

Another variation of SOFA can be used when you are close to the control and know approximately where you are. In this case, if your map shows terrain or human-made features that you can quickly find and use as attack points, go to the closest or most obvious

(findable) one. Be sure to keep your map oriented to the terrain. Remember, do not mentally force the ground and the map to match up—if your thought is that it almost matches up, then it probably does not, and you are setting yourself up to waste more time because you may not be where you hope you are. One of the most successful orienteers I have known over many years, Malvin Harding of Oregon, has a great ability to relocate immediately when he does not find the control on his first attempt. Mal wastes no time in aimless wandering. He goes quickly to a feature that he can find on the map and on the ground and comes precisely back to the control from that acquired location.

SOFA in Action

Look at the map in figure 6.4. Suppose you are on the map in the lower right corner, somewhere near the long line of cliffs. However, you are unsure of exactly where you are, and to locate the control (not marked on this map) you need that information. Your best choice is to

Figure 6.4 Apply SOFA when you are temporarily mislocated.
Courtesy of The USMA Orienteering Club.

stop, **o**rient the map, and find a **f**eature on the map (in this case, note the obvious trail to the southwest and especially the curve in the trail). Now, head southwest, which is downhill, until you come to where you can see the bend in the trail from higher up. **A**cquire that bend by going to it. Now you have relocated. Using CAR, go to the control from here.

If you see the depression but cannot find it on your map, consider that you may have made a 180 or even run all the way off the map! Go back to your last known point on the map and look in the opposite direction. Using your pace count to get a distance to measure on the map, and with the map oriented to the terrain, you may see the depression on the map in the other direction. If so, you made a 180 and you need to turn around. If all else fails, do not simply walk aimlessly or in circles, hoping to see something familiar. It is much faster to go back to your last known location and to start over.

Finally, here's one more consideration: Could you have indeed run off the map? Did your route choice take you close to the edge of the map? Might a 180 have taken you off the map? It is difficult enough to find relocation features using SOFA when you are on the map, but it is impossible to find them when you are off the map! If that nice depression is off your mapped area, it does you no good at all.

If you have run off the map, can you recover? Yes, but it is much more difficult, and yes, I have run off the map several times. Two things can help you immensely: first, if your thumb is still at the last point where you were certain of your location, and second, if you know how far you have gone from there (distance estimation by measure and pace). Why? Well, suppose you were near the edge of the map, marked your location at some place, and traveled 350 meters. Suddenly the map and the terrain no longer match up. Stop! Mentally draw a circle 350 meters around your last known location. If part of that circle is off the map, think about how you might have erred. Be sure, of course, that you really are off the map by trying SOFA. If so, could you have done a 180? Was your map oriented to north? Were you trying to use precision compass reading and drifted? If your answer to any of these is *yes*, then you have an idea how you left the mapped area and therefore you can make a plan to return.

By looking at that imaginary circle that has a radius of 350 meters, you can approximate how far off the map you are, which will allow you to estimate when you have returned to the mapped area, where you may be able to use the SOFA process successfully. If you made a 180, just reverse and go back to your last

known point. If you had the map with east at the top instead of north, you are 90 degrees off, which is harder to recover from but which you can figure out. If you may have drifted, it will help if you have studied which side you are likely to drift to (right or left) and can assume that you did so again.

If none of these tactics seems possible, carefully look at your map, which must definitely be oriented to north, and determine if there is a large feature that will relocate you if you go toward it. Many orienteering areas are surrounded by roads, and you are often given a safety azimuth, such as, if you are lost, go south until you come to the paved road. You may have to do so and either relocate from the paved road (which is usually on the map) or decide that you have lost so much time that you will just report to the finish line and do better at the next event. Be absolutely certain that you report to the finish line so that no search is organized for you while you are sitting in your car or the team bus, sulking because you failed to finish!

SUMMARY

The first of the five processes, orienting the map, is simple to master—just be sure the top of the map is pointing north and then move your body around the map to the opposite side from the direction you wish to travel. Now you will see features on the map and on the ground in the order that they appear. Practice orienting the map every single time you have a map of the terrain around you. It's fun and it builds skill and confidence. A second process, SOFA, is slightly more difficult but rarely used. If you find yourself often using SOFA to relocate, you are outrunning your orienteering ability! Slow down if you are competing. To practice recovering set yourself up to get mislocated by running into the terrain without looking at your map. After 15 seconds, stop and see if you can relocate. Go far enough sometimes to use SOFA. Be sure to practice recovery in a mapped area from which you can always find your way back out—in other words, practice recovering in an area where you know you can always head south and come to the road that goes to the parking lot where you left your car, for instance, or to the visitor's center (something you can always find). You will also find that as you master the skills, techniques, and processes, you will seldom need to relocate.

Two processes are not easy—simplifying the map and map memory—but they come naturally as you practice them and gain experience. You can practice both while sitting in a chair or out for a jog; you do not need to be on an actual course or in the area covered by the map. If you can train map memory on a practice map, you should become more skilled in less time. Finally, selecting a route is the key to your success, and like the last two, it can be practiced during map study without being outside. Be sure to practice correctly using CAR, which is more easily mastered by simple map study with no competitive pressure. In other words, learn to use CAR at home, not in the middle of a meet. To ensure success, be realistic. If you are not fit, select routes that go around hills instead of over them. If you walk every step, select direct routes whenever possible. In competition, remember the advice of a world-class athlete, Ted de St. Croix: "Select a route and stick to it!" Your experience, practice, and fitness will enable you to get better and better at executing these five processes and will place you on the award podium well ahead of your peers who do not have a system.

Ethics, Integrity, and Rules

Orienteering is a competition, testing your skill in navigating. As such, it has rules, ethics, and commonly accepted practices. This chapter is mainly concerned with integrity and fairness. Personal integrity is vital because unlike soccer, football, baseball, and other popular sports, orienteers are out of sight of the officials for most of the event. Section 35 of the rules, Fairness, sets the tone for all orienteering competition. It reads:

 All persons who take part at an orienteering event (competitors, organizers, team managers, and so on) shall demonstrate a high degree of fairness, a sporting attitude, a spirit of comradeship, and honesty.

Orienteering rules for the United States can be found at www.orienteeringusa.org/rules. The latest international rules can be found at http://orienteering.org. Do not be overwhelmed by the large number of pages. For one reason, the rules for foot orienteering, night orienteering, ski orienteering, and so on overlap and are repeated in each section. Another reason is that the rules that competitors, teachers, and coaches should master are not as numerous as the ones that apply to meet organizers, event controllers, and competitive mapmakers. You should begin with section 35, Fairness, and section 36, Equipment and Aids in the USA rules. Both are immediately important to you as a competitor, teacher, or coach. You may enjoy reviewing the categories of rules for items that interest you, such as National Rankings under the rules for Event Control (you do want to be number one in the nation, don't you?) or the rules for competitive courses under Technical Qualifications (how far do you have to run to win an advanced course?).

EXHIBITING INTEGRITY

Orienteering is founded on integrity. All competitors are shown the greatest respect because *it is assumed that you do not cheat*. Where else in life do you get that level of instant respect? Perhaps if you are a new park ranger, nurse, teacher, military officer, or doctor, but not in most businesses, so don't blow it. Integrity is so essential to the sport that if it is determined that you are cheating, you can be banned from competing! Although there is a nationally approved body of rules, competition for the individual is relatively simple. You report to the starting area on time. When told to start

and given a map, your race time starts. If you are running the most popular format (cross-country), your task is to visit each of the controls on your course in sequence, as fast as you can, receiving no intentional help from any other person. Your time stops when you cross the finish line. You are required to proceed by yourself.

 It is forbidden to obtain outside help or collaborate in running or navigation except in a noncompetitive class.

Integrity is so important because once you are out of sight of the start line, you are expected to police yourself and obey the rules. For example, if you need to relocate, use SOFA. You may not ask another orienteer to tell you where you are.

 A competitor shall not seek to obtain unfair advantage over fellow competitors, nor intentionally run with or behind other competitors during the event in order to profit from their skill.

There will be occasions when you and another orienteer may choose similar routes to the same control, but if you are seen running together through much of the course, or if your electronic punch times are close to simultaneous, expect to answer some tough questions. In other words, you must not follow other orienteers through the course, allowing them to do the orienteering while you just keep up.

Visit Each Control

You cannot fake it. Find and visit all of the controls or you don't get credit. As mentioned in previous chapters, to prove that you visited all of the controls, each control has either its own manual punch, much like a stapler with pins that make a distinct pattern on your scorecard, or an electronic punching (scoring) system that records and stores your time at that location automatically. Low-budget meets and some fun variations of orienteering may have something at each location for you to write down, such as letters, numbers, or historical facts (you will know this before you start). For the electronic scoring system, you wear a probe that contains a computer chip (called an *e-punch*, a *dibbler*, or a variety of other names) on your finger and use it to check in at each control. You check in electronically by inserting the probe into a hole in an electronic scoring device that is a timer. The electronic timers typically beep and flash a light to let you know you have successfully logged in. The term *punch* is often used for checking in because the old manual system forced small, needlelike pins through a paper scorecard to make a pattern—in effect, punching through the paper. Regardless, when you cross the finish line, you should have indisputable evidence that you found and visited every control even though no official followed you around the course. If you lose your scorecard or drop your e-punch (mine is on a cord that encircles my wrist), then the event never happened for you.

Punch Each Control in Sequence

With the manual system, you are on your honor to visit the controls in sequence. To avoid the temptation to go out of order, it is also incumbent upon the course designer to put the controls in a logical order for routes. Be aware that there may be officials on the course who can ask to see your scorecard to be sure the controls are punched in sequence. With the electronic system, you will be disqualified automatically if you electronically punch out of sequence. However, if you know you have punched out of sequence, such as if you somehow got to control 4 before checking in at 3, the electronic system will reset if you return to control 3, punch in, go back to 4, punch in again, and complete the course in the proper order from the missed control to the finish.

If you punch out of sequence with the manual system, you are on your honor to not only return to the control that you missed, but to proceed around the course from that control, going to the remainder of the controls in order. This usually requires that you return to the control that you accidently reached out of sequence. Suppose you punch your scorecard for control 4 and see that you missed 3. You go back to 3, collect that punch, return to 4, touch the control that you have already punched, and continue around the course. This is required even if you get to the last control and realize you never punched the first control (yikes!). Think of this experience as training and toughening yourself to be honest. In the orienteering world, strong competitors, no matter how good or bad, do not cheat. Wimps take the easy way. Should you accidentally punch in the wrong box, punch elsewhere on the scorecard and explain what happened at the finish before you hand in your scorecard.

With a manual punch, you complete the course by crossing the finish line. Be sure you do not run past the last control, which is often within sight of the finish line. Even if you can see that last control that you missed, once you cross the finish line you are not allowed to go back out on the course. If you do, you are breaking the rules and will be disqualified. With an electronic system, you finish by inserting your probe at one final timer at the finish line, so it is much harder to miss the last control.

Do Not Cheat

So, what is considered cheating? As mentioned earlier, running behind other orienteers so that they are doing all or most of the navigating is called *following*, and it is definitely cheating. Following is most obvious when seen by observers or when an orienteer's competitive time suddenly makes a dramatic improvement not warranted by any other data. Electronic punching can clearly show following. Moving a control or knocking it to the ground is obviously cheating. Intentionally searching for the controls in teams of two or more is cheating. Yelling to teammates or friends that the control is "over here!" is cheating. Yelling "Over here!" when the control is not actually nearby in order to mislead a competitor is both unethical and cheating.

In other words, when you are orienteering competitively, you are expected to exhibit good sporting behaviors while doing your own navigation, neither intentionally giving nor receiving assistance. This rule is often waived in training and occasionally in local meets, if the latter are for fun and not for competition. If the tone of this section on cheating seems overbearing, please take it as precautionary. Cheating in orienteering is not tolerated and consequently is not widespread. Orienteering is a great sport and we do not want to lose you or have you embarrassed because you were not aware of the rules and the consequences.

Intentional Versus Unintentional Help

Intentional help, where you ask another competitor for assistance (e.g., "Where is the control?") or follow another competitor on purpose, is forbidden. Incidental and unintentional help are not considered cheating. For example, three competitors arrive in the vicinity of a control at nearly the same time, but one goes left, one goes right, and one goes straight ahead. As long as this

The most blatant violation of following that I've ever witnessed occurred in the CISM (from the French for International Military Sports Council) World Orienteering Military Championships in Spain. One North African country known for its Olympic runners arrived with a full team and not one orienteer, as amply demonstrated at each practice. However, on competition day, as each runner on the team started, he simply ran to the nearest tree line where previous runners had disappeared (all competitors were on the same course) and waited for the next orienteer to come by. Then he latched onto that competitor. If his runner got passed during the event, he left the slower orienteer and followed the faster. This strategy was so unexpected that none of them got caught even though everyone knew what they were doing by the end of the day. It sort of worked. They finished somewhere in the middle of the pack while the U.S. team was farther back. However, no one was fooled that they could read a map and absolutely no one would trust those who cheated so blatantly.

is not a coordinated search, it is not likely to be cheating, but remember that you are to be quiet and not yell, "Over here!" What happens among experienced orienteers is that while each searches in her own pattern, she also keeps an eye (and an ear) out for a sudden change in behavior by any of the others. Why the ear? If you are hearing others move nearby and it suddenly gets quiet, it may mean the others found the control and left the area. When an orienteer spots the control, there is almost no way to hide the body language that practically shouts, "There it is!" And, no words need be spoken.

Likewise, you are allowed to look around and see what other orienteers may be doing in the woods near you. For example, you know you are close but you do not see the control; however, you do notice one or more people run by you purposefully, stoop over something you cannot see, and then run off at an angle. You may wish to check to see if they just punched the control that you are seeking. Beware, however, that often five or more courses are being run at the same time, so check the control codes carefully (they are given to you in advance as a separate clue sheet, as part of your map, or both). Chapter 1 revealed that each control has a unique identifier such as a three-digit number, and chapter 9 covers controls in depth.

Although they share a common point, these competitors are not on the same course and their routes will soon diverge.

Take heed: Do not come to depend on what other orienteers around you may be doing. For most orienteers, seeing others in the woods is a distraction that can break your focus on reading your map, counting your paces, or being aware of the terrain around you, especially if, like me, you are easily distracted. Marines often refer to *SA* (situational awareness or being situationally aware), which fits orienteering perfectly. Do not let other orienteers distract your SA!

Embargoes

When an area is going to be used for a championship orienteering event, it is usually embargoed for a year or more in advance. Embargoing an area means that orienteers are to stay out of that area—no hiking, running, hunting, training, or performing any other activity that takes you through the terrain on which the championship will be held. Generally, a new map will be made for a championship or an existing map will be expanded into new areas so that no competitor will be familiar with the terrain.

Prior investigation of the competition area is forbidden.

The area is embargoed because good orienteers can learn a great deal by walking or running through an area even once, giving them a decided advantage when they compete in that area—much as you would if you and I had a map of your neighborhood where you had lived for years and I had never visited, and we had a competition to find various locations on that map. Other things (such as fitness) being equal, you would be far faster than me. Even for events on existing maps, you are expected to stay out of the area before an event even if you've been there many times before. This is one reason coming events in a park are identified as specifically as possible, allowing orienteers to use the remainder of the park while staying out of the part used for the competition. However, on rare occasions someone cheats.

In a multinational military competition, two teams, including one team that we usually left well behind, suddenly caught up with our three-person team. At our look of surprise, one of their team members yelled out, "Follow the host-country team. They know the course!" In almost five decades of this military competition, every single host country, with two exceptions, has kept the course secret from all competitors, including its own team. The map is made in secret. The course is designed and set out in secret and checked by a trusted person (the technical delegate) from another country, who is also sworn to secrecy. (I was honored to be the technical delegate for Canada's superb course one year.)

Stunned, my teammates and I agreed to accompany the host-country team to see if they were really cheating, although we knew we would have to disqualify ourselves for following. The cheating team never opened the instructions at some controls. They ran straight to each location, which is impossible unless you are an orienteering psychic, and I've never met one.

However, a funny thing happened near the end of the course. Although following, I continued to orienteer. When they suddenly stopped in a clearing, looking bewildered, I realized they were lost. I quietly told my team to slip away. Unfortunately, the team that had alerted me to the cheating saw us leave and shouted, "There goes Ferguson! He knows where it is!" And, although I tried to lose them, the cheating team heard and followed. At the finish line, I immediately filed a protest about the cheating and turned in my own team for following.

What Happened?

As we warmed down, one of the U.S. coaches told us that everyone knew the host nation's team was cheating, just not how. Soldiers with radios manned several controls on the course and called in each team's arrival. The times were posted quickly. The host nation's chief of competition, a man of the highest integrity, watched in horror as his team's event-leading time and the times of two other teams were posted as simultaneous. To the team leaders from other countries, he said, "My team is not that good." Mortified, he left before his team finished. That team had course information in advance, probably through running the course several times before the event. Why did they suddenly stop in bewilderment at the clearing? Unbeknownst

(continued)

What Happened? *(continued)*

to them, the technical delegate, when vetting the course the day before the competition, discovered that the control was in the wrong clearing. He moved it to the correct location, which was not the one the cheaters had memorized. No one else knew it had been moved. Since they had not orienteered to the clearing, they were lost.

The international punishment must have been difficult to live through. No one spoke to the three cheaters, including their other teammates (who had not cheated). Interestingly, because of the moved control, they finished second. An extremely fit and near-world-class military orienteering team from Norway finished with the best time. When the first-place trophy was awarded, all of the other nations cheered wildly for the Norwegians. When the host nation accepted the second-place trophy, there was complete silence.

It did not end there. For many years everyone watched the teams from that nation to see if they might be cheating again. To the good, their embarrassed chief of competition made it his personal mission to improve orienteering in his military. From then on their teams did improve their times significantly without taking any illegal shortcuts. Other nations, seeing that country's long-term embarrassment, made sure their teams and coaches knew and followed the rules. The lesson here is that cheaters will probably be caught and the reputation of their school, college, or club (not to mention their own personal reputation) will be tarnished for a long time—severe (but appropriate) punishment for a lack of character.

ETHICAL ASSISTANCE TO OTHER COMPETITORS

Ethical assistance is mandatory in two cases: You must help if you come upon a competitor who admits to being hopelessly lost or if you find an injured or ill competitor. In both case cases the rules allow a sporting withdrawal for you. In addition, orienteering ethics provide that we treat the outdoors and its inhabitants with respect. See the following story for thoughts on when to give aid and, maybe, when to insist on helping.

Giving Aid to a Lost Competitor

Ethically, and in accord with the rules, if someone tells you he is totally lost, you must help him. You have an obligation to either help him find his way back to the start, forward to the finish, or in the direction of the safety azimuth. Use your best judgment as to whether you should accompany him or if you can simply give directions, but err generously on the side of safety. It is generally best to accompany them to safety, as I found out the usual way (see next sidebar).

Helping an Injured Competitor

As reported in chapter 1, helping an injured competitor, even though it costs you your race, is a time-honored tradition. It is part of our rules, our ethics, and our respect for others. It is also integral to our commitment to the safety of all competitors. Therefore, if you come upon an injured person while you are orienteering, you are required by tradition as well as by the rules and by common sense to offer any assistance needed to get that person to help. If you suspect internal injuries, do not attempt to move the person, but stay there and blow your whistle three times in quick succession. Repeat the three blasts as often as needed until others arrive. Then, mark your location on a map so that one of you can bring aid back to the correct location while at least one person stays with the injured orienteer. If the person can move but needs assistance, help him get to safety. If the person is lost and terrified, get him to safety. If he is lost but in control, use your best judgment. A beginner who is truly lost once may well get lost again, no matter how much he denies that possibility.

You will be given an honorable withdrawal from the event for helping someone in need, and what you will have done is far more important than any benefit

I came across a person new to the sport in the Hoosier National Forest in Indiana. She seemed confused, so I asked if she knew where she was. When she attempted to show me on the map, she was so far from her current location that I stopped to help. She said she wanted to go to the finish, so I had her turn around until she was facing up a road. I told her to walk to where the road curved to the left (you could see the curve about 200 meters away), at which point she would find a large trail going off to the right. She was to take that trail to its only junction and turn right, and she would be back at the finish in about five minutes even if she walked. I thought my instructions were clear (she repeated them and watched me show her on the map). Wrong!

Had I walked her in, we would not have spent the next seven hours looking for her. She never looked for the large trail to the right and she continued to run the trails deeper and deeper into the forest for several hours. The lesson here is that new orienteers may need more assistance than those who have orienteered several times, and they more than likely are embarrassed to ask for it. I should have taken a more active role in getting her to the finish. Since I ran more than 11 miles (18 km) of trails looking for her that evening, that lesson made a deep impression on me! A sheriff's volunteer found her asleep on a trail and brought her back on his all-terrain vehicle. When asked if she wanted to go home, she said, "No way, we have another day of training tomorrow!" Loved her spirit!

from finishing the course or even from winning. If you are that lost person who received help enabling you to complete the course, orienteering ethics require that you disqualify yourself at the finish by reporting that you received help. Just consider that day as a training day, not a competitive day. Receiving help is not forbidden, but receiving help and not disqualifying yourself is considered cheating.

An experienced orienteer helps a young child to relocate.

At the world championships in 2009, one of the top three competitors was injured during the competition. Two other competitors who were expected to finish among the top three stopped immediately to give aid to the fallen competitor, who was from another country. This was the final leg of the relay event, so at stake was not just the individual competitors' results but also the results for both of their countries' teams in the relay. They gave up a position on the medal stand to help an injured participant—a true display of the good sporting behavior expected in orienteering. Although I was not there, it was said that the winning team tried to decline the award, demonstrating the level of good sporting behavior in orienteering.

CARING FOR THE ENVIRONMENT

Orienteers follow the philosophy that they should take nothing away and leave nothing behind. So don't pick the flowers, do leave the birds and animals alone, and do pick up your trash. Though not a rule, being respectful of the outdoors is a major theme in orienteering culture. Orienteering USA's environmental policy is contained on its website under Land Access (www.orienteeringusa.org/mappers/land-access) and includes the following:

- Orienteering shall operate within all legal environmental standards and also within any framework agreed upon with land managers.

- No long-term damage to animals, plants, landscape, or archaeological features shall result from an orienteering event.

- Any temporary damage, such as plant trampling, should no longer be discernible after three months of a growing season.

- No litter, equipment, or extraneous material shall remain once a venue has been vacated.

- Where a venue contains vegetation, wildlife, or features of special sensitivity, event organizers shall cooperate with land managers to provide special protection.

The IOF has maintained an environmental policy since 1998, which is mirrored by the Orienteering USA policies.

A second way to respect the environment and also thank the various parks and public lands that let us orienteer is to volunteer for their projects. With a little instruction, some equipment and supervision, and a pair of work gloves, anyone can help improve trails in the park for half a day or help out with other nontechnical projects the park may not have the manpower to accomplish. In addition, our map-reading skills can be of assistance in various counts such as for finding invasive weeds. Finally, some parks have permanent orienteering courses, which you and your club or team can help place and map. Prince William Forest Park in Triangle, Virginia, has 30 maps of permanent controls that park visitors can check out to improve their navigation skills. To avoid wear and tear on the terrain, the park uses the even-numbered maps one year and the odd-numbered maps the next.

ETHICAL USE OF SPECIAL EQUIPMENT

Orienteers are not allowed to use any equipment that assists in navigation other than map and compass. For example, you may not use an altimeter. An altimeter could be used to determine the height of the feature you are on so that you could calculate your approximate position from the contours on your map, helping to locate where you are. You also may not use a GPS unit to relocate once you have become temporarily mislocated. Although the following is currently a rule now, please be aware that it is under discussion by the Board of Directors for Orienteering USA.

 The use of any navigational aid other than a compass is prohibited (e.g., transport, electronic apparatus, radio, pedometer, altimeter).

GPS Devices

The value of wearing a GPS tracking device while you are orienteering, particularly one that has a covered face and cannot help you navigate, is the most efficient mechanism to record your routes. The IOF has banned the use of any GPS-enabled device with a visible screen, and such devices are banned in the United States by the rule prohibiting the use of any navigational aid other than a compass.

In rare instances you may be able to wear a GPS-enabled wristwatch if given permission by the meet director, but you will be on your honor not to use it for navigational purposes during the race. The newer GPS-enabled watches not only calculate the total distance you have traveled but also plot your entire route after you have completed your course. Being able to review your routes afterward, particularly your poor route choices or route executions, is excellent feedback for working on your weaknesses. Quantico Orienteering Club periodically takes a number of Garmin 205 watches to local meets and loans them out. Then one of the club members posts routes and times using RouteGadget (see chapter 10) so that there is no doubt exactly where you went and how long it took you to get there.

Cell Phones

Generally you are not allowed to carry any equipment other than a map, watch, whistle, compass, and clue sheet (which describes the controls). You can, of course, carry water and snacks such as energy bars. The prohibition includes cell phones because many are GPS capable. Should you wish to carry a cell phone for safety reasons at a meet, ask the meet director if carrying one will disqualify you. Some older electronic punching equipment can be wiped clean by a cell phone signal, so make sure such older equipment is not in use. When Coach Turbyfill and I teach orienteering, we encourage our students to carry cell phones for safety reasons (most are just learning to orienteer). However, be aware that because much orienteering is done in state and national parks, cell phone coverage is often spotty at best.

To sum up, you probably do not need a cell phone at a meet, but if you are a beginner, by all means ask for permission to carry one if you want its security or if you have a health problem that might occur during your run (see chapter 8 about beginning courses, which should reassure you that you do not need to carry one). In those rare instances in which we have to search, the missing people usually were trying to do courses that were too advanced for their skills, and almost to a person, they did not listen to the meet director's instructions, such as to use the safety azimuth or to find a road or trail and stop moving. Taking a cell phone along when you are learning to orienteer or when you are training in a new place makes good sense, but you should not need one at a meet.

Pedometers

Although you are not allowed to compete using a pedometer, it can be useful for training. It is helpful to

Cell phones helped me find another missing orienteer from that same class we taught in Hoosier National Forest in Indiana. When one beginning orienteer did not return within the allotted time, we called her cell phone and she described where she thought she was. She was 600 meters from her projected location, but her description got me close enough to hear the three blasts of her whistle. I answered with two blasts of my own (meaning, "I'm coming to you."). Our safety plan included writing down the cell phone numbers of all the students and giving them our numbers. It paid off; we picked her up just before dark.

It is rare to have to look for a student at any of our classes and events, but this class represented four schools so it was unusually large, young, and inexperienced. There was one more partial rescue with this class. Two boys had joined up to locate their last control as darkness was falling, well after their three-hour time limit had expired. We finally reached them on a cell phone and told them to stay at the control, which was near a road. My wife then drove closely enough for them to hear her horn and see her headlights, and they moved quickly to her car. You can bet we made the point several more times that there is a reason we have a time limit for our events, and if you go over that limit you cause a great deal of work and trouble, not to mention the worry. They seemed to get the message. They had been outside of cell phone range until they suddenly got a signal (which you simply cannot count on in many parks and forests). The good news is that we were able to show them the way using a car horn and headlights, neither of which is probably in anyone's safety plan. As a very resigned college professor once said to a student who wanted to write more than the required number of pages: "Genius is allowed." When there is an emergency all manner of unplanned responses may help, including headlights and a car horn.

know approximately how far your typical route selection takes you from the optimal route choices upon which course distances are computed. Several years ago I wore a pedometer for various training meets with the meet director's approval and my word that I would not look at the pedometer until I had crossed the finish line. My route choices averaged 24 percent longer than the optimal routes as computed by the course designer. Had I been fitter, I might have gone over some hills that I went around, but it was useful to know that I was moving a bit faster than I had thought (based on dividing my time by the optimal course lengths). It also encouraged me to study my process of route selection to determine if I was going too far out of the way simply because the running was less steep or the terrain was easier to follow. My conclusion was that I was going a bit more out of the way because I felt I was in better contact with the terrain—another way of saying that often I took a longer choice so I could get to the control faster (by not losing my way).

SUMMARY

Having studied the tools, skills, techniques, processes, and rules of orienteering, you should be fully prepared to train and to compete. You should understand the concept of fairness and competing with a sporting attitude. *Following* has been defined and you are aware that it is perhaps the most common cheating temptation that you must avoid. A number of other forbidden practices are spelled out as well. You know that it is OK to observe what others are doing around you but that you must do your own orienteering.

Orienteers respect the environment and build goodwill by helping those who manage our parks. There are a number of specific rules that forbid certain equipment, but you know that in general you are to use no equipment as a navigational aid beyond your map and compass. Cell phones are of particular interest, and you have learned that they may be prohibited at larger events and at those using electronic punching (because they can wipe clean the stations at the controls). You also know cell phones can enhance safety, particularly for beginners, and that there are procedures for obtaining permission to use them. You have learned there are times when you must stop competing and render assistance and there are guidelines for when and how. You also know how important personal integrity is to orienteering. You should be aware that orienteering membership is in that small class of sports that introduce honor right up front in the expectations for all competitors, teachers, and coaches! Now it is time to move on to getting ready for your first meet.

Preparing Before an Event

Chapter 8 helps you prepare before an event. It begins with finding an event and explains the level and difficulty of the courses to help you choose the correct one. Thoughts on gathering your equipment and dressing comfortably precede the most important piece of information at any meet: your start time. Should you go to a large meet for which you must preregister, the meet packet, course setter's notes, and map scales are explained and their importance emphasized.

FIND AN EVENT

First, find an orienteering event; then, determine whether you can just show up or whether you must register beforehand. You have to enter some meets in advance so the organizers will know how many maps to print (among other administrative necessities). Therefore, start your preparations by finding an orienteering event and, if required, by letting the organizers know that you (or you and your team) are planning to come. This is particularly true of events organized by smaller orienteering clubs or teams. For a large club, the meet director will often bring lots of maps and can provide for whoever shows up and wants to orienteer, but do not take that for granted. You are expected to provide full information in advance to the meet organizer. In particular you should give the number of participants on your team and the possible courses they will run.

The first step is to go to the Orienteering USA website at www.orienteeringusa.org and click on "Come Try Orienteering" or the Orienteering Canada website at www.orienteering.ca/events/upcoming-events/. On the U.S. site, clubs are listed within each state. Click on the nearest club and find its schedule on the menu. Canadian events are listed by province—and there is absolutely superb orienteering in Canada! Click on *Quebec* and you can find events in the Montreal area, and you can find events in the Ottawa and Gatineau area on the Ottawa website. What you need to know is generally written in English, but Orienteering Quebec provides an opportunity to use your French as well. Orienteering Nova Scotia, to mention another excellent Canadian website, lists information for five orienteering clubs active in Nova Scotia.

In short, orienteering clubs are all over the United States, Canada, and the rest of the world. And remember, a club may not be close to you, but it may have meets in your area. In the United States, DVOA hosts meets in Delaware, Pennsylvania, New Jersey, and Maryland because it has members in all four states. The DVOA website also lists nearby regional meets and national meets of interests. The Bay Area Orienteering Club (BAOC) in San Francisco may host meets in both California and Nevada. The Columbia River Orienteering Club (CROC) in Portland, Oregon, has meets mainly in Oregon, whereas the St. Louis Orienteering Club (SLOC) lists links to regional clubs such as Cincinnati, Colorado, and Chicago. The Georgia Orienteering Club (GAOC) hosts the Navy Regional JROTC Orienteering Championship as well as numerous local meets and a national A-meet most years. Many other clubs provide similar information as well as e-mail contact information.

If there is no Orienteering USA or Orienteering Canada event close to you, check for other possible orienteering sources. A good place to search is the website for high schools with orienteering teams. Most U.S. high school orienteering teams are associated with the JROTC. Units that are close to one another often stage weekend meets and, if asked, may allow unaffiliated competitors to enter their meets—but be sure to ask in advance! South Carolina has no Orienteering USA club at this time, although there are active clubs close by in North Carolina and in Georgia. There are, however, a good many orienteering meets within South Carolina organized at the high school level. Canada is a bit more organized at the national and provincial level, but in both countries you may find web pages that have not been updated in a timely manner.

CHOOSE A COURSE

Orienteering courses in the United States (but almost nowhere else in the orienteering world) are commonly named by color based on their length and degree of difficulty. Beginning courses in the United States are white and yellow and are not technically difficult. The orange course is an intermediate course with more technically difficult controls than the beginning courses. The more advanced courses are brown, green, red, and blue, with blue being the longest and having the most climb. Canada, on the other hand, uses the more widespread numerical designations ranging from 1 to 10, with the smaller numbers equal to U.S. white and yellow courses and course 10 much like the blue course.

Courses in both countries are further broken down into men's and women's courses, and both countries divide their competitive ranks into age groups. For example, a 35-year-old male in the United States would compete on the red course, which is also the championship course for a 21-year-old female. In Canada, the same man would run course 9, as would the 21-year-old woman. Allowances are made in both countries for levels of skill; for example, that same 35-year-old man, if new to orienteering, could run the orange course in the open category. Canada allows meet directors to have beginner courses if they desire, and both countries allow wayfarers (people who want to tour the courses without competing). Finally, both countries sometimes have elite courses open only to the most advanced competitors.

How does the beginner know which course to choose? If you have never orienteered or if you orienteered so long ago that you don't remember much about it, by all means start on a beginner course. If you feel you are competent with map and compass—perhaps you are a park ranger, a search-and-rescue professional, or a recce Marine such as Major Hardin in chapter 1—start out on a course rated no more than intermediate. My wife, Linda, and I used to host local meets at F.D. Roosevelt State Park in Georgia. Because Fort Benning, which hosts the Army Ranger School, is within easy driving distance, we frequently had Army Rangers show up at registration with the demand, "Put me on your hardest course!" We did that the first time, and true to Major Hardin's experience, none of the Rangers returned within the three-hour time limit. After that first meet we put them on a beginning or intermediate course with a promise of a free advanced course if they found it too easy. We never had to pay up. The purpose here is not to denigrate Army land navigation training but to point out that orienteering skills, techniques, and processes take the sport to a whole new level for which your background with a compass and perhaps a 1:24,000 map have not prepared you—so start easy and work up.

The following description of beginning, intermediate, and advanced courses uses the U.S. color system but equates equally well with the numerical system used in Canada and most of the world. For comparison, go to www.orienteering.ca/resources/guidelines/ to review the Canadian course and category guidelines for Canada Cups: championship events (10 courses) and smaller events (7 courses). Then simply line up the numerical scheme with the color scheme and the descriptions will apply equally.

Beginning or Novice Course: White

The initial beginning course in the United States is the white course. A white course is 2 to 3 kilometers in length and has little climb (introduced in chapter 2, *climb* is a measurement of how much you go uphill if you walk or run an optimal course in a straight line). White courses typically use paths, roads, or handrails as the most direct route to each control. If a white course has to depart from a trail, power line, or stream to cross through a section of woods or brush, the route is marked with strips of tape to keep the beginning orienteer on course. Generally, on a white course the only decisions you have to make are whether to go straight ahead or to turn left or right on a path, road, trail, or stream. No good course will require you to go backward (unless, of course, you jog past the control and have to return to it).

The two skills required on a white course are precision map reading and, of course, distance estimation by measure and pace. As discussed previously, when using precision map reading, you must orient the map to north and move your body around the map on the opposite side from the direction of travel, keeping the map always pointing north. In addition, you should use the technique of collecting features by thumbing along, placing your thumb on the map at the last place you knew for sure where you were and leaving it there until you get to the next place (the next control, a sharp bend in the trail, a bridge over a stream, and so on) where you are again sure of where you are, both on the map and on the ground. Even if you think you know what you are doing, it is wise to start orienteering on a white course to familiarize yourself with these elementary but important tools, processes, and techniques. You will continue to use them as you progress to longer and more difficult courses. On the white course you will use your compass chiefly to orient your map and to be sure that you start in the correct direction.

Beginning or Novice Course: Yellow

Once you feel the white course is no longer a challenge, it is time to move up to the yellow course. Orienteers measure the challenge of a course with a saying: "You break 10 or win." This rule of thumb means to move up to the next level of difficulty when you are running faster than 10 minutes per kilometer or when you are consistently finishing in the top three of your age group. Yellow courses are 3 to 5 kilometers in length, although 3 to 4 kilometers is more common. They may also have a bit more climb, although by international rules, climb should not exceed 4 percent of the length of the course (this is occasionally waived by necessity in hilly terrain). Yellow courses take orienteers off paths and roads into the woods and fields (but not far from the linear features). To the two skills of the white course, precision map reading and distance estimation by measure and pace, you now add rough compass reading. Again, you must orient the map and use the technique of collecting features by thumbing along, but now you can guide yourself off the trails by using rough compass reading (you should not need to go far) or precision compass reading and by keeping a careful pace count after measuring the distance on a map.

Intermediate Course: Orange

The orange course is the introduction to the more advanced orienteering that occurs as you leave the comfort of roads, trails, and paths and navigate through the woods. The skills, techniques, and processes are the same as for the advanced courses (see the next section), but the orange course is shorter (4.5-7 km, although most orange courses should be closer to the minimum distance) and the control locations are less difficult technically. Most controls are located on a large feature or on a small feature that is on something large. For example, it is not unusual on an orange course to find a small boulder that is sitting on top of a large hill. From a process standpoint, route selection starts to play a much more important part on the orange course. A good orange course should offer more than one good route choice for many of the legs between controls and should have longer handrail options on most legs.

Advanced Courses: Brown, Green, Red, and Blue

To navigate an orange course and any of the advanced courses (brown, green, red, and blue), you will now call upon all five skills (precision map reading, distance estimation by measure and pace, rough compass reading, rough map reading, and precision compass reading), the five techniques (finding attack points, aiming

off, collecting features by thumbing along, catching features, and following handrails), and the five processes (orienting the map, simplifying, selecting the route, developing map memory, and relocating).

Every single course, regardless of difficulty, requires that you keep the map oriented and that you thumb along. However, on the intermediate and advanced courses, route selection comes significantly into play. Route selection begins with your objective; in other words, starting with the **c**ontrol. Next, determine the **a**ttack point, and only then decide on your **r**oute. As you have already learned, the useful acronym for this effort is *CAR*. Depending on the map and ground, you also may use all of the orienteering techniques of finding attack points, aiming off, catching features, collecting features, and using handrails. Moving at race pace may now require relocating yourself through the process of **s**topping, **o**rienting the map, locating a terrain **f**eature, and **a**cquiring that feature on the map (SOFA). Remember not to sweat it if you are temporarily mislocated; everyone has been or will be at some point. It is how fast you recover that will determine if you are in contention for a spot on the podium.

Hopefully this explanation of the various courses has given you enough information that you know what course you wish to run when you actually enter the meet. Let's get back to meet preparation and what to bring with you.

GATHER YOUR EQUIPMENT

Before you leave home, be sure that you have a watch, compass, and whistle. If you don't normally wear a watch, buy a cheap watch just for orienteering. Also buy a whistle (see chapter 2). A whistle can save your life should you become immobile or totally lost, so you need to buy a pealess safety whistle. A pealess whistle has no moving parts (no pea in the middle), so it works when wet. If you don't have a compass, check with the meet-information contact person to see if you can rent a compass at the meet site. Quantico Orienteering Club rents compasses at its meets, but because the rental fee is nominal and the compasses are expensive, you may be required to deposit your car keys or driver's license until you return the compass. Should you own an e-punch for electronic punching, be sure to take that as well. If you don't have your own, you can rent one at most meets that use electronic punching; again, it is useful to find out ahead of time. As with the compass rental, expect to leave your driver's license or car keys until you return the e-punch. Should you lose either, expect to pay for it before your collateral is returned (in other words, take enough money or your checkbook).

It is good to have your own compass. After falling and breaking a couple, I now carry two! Half a dozen times, someone at the start line who suddenly realized she had forgotten to bring a compass has been lucky enough to borrow one of mine. If you do not know what compass to buy and if you can rent one at the event, rent one and ask about compasses after the event. Most orienteers will proudly show you their compasses and tell you why they chose that particular one. You need a watch because nearly every orienteering meet in the United States has a three-hour time limit for being out on a course. You can buy an acceptable watch for a few dollars—just keep it in your orienteering bag. Be aware that some meets that use electronic punching do not allow you to carry a cell phone because it can turn off older e-punching devices and because many cell phones have GPS capability. Therefore, your cell should not be your means of knowing the time because generally you won't be allowed to carry it. Besides, it is easier to glance at your watch than to drag out your phone (and risk losing it).

At the risk of sounding overly stern, let me make a point about when having fun orienteering must absolutely stop in consideration of others. It is the height of selfishness and rudeness to stay out on your course for well over three hours just because you are having fun and you want to find all of the controls. You are highly likely to set off a massive search, pulling people off other duties to look for you, and no one is going to be happy to see you at an orienteering meet again. It is even more horrendous (and selfish) to leave the course without checking in at the finish so the meet officials know you are safe. At some point your failure to check in automatically triggers a search. Unless you or someone else can confirm that you returned safely, the meet organizers are obligated to drop everything and search

If you psych yourself out because of poor preparation, you are unlikely to start, run, or finish well. Just ask the interscholastic champion who won at his first attempt, lost badly at his second attempt, and won handily at his third and final time. Why did he lose so badly in his second attempt? His orienteering skills did not diminish before the middle championship, but his concentration did. As he said later, he lost in no small part because he could not find his orienteering shoes before the race (he had left them at home). With the missing shoes on his mind, he walked away from his car without his compass, only realizing its absence after a long uphill walk to the start line with no time to go back to the car. Able to borrow a compass from another competitor, he appeared cool and in control. However, he confessed later that he was so upset on the inside that he ran right by the first control. Then he compounded the error by recovering so poorly that he made a 15-minute error—pretty hard to overcome at a championship. The moral of the story is good event preparation allows you to focus on the orienteering. By the way, he is now perhaps the best U.S. orienteer in his age group and he has the potential to be a world-class orienteer—so did he ever learn! For years, I used an index card when I packed for a meet. It listed my orienteering suit, gaiters, two compasses, whistle, shoes, socks, sweat band, and watch, among other items. It seems simple to remember, but I was very competitive and wanted nothing to disturb my concentration.

One other aspect of meet preparation that is often overlooked is how long it will take to get to the meet site and how tired you are likely to be upon arrival. One elite West Coast orienteer entered a meet in Canada that was a nine-hour drive from his home. He worked a full day and then drove most of the night, arriving at the meet site just before he was due to start. With no time to clear his head, rest his body and mind, or get on the map (i.e., thinking about orienteering versus worrying that he might be late and miss his start time), he ran more than 1,600 meters past the first control (nearly a mile!) before he was able to slow down and locate himself. At that point, he realized what a bad day it was going to be, so he went straight to the finish, let the meet officials know he was DNFing (*DNF* stands for "did not finish"), took a long nap, and drove straight back home. As they say in business, "Sleep is a weapon. It will hurt you if you don't get enough!" To do your best in orienteering, you should arrive well rested on the day of the meet, clear your mind of all distractions, and think orienteering.

for you. You must make every effort to be back at the finish within your time limit (usually three hours) and never, ever fail to check in at the finish before you depart the meet site. I do not mean to be off-putting, but this breach of good sense is so important to avoid. On the good side, all courses are designed to be completed in well under the announced time limits, so just be sure that you do not tackle a course that is beyond your physical or orienteering capability. Should you find that you are in over your head, then keep up with the time and graciously go to the finish when your time limit expires.

DRESS PROPERLY

You should wear older clothes that you are willing to get muddy, wet, and perhaps snagged on a briar or two. Military clothing such as fatigue, utility, or battle dress uniform (BDU) pants (the name depends on the service) work well for the beginner, but unless you are JROTC, an entire uniform is heavy and is generally uncommon in orienteering. Likewise, an old pair of jeans will work, but keep in mind that jeans are cotton, which can tear and rip easily, and will wick heat away from your body when wet—worth remembering in cold weather. Old running shoes or light boots work well, too. Taking a change of clothes for after the event is a good idea, and always leave an extra pair of dry socks and a small towel in the car or bus for postmeet comfort. Finally, have some water, a sports drink, and food back at your car with your dry socks. Fruit is excellent to restore your energy. Should you have the good fortune to attend a national A-level meet, you may find an orienteering vendor or two from whom you can buy an excellent compass and any other equipment, from thorn gaiters to a ripstop O-suit to special orienteering shoes. Several vendors are also listed on the Orienteering USA website at www.orienteeringusa.org (type "O vendors" into the search field).

Figure 8.1 shows an orienteer in an O-suit with gaiters, compass, and so on. To orienteer well, you do not need any of this gear except for the compass, watch, and whistle. And, no one much cares what you wear so long as you do not resemble a moving control. Orienteering is a very egalitarian and unassuming sport.

One other thought: Once you begin to accumulate some orienteering gear (such as a watch, a couple of compasses, an e-punch, some spare socks, maybe an O-suit, and a favorite pair of orienteering shoes),

Figure 8.1   Plan ahead! Wear proper clothing and equipment. Have your clues, e-punch, and compass safely attached to your hand and wrist, and your map in a map bag. Don't forget your emergency whistle!

seriously consider getting a specific gym bag or backpack in order to keep everything in one easy-to-find place. Then, make it a habit to repack everything in that bag as soon as possible after the event. For example, your compass and e-punch can go in as soon as you get back to your car or bus, whereas your O-suit and even your favorite orienteering shoes may need to go through the washing machine before you load them into the orienteering bag. It is smart to place contact information (name, address, phone number, e-mail address) in a zippered compartment or a sealed plastic snack bag inside your orienteering bag. Carry a plastic grocery bag or two for holding your wet shoes and clothes until you get home. Although not necessarily an irreversible mistake, you can upset your entire mental preparation if you arrive at a meet only to find that your compass, your probe, or even your entire bag is back at your house.

KNOW YOUR START TIME

Once you have located a meet and figured out how you will get there, the most important meet information to determine is your start time. If you must preregister for the meet, your start time will likely be posted online or at the meet site. In the latter case, you need to know when the first competitors are starting so that you arrive in plenty of time to get your start time and prepare to orienteer. If meet times are assigned only at the meet, then your first action upon arrival is to find out when you start and commit yourself to meeting that start time. Along with your start time, you also need to know how much time it takes to walk or run to the starting place. This information is usually online or clearly visible when you register.

Meets generally have three to five (or more) courses starting simultaneously. Therefore, meet directors usually start the last competitors no later than 1:00 p.m., with everyone having a three-hour time limit for completing the course. Starting the last competitor by 1:00 p.m. gets everyone back to the finish line before it gets dark. The three-hour time limit is from the time you start, not from 1:00 p.m. Because safety is a major concern, you are required to return to the finish after three hours whether or not you have completed your course and to report to a meet official that you are back—*especially* if you did not finish the course. That way, the meet administrators know you have returned safely and do not have to mount a search for you as a missing person. If you want everyone at a meet angry with you (and probably your school and your coach), forget to report in and go home! If it cannot be absolutely confirmed that you are safely back, a search has to be made to ensure that you are not lost or lying unconscious somewhere on the course. Again, if you do not complete your course within the time limit, be sure to tell a meet official, preferably an official at the finish line, that you have returned safely and did not finish your course. Make sure that person writes down your name or your bib number (if you are issued bib numbers), and then do not go back out on the course. Once you complete a course or withdraw, the rules do not allow you to go back out on the course except to render assistance to an injured or sick person or to help conduct a search. Note that you do not go back out on the course

to conduct a search on your own but only as assigned by meet officials in accordance with their safety plan.

If the meet starts at 11:00 a.m., competitors can usually start until 1:00 p.m., and each person who is on the same course (orange, for example) starts three minutes apart (so you won't be forced to follow each other); this means, however, that only 41 people can start on any course in the two-hour time period. Consequently, if you have a start time of 11:27 a.m. and you are late and miss it, there may be no slot to start you until 1:00 p.m. (and only then if the meet organizers are willing to extend the start times just for you). If you do have a good excuse, by all means tell the starter, but remember that the starter is trying to keep everyone safe and the competition fair. Finding out your start time and arriving in plenty of time to be ready are your most important tasks before you orienteer. If the meet uses electronic punching, changing a start time may be easier, but only if a new slot is available, so find out your start time and be there! One recent North American Championship had so many competitors sign up that the meet director announced prior to the meet that there would be no changed or late start times. Such an announcement is unusual in the United States, but it reemphasizes that it is your responsibility to know your start time and to be at the starting line on time.

The weather at the Georgia Navigator Cup started out sunny and warm for the majority of the start times in January 2002. Therefore, most orienteers started the course in light clothing. An unexpected front arrived, bringing cold, driving rain. More than 100 people quickly got very cold and wet, with some chilling dangerously close to hypothermia (hypothermia is always serious and can be deadly). Fortunately, every runner who quit the course checked in at the finish line and those whom the organizers had to find and bring out of the woods were also reported to the finish-line crew. In less than an hour, all competitors were accounted for and the most seriously cold ones were being warmed and dried, averting what could have been a disaster. Always, always check in!

PICK UP YOUR MEET PACKET

More formal and organized meets requiring preregistration generally have a large envelope for each competitor. That envelope is called your *meet packet*. On the outside of the envelope you should find your name, start time (or times, if you entered more than one event at the meet), and perhaps information about money due for an entry fee or lunch and whether you purchased a meet T-shirt.

Inside the packet, you may find such useful information as the course setter's notes, how long it takes to walk to the start from a common point such as the parking lot, the safety azimuth or directions, the time limit on the course, the scale of the map, any nonstandard map symbols, your bib and competition number, and even clue sheets for each event. (Clue sheets are discussed in chapter 9). Obviously, you want to arrive in plenty of time to read and thoroughly understand your meet packet. To plan your preparation, work backward from your start time to allow plenty of time to get to the start (about 10 minutes early).

For more formal meets, there should be online instructions about where and when you can pick up your meet packet. If your packet contains a bib number, as it should for national A-meets, immediately mount it on the outside of your orienteering shirt. Packets with bib numbers usually contain safety pins. If it is cold and you are wearing a coat, you will more than likely warm up quickly once you start moving, causing you to unzip it or take it off. Regardless, the bib showing your orienteering number should be plainly visible at all times, so think about its visibility before you stick the bib on the outside of a coat that you may end up wearing around your waist. Competition photographers can more easily identify you by your bib number. Likewise, as you dash with aplomb into the finish chute, those working the finish will identify you by your bib number. And, finally, if there are marshals on the course, they too will identify you by your bib number. In larger meets or those hosted by larger clubs, your registration packet may also contain an e-punch if you rented one. In that case, you use the e-punch to record your visit to each control as well as at the last timer at the finish line. If you own your own e-punch, just be sure you have it at the start. As noted, e-punches can be rented but are expensive compared with the small rental charge, so be prepared to hand over your driver's license or car keys as collateral.

For less formal meets, the same information as in the meet packet may be posted online along with the directions to the meet site. Or, upon arrival, you may find several copies of the information set out on nearby picnic tables or stapled to a nearby post. Finally, when you check in and pay your fee at a local meet, you may not get a meet packet. Instead, you may be told useful information by the people handling your registration or referred to another meet official who provides that information away from the occasional chaos of registration.

Course Setter's Notes

The course setter's notes are well worth studying. The course setter has visited all of the controls and is familiar with the mapped area. Her notes describe the terrain and any features out of the ordinary. The notes will also tell you how terrain may change from one part of the map to another and how recent weather may have affected the appearance of water features.

Here is an example of the course setter's notes from a meet at West Point, New York:

> **"West Point exhibits many of the characteristics of the Hudson Highlands. Significant cliffs and rocky areas are present throughout the map. Please exercise caution throughout your course. If damp or wet conditions are present, much of the area will be quite slick. Please exercise caution if this occurs. The map is bounded by roads; do not cross a major road near the edge of the maps as it will *not* be beneficial to your race."**

From these notes, the orienteer would know to wear appropriate shoes. For example, orienteering shoes with spikes are quite slick over rock faces, so an old pair of running shoes may provide better traction.

Here's another example, this time from a ski orienteering meet at Laurel Ridge State Park in Pennsylvania:

> **"The map scale will be 1:7,500 with 5-meter contours. You are encouraged to try both the A and B courses, with the B course first. Obey the purple arrows that denote one-way trails (hills). Do not ski on these marked trails in the opposite directions. Signs posted**

at the bottom of the hills will also warn you. The map currently shows only contour lines, ski trails, major vegetation boundaries, and manmade objects. Ski trails are drawn as green lines: Dashed green lines mark a good track made by a snowmobile, usually 1 to 1.5 meters wide; solid green lines denote a fast, skateable track made by a snowmobile, usually 2 to 3 meters in width; and wide solid green lines mark a very fast and wide (more than 3 meters) track. Due to the expected snowfall, the mapped trails may be actually groomed differently (e.g., narrower or in an extreme situation, not at all)."

Again, this is all good information to know before you put on your skis.

Finally, here's one last example, this time from the West Coast:

"Come join CROC on the banks of the Clackamas River at Milo McIver State Park near Estacada (Oregon). Our easier courses will be generally flat, but expect to do some climbing and occasional bushwhacking on green. (No worries, poison oak and stinging nettle can be avoided.) McIver State Park is a 1,680-acre state park with many miles of trails winding along the Clackamas River. The park is very accessible yet large enough to give participants a feeling of 'getting out there.' There is a nice mix of paved paths, open grass, and wooded areas. The terrain is both flat and hilly. Most of the orienteering route choices will include trails due to thick vegetation. The advanced course will be designed with the challenge of multiple route choices for most legs and will be a little longer than typical."

Map Scale

One piece of information that you want to get quickly (after getting your start time) is the scale that will be used on your map. If you are running an advanced (red or blue) course, the scale will probably be 1:15,000. If you are on the other courses, it may be 1:10,000, and if you are doing trail or sprint orienteering, it may be 1:5,000. Ski orienteering may be 1:7,500. Why can't you assume what the scale will be based on the color of the course? Although it is fairly safe to do so

in a national meet, never assume that what has been published is accurate, because running with the wrong scale is a sure recipe for disaster. There could have been last-minute changes that were not published. *Always* ask what the scale is for your course, and then check your map (the scale is usually printed on each map). Also, at local meets, the host club or team may have a large supply of maps of one scale or another (often 1:15,000) that they are trying to use up to get back their printing costs, so everyone will use that scale, no matter the course.

You need to know the exact scale for your course so that you show up at the start line with the corresponding scale easily accessible on your compass—not somewhere else (too many things to handle and possibly drop). Most orienteering compasses come with a 1:10,000 scale, which matches the millimeter or centimeter scale and is normally useful for everyone except runners on a red or blue course. Some orienteering compasses come with a removable scale (see figure 8.2), allowing you to easily interchange a number of scales on one compass.

Maps are often copied at local meets (versus being printed), so you need to be aware that copying can distort both the map and the scale. If the map was distorted when copied (made larger or smaller), the scale that was copied at the same time still works even though it will not exactly match up with the permanent scale on your compass. If your compass does not have the correct scale, there is an easy fix. Find a piece of athletic tape (duct tape will work but can leave more residue than athletic tape), cut a narrow piece to lap over both sides of the front of your compass, and stretch it on tightly. Now find a red pen that won't smear easily (any color will do in a pinch) and a compass or map with the correct scale and copy it onto the tape on the front of your compass. As an extreme example, suppose a meet official decided to increase the size of the map by copying it 100 percent larger. If that map was previously at a scale of 1:10,000, it has now been changed to a scale of 1:5,000 no matter what it says in the map legend (which is also twice as big). So, it is smart to match up the scale on your compass with the scale on the map. If they differ, go with the map scale.

Finally, any meet that does not use electronic punching will use paper or Tyvek scorecards. Tyvek resembles paper but is a synthetic material that does not melt, or blob, when it gets wet. Chapter 9 covers the preparation of your scorecard and steps to ensure that you do not lose it on the course.

Figure 8.2 Note the difference in the interchangeable scales for the baseplate compass compared to the printed scale on the thumb compass.

VIEW THE FINISH LOCATION

Quite often the finish area may be close by parking, registration, or the start. If the finish is visible without going onto the course, it is not against the rules to take a look. To cut down on the logistics of people and material, the start and the finish can be in the same place (you simply start out one way and finish from the other direction). If so, it is perfectly acceptable to walk over to the finish area (do not enter the course, however) and look for the last control. It may be readily visible because many meet directors use colored flags like the ones you see at used-car lots or brightly colored plastic tape funneling competitors from the last control to the finish line. Checking out the location of the last control, if plainly visible to any competitor, is ethical and is not considered cheating. Just remember that the last control has to be available for all competitors to see, which it often is. Do this because you are probably going to be tired coming into the last control and it is helpful if you have a mental picture of what you seek. Seeing the last control before you run may save a few seconds in your run. Many competitions have been decided by a few seconds (or even by one second), so take a peek if the opportunity is there.

STUDY THE COMPETITION MAP

If there is an available copy of the competition map, by all means examine it as closely as time permits. If there is a single copy, perhaps hanging on a string at the start, orienteering culture requires that you share. If only one or two people can view it at one time, limit your study time to a minute or less if others are waiting. Then, move out of their way. The first items of interest on the map are the small features in the legend. The time to discover that the green *X* on this map is an evergreen tree is now, not after you are on the clock, running the course. Be sure to check out the map legend for any unusual features of that particular map. Just as a legend can be a story, so the legend of a map is the story of the map. Next, look at the boundaries of the map to determine if there is any place you could easily run completely off the map. When you are on the map, it is hard enough to find the markers. When you are off the map, it is *really* hard to find the markers—how about impossible?

Next, look at the water flow patterns. Which way does water flow through the terrain? If you know where the water is and how it flows, you should have a good feel for the rest of the terrain, particularly for determining which contours are showing you up and which are showing you down. (Remember the discussion of up and down from the descriptions of landforms in chapter 3 and how to recognize whether you need to go up or down.) Most importantly, you should study the map to locate hilltops and other higher ground such as spurs and then observe that water would flow down from the higher ground to lower areas, especially to streams. If there is sufficient time to look at any linear features, look at railroads, roads, and trails in that order. Finally, check the scale on the map one more time, especially if it is the competition map. It is possible that you will have the same map with a different scale, though generally what you are shown is similar to what you will use.

You have another possibility for useful map study if you happen to have an older map of the event location. Many large meets are held on maps that have been used before or new maps that are similar to older maps nearby. There will be more about what to study from such a map in the following chapter, and, yes, it is ethical and it is not against the rules. To be fair, you should have obtained the map in a manner that anyone else could have, such as entering a past meet in the area where the meet was open to all comers or downloading it from the Internet. By contacting the event organizers, you may be able to buy a map that will give good information about the competition terrain. Such maps are often posted for sale as part of the registration process for national meets and are a wise purchase for review, particularly if you have not orienteered there before.

Finally, many national meets recognize the advantage that local orienteers have from familiarity with the terrain and will host model events on the Friday before the meet (two-day meets normally start on a Saturday). The model map will be of similar terrain to the competition map and will be marked with controls in similar locations to those of the event. Competitors go out to the model event on their own time and walk or run all or part of the marked course, paying particular attention to the terrain to get a feel for what they will encounter during the event. This is excellent no-pressure preparation and can be enjoyed with one or several competitors while discussing techniques and thought processes appropriate for the model map terrain.

SUMMARY

Why is thorough preparation so important? Preparation matters because orienteering is between you and the course—not the other runners and not the clock. From this chapter, you know how to find an orienteering meet. You know that having your orienteering gear is essential to your mental preparedness. You know what to wear and what equipment you need to compete. You have an idea of what course to run based on your ability and experience, whether you are on a course in the United States, in Canada, or somewhere around the world, and you know that the most important piece of information about the meet is your start time. Let's move on to chapter 9 and get ready!

A good tip for the prepared orienteer is to make a checklist of what you will wear and carry to an orienteering meet. If you are on a team or in a group, this can be a group activity. Once you have your list, put your orienteering essentials in a specific backpack or gym bag, preferably one that is clearly marked "orienteering" or that does not look like your other bags. The coach or teacher should also check to see that all of the orienteers traveling to the meet have a compass (or money to rent one), a watch, and a whistle and that they know their start times if these are available beforehand. Coaches and teachers should be sure their orienteers also know how much time is needed to get from the parking lot or assembly area to the start line.

Get a meet packet from a meet (or download one) and go over the contents and information with the orienteers, particularly the course setter's notes. Explain again why it is so important to stay within the time limits for any meet. Once at the meet, take the group to the finish line if that area is open to everyone and go over the competition map if one is available. If a copy is available ahead of time, go over it en route to the meet. And, of course, do the model event if one is offered. The coach or teacher should help competitors decide which course to run at which level of difficulty. It is discouraging to fail to complete a course that is too difficult and very unfulfilling to run one that is too easy.

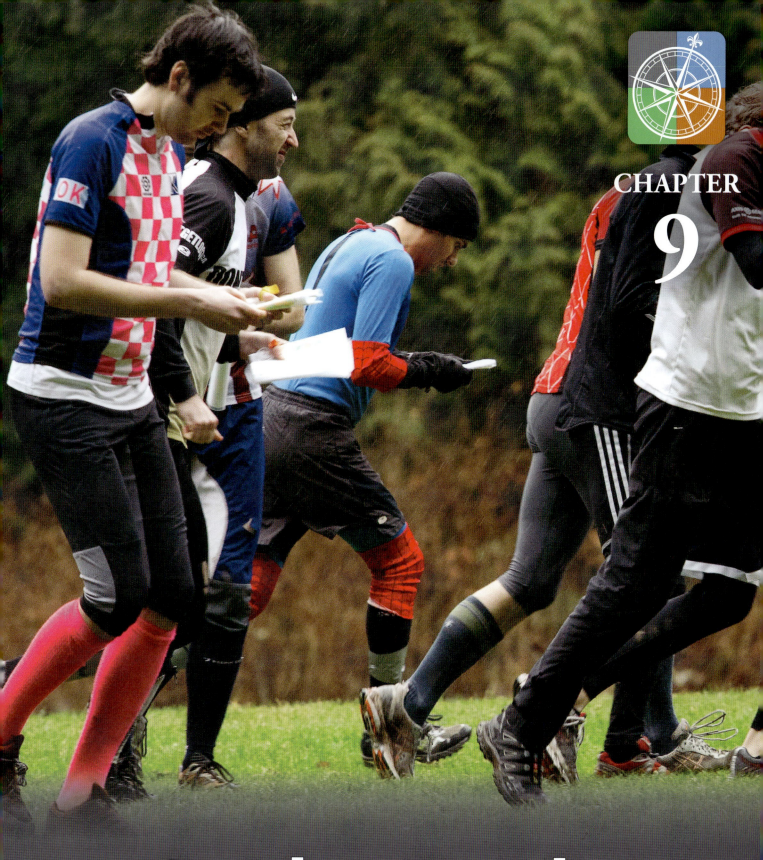

Getting Ready
to Start Your Course

Chapter 8 has prepared you for a meet. You have rented or brought your compass and it has the correct scale. Your whistle is in your pocket or around your neck and you know the three-blast code. You have read the meet packet and know the unusual terrain features from the course setter's notes. You are dressed properly for the weather and the briars and you have carefully reviewed a copy of the competition map. Your bib is in place for all to see. You are ready! What are the next steps to take?

STUDY YOUR CONTROL DESCRIPTION SHEET

Early on we said orienteering is much like solving a mystery and, as in a mystery, orienteering uses clues—at orienteering meets you receive a control description sheet, commonly called the *clue sheet*. It is either in your packet or at the start, and it serves to identify each control by the feature where it is located (the main clue is the feature, such as a reentrant junction or a hilltop). If there is a clue sheet in your packet, you want to study it in advance so that you merely have to glance at it as you orienteer. Additionally, there is information on the sheet that you may want to transfer to your scorecard for manually scored meets.

The clue sheet describes the feature that is in the center of each numbered circle. In other words, it tells you exactly what feature you will find at each numbered control. The circle number is on the map and matches the control number on your clue sheet. A marker (usually orange and white) positively identifies each control with a specific control identifier (sometimes called the *code*) on your clue sheet. For example, control 1 may be identified as *AA* and located on a hilltop. Control 2 might be identified as *129* and also located on a hilltop. (Do not expect the control identifiers on your course to be numbered consecutively—in practice, several courses may share a particular control.) Having a unique code on each control marker ensures that when you find the control labeled *AA*, you know you have found control 1 and not control 2, which is also located on a hilltop. Control identifiers can be numbers or letters and do not have to be in any certain sequence, but they should be unique in order to control or identify each location. Note that you can have the same feature several times on a course, but each time it will have a uniquely coded marker so that

you know precisely which control you have found. The clue sheet may provide additional information such as which feature you're looking for—it will tell you that you are looking for the southernmost feature or the one in the middle. It might also tell you that the control is at the top of the feature (e.g., reentrant) or at the foot of the feature (e.g., cliff).

You should study clue sheets at home or in the classroom so that you are not mystified halfway through a course by some symbol or indication that you have never seen before. By the way, it is considered acceptable to ask others at the start line what a symbol means; however, it is not permissible to do so once you are competing. More information on reading clue sheets is at www.williams.edu/Biology/Faculty_Staff/hwilliams/Orienteering/clues.html. There may be more than one clue sheet in your packet, especially at an A-meet. An A-meet may easily have three or four events, such as a sprint, a trail-O (trail orienteering), a medium distance, and a long distance. Each will have its own clue sheet.

Using the Clue Sheet

Take a look at the left column of the clue sheet in figure 9.1. (In a competition, your clue sheet should be identified by your course, whether it is a number as in Canada and Europe or a color as in the United States). The first necessity is the number of the control, such as control number 1, 2, or 3. Remember, if you are on a cross-country course, you must take the controls in sequence; thus the numerical order. The second bit of important information is the control identifier. It may be a number, a letter, or any combination of numbers and letters. Why is the control identifier so important? Can't you just run to the center of the circle? The answer is that there may be five or more courses in the woods in addition to your course and some controls are bound to be on similar features. Should you come to a control that is on a similar feature to the one you seek, you can confirm that you have found the correct control by checking the control identifier. A complete description of all of the information found on a clue sheet can be found at www.orienteeringbc.ca/sage/IOF_Control_Descriptions_2004_long.pdf.

The third important piece of information is the control description. If you are on a white or yellow course, the control description will be written out for you. If you are on an advanced course, the control description will be in the IOF symbols. The IOF

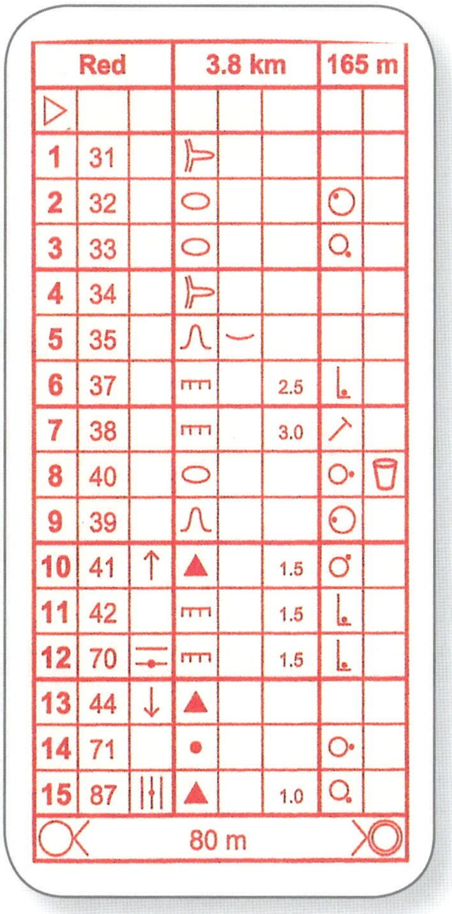
Red
3.8 km
165 m
1 31
2 32
3 33
4 34
5 35
6 37 2.5
7 38 3.0
8 40
9 39
10 41 1.5
11 42 1.5
12 70 1.5
13 44
14 71
15 87 1.0
80 m

Figure 9.1 Sample clue sheet.

Courtesy of The USMA Orienteering Club.

> At my first meet with more than one course, I stopped counting my paces as soon as I saw a control. To my unhappy surprise, it was not mine! Despite a great deal of evidence right before my eyes, I never realized I was competing in an event with multiple courses—yes, I've made every mistake in this book. I checked two other controls before I found the correct one—a totally avoidable waste of time!

control description symbols can be found at http://orienteering.org/wp-content/uploads/2010/12/IOF-Control-Descriptions-2004.pdf. The symbols at that site should be what you read on the clue sheet. However, should you advance to making orienteering maps, review the slightly different symbols used in mapmaking at http://orienteering.org/wp-content/uploads/2010/12/International-Specification-for-Orienteering-Maps-2000.pdf.

The control description tells you exactly the feature you are seeking, whether it is a hilltop, a trail junction, a reentrant, or any other feature. Any further data about that control is designed to give more and more precise information to pin down exactly which feature, perhaps of similar features (remember parallel errors), is the one with the control. The clue sheet should also indicate the water controls, where you will find cups and water to drink. Water can also be placed at obvious places such as trail junctions. If so, these will be marked on your map.

Carrying the Clue Sheet

Affix the clue sheet to your body in a manner that makes it easy to read. I prefer to have it on my left arm inside a plastic cover. Orienteering clubs often print the clue sheet on the map itself, which is good because you won't lose it as long as you hang onto the map. I still attach the clues to my left arm to avoid having to unfold my map (see the next section) just to read

Clue Sheet Tips

1. An upside-down six looks like a nine and an upside-down nine looks like a six, so be sure you are going to the correct control! Rather than turning the map around to view the clues when I'm running south, I simply look at the clue sheet taped to my arm.
2. If you are using a scorecard, write the control identifier and the IOF symbol for the control description on the scorecard under the control number. That way when you are punching the correct box on the scorecard, you have one more chance to compare the control identifier you sought with the one you found.

the clues. Remember that the top of the map is north. Therefore, any writing on the map will be printed so that it is right side up if you are on the south side of the map. Should you happen to have your body on the north side of the map because you are running south, then the clue sheet and all of the numbers will appear upside down.

FOLD YOUR MAP PROPERLY

Most orienteers fold their competition maps. There are good reasons to do so, but note that a folded map will hide the clue sheet for at least half of the course and probably more. If you do not carry your clues somewhere besides on the map, you will waste precious time unfolding the map every time you need to check the clues. Why fold the map at all then? If you are running from control 5 to control 6, it helps to focus your

When properly folded, the map is held in the direction of travel with the top of the map oriented to magnetic north.

attention if you fold the map so that the route from 5 to 6 is centered. That way you do not have to constantly search the map with your eyes to find the area between 5 and 6. Also, your thumb should be moving between 5 and 6 as you pass features that tell you exactly where you are, and your thumb has to be able to reach that part of the map. Second, a folded map is easier to carry in one hand and does not seem to catch on branches, briars, and vines as easily as the unfolded map does, so you rarely drop it. Orienteers who use a thumb compass usually keep the compass and the map in the same hand with the compass over, beside, or close to the route. Obviously you must fold the map when using a thumb compass or you cannot get the compass close to the route if your route is away from an edge. So, although there are good reasons to fold the map, if you do, you should be sure the clues are easily available by writing them on your scorecard or attaching them in some fashion to your arm.

SCOPE THE MAP

Just as it is permissible and desirable to locate the last control ahead of time so long as that control is in plain sight for everyone to see, it is also ethical and smart to look at maps of the event area ahead of time. Making a new map for a national championship is the rule (versus using an existing map). The area covered by the new map is normally embargoed for at least a year before the championship, meaning you cannot walk, run, or orienteer in the embargoed area. An embargo is another way of saying that orienteers should stay out of the championship area so that no one has the unfair advantage of recent knowledge of the terrain. Similarly, you should not view a copy of the new map unless it is freely available to all competitors. However, it is excellent strategy to review any other existing map of the area in which you will orienteer. Such maps can be found in a variety of places. You may be able to buy an existing or nearby map when you register for the event. If so, buy one and study it before you compete. If no maps are for sale, there may be one or more copies posted at the registration site. Arrive early and study them. If you or your friends have orienteered in that area before, one of you may have a copy of the previous map in your files (it is a good idea to keep copies of all your maps with an index to allow the easy retrieval of the right map when you need it). Finally, you may be able to download or purchase a nonorienteering map (especially of a park or national forest), which could be valuable as well.

Map Clues

Let's assume you have found an existing map. What exactly about the map is important? At the beginning of this chapter we started with the clue sheet, but there are other helpful indicators or clues, such as the actual shapes and sizes of the features, that come right from the map. You can get a feel for some of these by looking at a map in advance, and others will become obvious as you actually orienteer on the map. For pre-event map study or at the event, a useful clue for a linear feature is the direction of that linear feature. Studying the map before the race reveals the general direction of linear features. In addition, the exact direction of a major linear feature such as a highway or river may jump out at you in prerace map study. Put your compass on the feature on the map (i.e., align your direction-of-travel arrow and rotate your bezel to line up the north orienting lines) to get its direction. Also do this for any other significant linear features, such as a trail that runs north to south. Should you encounter any of these pre-noted features during the competition, they will be useful as navigation and directional check points.

If you are already out orienteering on the terrain and encounter a significant linear feature and you want to know if it matches one you see on the map, pick up your compass from the map and sight down the feature to make sure it runs in the correct direction. (You can make good time running on a trail, but if it is not the correct trail, you may be losing time moving away from the control.) To sight down the feature (let's assume it is a path that runs west to east), you face one direction on the path, pull the compass away from the map and into the middle of your body, and turn the bezel until the red end of the magnetic needle is aligned with the north magnetic orienting arrow inside the bezel. Without moving, note where the direction of travel arrow is pointing. In this instance if you are facing east on the path, the direction of travel arrow will be pointing east, which is 90 degrees. Without moving the bezel, now place the compass back on the map with the direction of travel arrow pointing down the path on your map (in this case pointing east on your map). If this is the path you think it is, and you have done this procedure correctly, then the north magnetic orienting lines inside the bezel should line up with the north magnetic lines on the map. This is easier to do than it is to describe! It quickly becomes second nature and you will even learn to estimate the approximate direction of a stream or trail that is only rarely a straight line. Carefully look to

be sure there are not similar parallel features to the one you have found but which may later swing away in a direction you do not wish to go. If everything lines up, you have identified the linear feature and can use that information in your navigation decisions.

A well-drawn orienteering map can also provide definitive information because it presents almost the exact shape of the features. Another clue can be the slope of the land as shown by the contours. It is possible, unfortunately, to misread contours so that you see a reentrant as a spur and a spur as a reentrant. Therefore, look for a nearby stream or hilltop to be sure you should be going uphill, downhill, or relatively level. There can be negative clues or indicators during orienteering as well. For example, you may come to an easily recognizable feature on the ground that is *not* on your route on the map. When that happens, stop, locate the feature on the map, and figure out where you are. Figuring out where you are, which we refer to as *relocating*, uses the SOFA process from chapter 6.

Legend

Another great source of information from the map is the legend. If the orienteering map has a legend, read it first specifically for the little symbols that may be unique to that particular map. Having seen maps and legends in this book, you know what a legend normally contains. What you now want to know is what is different about this map. Generally speaking, if the map uses special symbols (remember the flat places on the DVOA map where charcoal was made in chapter 3?), those symbols are likely to be the small *x*s and *o*s with the occasional sideways *t* for a downed tree. Pay particular attention to the color of these symbols. For example, a black *x* is a human-made feature. A brown or green *x* would then indicate a special feature on the map. It is also possible that if the map you review is old enough, the feature may still be listed but has changed color! There is a map in Maryland in which the oldest version shows rootstocks in green, but the most recent version shows those same rootstocks as brown. (A rootstock is created when a tree topples so that its roots stick up into the air at least 1 meter high. One problem with rootstocks is that they deteriorate over time and may be harder to see as a distinct feature on the ground in 5 to 10 years. Another problem with rootstocks is that a strong windstorm can create new rootstocks after the map has been drawn, leaving the orienteer to decide which rootstocks are mapped and which are not.)

Contours

Another important piece of information on the map, usually printed right under the scale, is the contour interval. Chapter 3 mentioned that the contour interval tells you how far apart the contour lines are (see the Bull Pond map, figure 9.2). If the contour interval is the standard 5 meters (16.4 ft), then each brown contour line on the map represents about 5 meters either up or down from the contour lines on either side (or just one side for a hilltop).

So, how is this information useful? If you are standing at the foot of a 50-foot (15-meter) hill, then it should be shown on the map with three contours. If the contour lines on your map suggest that the hill is a lot higher than 50 feet, then you know you are at the foot of the wrong hill! Also, contour lines that are close together warn of steepness, whereas contour lines that are far apart represent gently sloping or even virtually level terrain. Contour lines that are very close may indicate a dangerous or unsafe area that you should orienteer around versus climbing up or sliding down.

Be aware that contour intervals vary, and the contour interval for a specialty map may also differ. For example, the IOF specifies a contour interval for sprint maps at either 2 or 2.5 meters. In very flat terrain, such as Florida (see the Moss Park/Split Forest map, figure 9.3), you may see a 1.5-meter (about 5 feet) contour interval. Such a small distance between contour lines usually means that the gentle slope of the land may not give good information about your location. The contour interval and the scale are printed on most orienteering maps whether or not any other part of the legend is printed there. Wouldn't you like to know this type of information ahead of time (particularly if you are using collecting features as a technique) rather than figuring them out as you orienteer?

Map Boundaries

After thoroughly perusing the legend, check the boundaries of the map. Are there places where the map boundaries are not distinct—that is, places where careless orienteering might take you completely off the

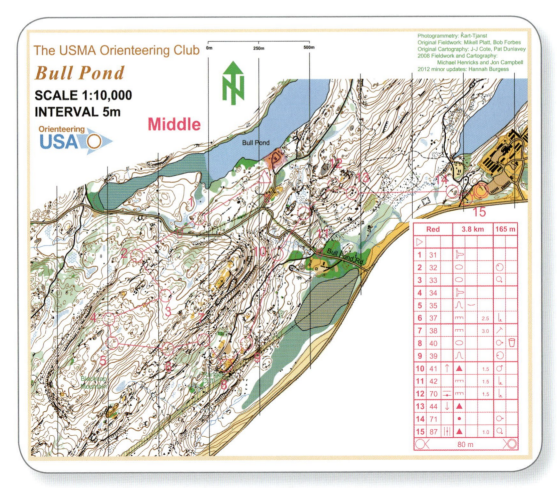

Figure 9.2   This sample West Point map shows a standard contour interval of 5 meters (16.4 ft).

Courtesy of The USMA Orienteering Club.

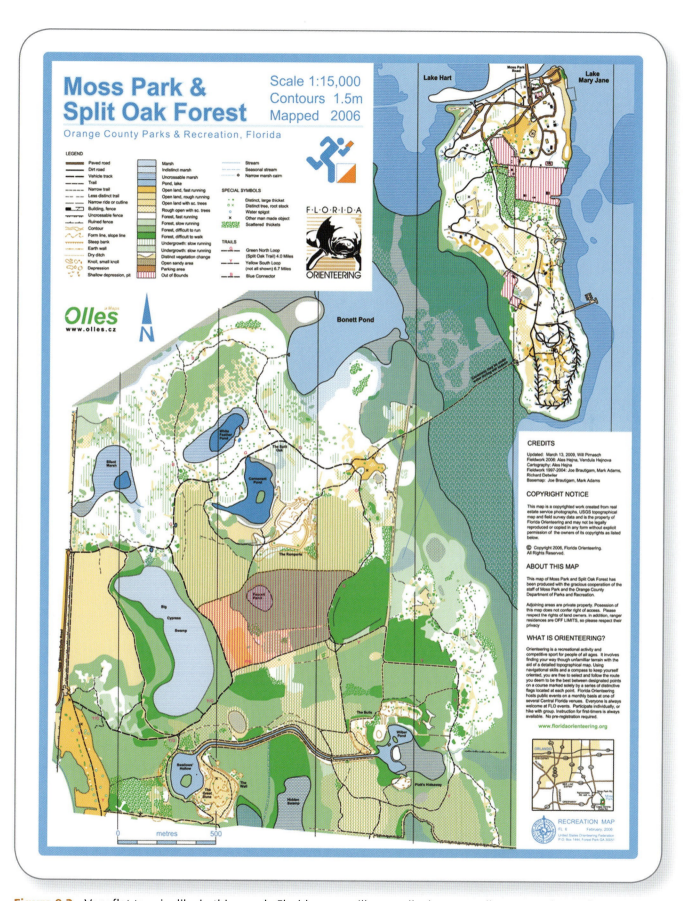

Figure 9.3 Very flat terrain, like in this sample Florida map, will generally show a smaller contour interval.

Courtesy of Florida Orienteering—www.floridaorienteering.org.

Early in his orienteering career, one of Coach Turbyfill's teammates ran as quickly as he could to his next control, which was hung in a lone tree at the foot of a cliff. Paying no attention that he was approaching from the top of the cliff and too focused on his map, he ran straight off the top, falling some 10 meters down through the tree, which fortunately broke his fall. He tumbled to the ground at the feet of another orienteer who stood there in total astonishment as she waited to punch her scorecard. Brushing himself off, he said, "Good morning," and rushed off to find his next control. Seeing his USMC orienteering suit, she is reported to have muttered, "I heard Marines were crazy and now I've seen it!" The point is to pay attention to your contour lines so that you know whether to go up or down, and also to know the symbol for a cliff (chapter 3)!

map? If so, you want to be very focused on the map in the event that any of your routes go through those areas. A distinct and easy-to-find boundary would be a road, a long fence, or a significant water feature. An indistinct boundary could be in the middle of the forest, on the side of a hill, or among numerous parallel features. Remember, relocating yourself or finding control markers can be difficult when you are on the map, and it can be near impossible when you are off the map!

Earlier we mentioned downloading or purchasing nonorienteering maps of areas where you will be orienteering. Those maps can be useful for knowing where boundaries are located, especially if the boundaries are close to the orienteering area. For example, let's say you notice before the event that the park map shows a paved road all along its western boundary. During the event, you drift west and suddenly find that paved road. Even if you are off the orienteering map, you know enough to head east until you can relocate.

Hydrography

The third step after checking the legend and the map boundaries is to study the hydrography on the map. Hydrography is the science of the measurement, description, and mapping of the surface waters of the earth with special reference to navigation. So *hydrography* is not only a great orienteering term to know, it can be a significant piece of information about the map. Hydrography shows you how the water flows. You may say that obviously water flows downhill, and you'd be right, but it is not always easy to read contours to distinguish downhill from uphill on your orienteering map. If water is down, then everything away from water is up. Thus, if you can locate water such as in a stream or pond, it is much easier to read the contours

by working uphill from the water or downhill to the water. Doing this ahead of time through map scoping may save you seconds or even minutes during your orienteering. Your intent is to know how the water flows through the area to give you a general sense of what it will feel like and look like to orienteer in this terrain.

Linear Features

For your fourth item to study, look at the main (large) linear features on the map. How do they run? Remembering that streams can be linear features, does the hydrography reveal that the water flows generally from east to west (or in any other direction)? Do the spurs generally run in a certain direction as well? Are there roads that might be useful as boundaries and handrails? Is there a railroad track or are there power lines that could help you navigate? Should you be on the Umstead State Park orienteering map in Raleigh, North Carolina, you will wish to pay attention even to the runways at the Raleigh-Durham Airport. Airplanes, which you can see from the park, take off and land in line with the runways, and that could be useful information if nothing else is working for you.

Intricate Trail Networks

Fifth, look for trail networks, especially intricate networks that include trails intersecting frequently and running in various directions in the mapped area. Trail running can be the fastest way to navigate, particularly in areas of thick undergrowth, limited visibility, and difficult footing (e.g., mud, fallen timber) and in flat areas with few collecting features. However, intricate trail networks can be confusing. (Is that the third trail to the left or the fourth that you're using as an attack

I once transposed the contour lines in a CIOR competition in France so that I ran past the hill upon which the control sat (mocking me, I'm sure, as I charged by) and on to the small valley on the other side. My team and I (CIOR competition teams are made up of three people, one of whom is the orienteer) wasted 20 minutes searching that valley before I realized my mistake. Before that error we were in great position to be a top-10 finisher, and I aced the rest of the course, but that didn't matter—there was no way to make up the unnecessary loss of time. The error was unnecessary because based on my misreading of the contours, I had been so sure the control was in the valley that I had ignored my pace count as well as how closely a river flowed by on our side of the valley. Either clue would have sent me to the top of the hill! By now you have figured out that I have made every mistake of which I warn you. As I look back over my orienteering experiences, I wish I'd had this book decades ago!

point or collecting feature?) So, if there are intricate trail networks in an area and you can study them ahead of time, you may be able to use the trails to your advantage rather than getting disoriented in their complexity and wasting valuable time relocating.

As you study such fine details as an intricate trail network, get a feel for the map in general. If you have never orienteered at West Point or in Florida or Houston, for example, you may be surprised by the unusual terrain. The academy-produced maps at West Point are superbly detailed, but during a first look at one, most orienteers are shocked by the plethora of rock features, from boulders to cliffs (see figure 9.2). The map has far too much black on it! If you orienteer at West Point, you are going to see tons of rock features and you'd best be prepared to tell them apart and to pace carefully.

In looking at a Florida map or one for Houston, Texas (see figure 9.3), most orienteers wonder what happened to the contours. If the land is relatively flat, as it is in Florida and parts of Texas, the orienteering map will have few, if any, contours, and the contour interval may be a meter or less. Therefore, if you depend on the rise and fall of the ground to tell you where you are on the map, you'd best look for other features such

as vegetation boundaries, trails, and streams, and, as always, use your distance estimation skill.

Feel the Terrain

You have now read the legend, checked out the boundary areas, followed the hydrography, noted the main linear features, and paid attention to any intricate trail networks and other unusual features. What is the ultimate goal for all of this information in your mind? To quote noted orienteer and rogaine organizer Malvin Harding, "Go from seeing the map to feeling the terrain." Wise advice from Mal, and the better you do it, the faster you will orienteer. In other words, when you see contours forming a hill, imagine a hill in that shape in your mind. Then when you run to it, the hill will be familiar and you will know that you are in the right place because it looks right and feels right. (Note: *Rogaine* once stood for Rod, Gail, and Neill, who popularized the sport in Australia. Now few remember that, and rogaines are known as **r**ugged **o**utdoor **g**roup **a**ctivities **i**nvolving **n**avigation and **e**ndurance. They are long orienteering events, often lasting 24 hours, that are great training for orienteers and particularly for adventure racers.)

When you decide to run on a trail, always get a rough bearing off the map and check it with your compass against the azimuth of the trail to be sure you go in the correct direction. If trail running can move you quickly toward your control, the reverse is that it can take you just as quickly in the wrong direction. It is not a good feeling to run 300 meters in the wrong direction, only to turn around and retrace your steps. You know that you have lost time and that you are wasting energy every step of the way.

PREPARE YOUR SCORECARD

The strength (in members and volunteers) and wealth of the orienteering club staging the orienteering meet often determines whether the meet will use electronic punching or paper or Tyvek scorecards. You are wise to prepare for both possibilities. The scorecard is part of your plan for how you will proceed because it lists the sequence of controls. It was noted earlier that unless you are doing score orienteering, where you find as many controls as possible within a time limit, you must take the controls in order. Your scorecard gives you that order. In addition, your scorecard is your record of having visited each control. Table 9.1 explains what information you should put on the scorecard, where you should put that information, and why the information is there.

In many events using scorecards, the first four items may be printed on the card for you. The last three rows on the card will not be. All of the information on the card is your responsibility. Make sure the printed information is correct, and make any corrections before the race starts. All the information you have to enter yourself, including the information in the squares, is your responsibility (see figure 9.4).

You must be careful not to lose the scorecard on the course. It sounds simple, but almost every orienteer who's been at it for any length of time has lost a scorecard and been disqualified for lacking proof of visiting all the controls. Let's make this clear: If you do not return with your scorecard, the event never happened for you!

There is one rarely executed exception to this rule. Should you lose your scorecard between the start and control number 1 (or any time thereafter if you are willing to return to control 1), you could conceivably run to the center of each circle on your map in the proper sequence, hope or determine you are in the correct place, and punch the side of your map at whatever control you found, again remembering to keep the punches in order on the side of your map. Once you traversed the entire course, you would have a record on your map, which would be acceptable at most finish lines. However, your navigation would have to be perfect since you would not know any control identifiers (unless you carry a separate clue sheet) and would simply have to decide that you were at the correct control each time. As more and more clubs change to e-punching for every meet, this is an increasingly unlikely scenario.

Attach the scorecard to your body or clothes with some type of fastener. I pin my scorecard to the bottom of my orienteering shirt using at least three safety pins. Some orienteers place the scorecard in a small plastic bag and tape the bag to a sleeve, and others hang it in a plastic bag around their neck. Use any secure means that works for you in order to keep your scorecard. What you do not want to do is carry it loose in your hand, because sooner or later you will drop it. Nor do you want to put it inside a waist pack, zippered pocket, or any other place where it is difficult to

Table 9.1   Scorecard Preparation

What	Where	Why
1. Name	In name space	This card belongs to whom?
2. Course	In course space	On what course?
3. Category	In category space	Which category?
4. Start time	In proper space	When do you start?

5. Correct control
   a. Code
   b. Clues
   c. Punch
	In squares	Which one is your control?
		What are you looking for?
		What is the proof that you were there?

pull out when you are ready to punch in mechanically, unless, of course, you are in no hurry. Where seconds count, you should have the scorecard easily available as you approach the control. You lose valuable time if you must fish it out of a zippered pocket every time you punch.

Even with electronic punching, there will be a manual punching device at each control (on rare occasions a battery can fail on an e-punch receptacle, requiring manual punching). For such an occurrence, use the manual punch to make a mark somewhere on one side of your map.

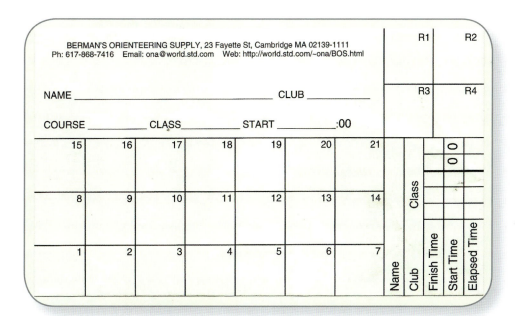

Figure 9.4 Sample blank scorecard.

Reprinted, by permission, from Berman's Orienteering Supply.

The CIOR military competitions for reserve officers always include an orienteering course. At a competition hosted by Canada, I served as technical delegate, which means that prior to the event I checked all the venues of competition—shooting, running and swimming obstacle courses, first aid, and, of course, orienteering. Norwegian teams are always strong in orienteering, but somewhere along the course, the best Norwegian team lost its scorecard (practically unbelievable for such experienced orienteers) and was disqualified. Doing well in orienteering would have positioned them to win the overall championship if no other team beat their time.

The Norwegian team immediately appealed on the grounds that they could completely describe all 23 controls, thus proving that they had been to each one. I was called before the appeals jury because I had repeatedly vetted the course to be sure that it met standards and I, too, could describe every control from memory. Slowly and carefully for half an hour without looking at a map, the Norwegians perfectly described each control. I had my map to double-check and marveled at their amazing recall after only one trip around the course. I truthfully told the appeals jury that, in my opinion, that team had visited every control. Unfortunately the rules allowed for no wiggle room and their time was thrown out. This illustrates two lessons: First, take good care of your scorecard or it may end up disintegrating slowly in the woods, and second, you will become proficient at what may seem quite difficult to you now. After orienteering for just a short while, you will be able to describe each control you visited, naming your attack point and analyzing your route choices.

Manual Punching

The manual punch will be plastic, often bright red, and will somewhat resemble a stapler (see figure 9.5). I wear my scorecard near my waist because the punch is hanging from a string and I can pull it to my scorecard easily without wasted motion or time. If the scorecard is around your neck, you may have to squat or kneel to validate your scorecard.

The scorecard has numbered boxes. When you get to the first control, for example, you place the scorecard into the pincher end of the punch and press the pins into box 1 on your scorecard. The pins on the punch will make a number, letter, or pattern that has been recorded for that control, providing proof that you were there. You proceed around the course recording the mark of each punch in the correct box on the scorecard. Should you accidentally punch in the wrong box, punch elsewhere on the scorecard and explain what happened at the finish before you hand in your scorecard. Should you forget to punch at a control, you can only complete the course by going back to that control and punching your scorecard. If you do lose your scorecard and you have been out less than three hours, either look for it (remembering where you last had it, which should be somewhere between the control where you now need it and the last control where you punched) or complete the course without it (but punching the edge of your map in the generally vain hope that someone will bring in your dropped scorecard). If no one returns your scorecard, as is likely, just call it a training day. Regardless, get to the finish line by the time limit. As noted earlier, should you lose your scorecard before reaching the first control, you may be able to complete the course by punching in order around the side of your map as proof you visited every control.

Electronic Punching

Whenever you orienteer using electronic punching, you are in for a treat. It is a good idea to go over in your mind what will happen. First, you either have your own e-punch (also called a *stick*, *dibbler*, or even *probe*) or you must rent one at the event. On most entry forms you will be asked for your e-punch number. Second, when you get to the start area, find the clear and check devices. They look just like the timing devices at each control and should be marked *clear* on one and *check* on the other. They will not be hidden. You use them

Figure 9.5 Manual punch: *(a)* a check-in sheet with a manual punch hanging from the control marker and an electronic punch receiver; *(b)* or shown with an e-punch receiver.

At the Control

1. As soon as you see the control you are approaching, and you feel sure it is your control, use CAR to determine in which direction you will depart the control area. (I tend to think of going right, left, or ahead instead of a cardinal direction such as east.)

2. Look ahead for your route choices (using CAR) whenever you come to part of your route that is easy running (e.g., a trail) or where you have to walk (e.g., uphill). You don't need to make the final route selection, although that can be good, too—just get an idea of what you will do at the next few controls.

3. Move away from the control as quickly as possible. One of the easiest ways to locate a control precisely is to see another orienteer standing where you think (or hope) it may be, obviously planning how to proceed to the next control. Don't make that mistake! Do your planning in advance so that after you punch in, you leave immediately. Do not stand by the control and give the location away to the competition. Move away as fast as you can!

in order. First, insert the e-punch into the clear device until it beeps and a light flashes. Then move over to the check device and repeat. The check device ensures that your e-punch is clear and ready to receive new data during your run. If you do not get a beep and light, you may well have a defective e-punch (you definitely do if everyone else is able to clear and check) and must replace it.

Your e-punch has signaled that it works. How do you carry it? The e-punch should come with a stretchable fabric circle that holds the device and can be tightened on one of your fingers. This elastic band can break, loosen, or come unfastened, so it is a great idea to back up the band with a wrist string that can be snugged (see figure 9.6). Should the band slip off, the wrist string will keep you from dropping, and possibly losing, the e-punch. Some have laughed at those of us who wear wrist strings (sometimes called *dummy cords*). Others have cried when they lost their e-punch after an unexpected fall or when the catch failed and the e-punch dropped silently to the ground and beneath the leaves.

Decide where to wear the e-punch and slip it on your finger. I wear it on the forefinger of my left hand. I also hold my map in my left hand (my compass is in my right hand, secured to my right wrist by a wrist string). Since you only need the e-punch at the control, mine is out of the way under my map until I arrive. In the last few steps, I reverse my palm and clinch three fingers and my thumb into a fist. The e-punch, which is on my forefinger, now sticks out. Then I simply insert it into the hole in the timing device until I hear a beep. Having done this hundreds of times, I rarely watch for the flashing light but am already checking my compass to be sure I start away from the control in the correct direction.

Figure 9.6 An e-punch should be held to the finger with a finger band and also secured to the wrist with a string to assure it will not drop off while competing. Replacing a lost e-punch is costly and may result in a lost race. This e-punch is shown along with a plastic holder for containing the competitor's course clues.

TEACHING TIPS

As an orienteer, teacher, or coach, there is a lot you can do to master this chapter. First, be sure everyone has a copy of the control descriptions from the IOF and has read or heard how to use a scorecard. Then master the symbols by turning the sheets over and trying to stump each other with the symbols. Likewise, make a paper copy of a map and have everyone fold it to best show the route and terrain from one control to another. So that everyone folds to show a different leg of the course, one person can fold to show the route from control 1 to 2 while another can do 2 to 1 or any other variation and then let each other see how you folded the map. Give everyone a copy of a map with a legend (hopefully a color copy) and take turns answering the question, "What is important?" (Here's a hint: linear features, hydrography, and map edges where it would be easy to run off the map. For a second hint, name as many linear features as you can from the map, such as trails, roads, waterways, and ridges.) Finally, take a scorecard and take turns filling in the blanks by locating features on the map as control points and then listing and describing them with the correct control descriptions and in the correct sequence on the scorecard.

One other thought, coaches: When you instruct your team that if they lose their scorecards they should treat the event as a training day, stress that it is a *hard* training day. They should not just walk in; they should practice skills, techniques, and processes *at top speed.* Since they are already disqualified, a few more mistakes won't matter, and many will be amazed at how well they can orienteer at top speed—exactly what you want them to learn. Surprisingly, then, losing a scorecard, while disappointing, may be of much more future benefit than completing that day's course.

SUMMARY

Now you are at an orienteering event and your scorecard is filled in and firmly attached to your shirt—this event definitely is going to happen for you. When you opened your meet packet in chapter 8, you pulled out the control description sheet, or clue sheet, for your course, and if the event is not using electronic punching, you wrote the control identifications in the boxes on your scorecard under the correct control numbers. Because you are familiar with the IOF control symbols, you may have drawn them in the boxes as well. The clue sheet is taped in clear plastic on your arm for easy reference.

You have scoped an old map of the orienteering area and carefully examined a newer map that was posted for all competitors. Examining the legend of the map, you are prepared for any unique symbols, such as a green *x* for a certain kind of tree, and you know the competition map scale and the contour interval. You paid particular attention to the hydrography and to map boundaries (just in case your course goes near an indistinct edge of the map). You also carefully noted the linear features, especially any trails and trail networks, and now have a feel for the terrain. You are generally going to recognize when the ground should be going up, going down, or remaining flat. You know whether to expect lots of rock features such as boulders and cliffs (any West Point meet); lots of small depressions (the kettles of Kettle Moraine) left behind by glacier action in Wisconsin; the flat lands around Houston, Texas, and in Florida; or the steeper terrain of Lake Tahoe. Finally, if you are fortunate enough to be at a meet with electronic punching, you know how to clear and check your own e-punch or the one you rented. You also are ready to carry that e-punch because you bought a dummy cord and you know how to use the e-punch to check into each control. Yes, you are ready to go orienteering!

Running the Course

In past chapters you have studied the tools, skills, techniques, and processes of orienteering. You know how to read a map and use a compass. Now you are at a meet and you are ready to go. Chapter 10 takes you to the start line and tells you what happens there and what you need to do to start your race. There is an art to orienteering, whether it is how to proceed to your first control or how to punch in or log in once you find it, and these moves are explained. Chapter 10 also covers how to avoid a common error at water points and how to finish your race (before you go to the award ceremony to receive your medal). Finally, it discusses what to record on your map at the event and what to record at home so that you (and your teacher or coach) can analyze how and what you did so that you can train to improve your times. Remember the old saw, "Train to your weaknesses. Compete to your strengths." Good records will reveal both your strengths and the areas you need to improve.

AT THE START LINE

Clear your e-punch before you start or check to be sure you have the correct scorecard. At many start areas your course map will be in a box of like maps (e.g., all orange in one box, all red in another). Often there is a waterproof pen as well; if so, take the time to write your bib number on the back of your map (remember not to turn the map over until you are told to start), or if your map is in a plastic bag (as preferred), write on the plastic. I also add my name. This takes seconds and makes it easy to find my map after the event. Maps at national meets are normally taken away from you at the finish line until every orienteer has started so that no one can get an unfair advantage by seeing a map of the course before starting. This is particularly important if the start and finish are close together. After everyone has started, the maps are set out in piles, and you can pick yours up. At local meets you normally keep your map after your run.

At well-attended meets, there may be two courses of the same color, such as green-X and green-Y, usually divided into a women's and a men's course—both equally difficult and equally long. (Color-coded courses, such as green, are used mainly in the United States and in local meets in England. In Canada and many other countries, courses are number coded.) If there are *X* and *Y* maps for your course, be sure you get a map from the correct box (you find out which course you are on when you register). Never forget that meet personnel can make unintentional mistakes when boxing up maps. Before you have placed your number and name on the back of your map, hold it up facing away from you and toward the meet official standing at the start. Ask if the map you are holding is the correct one. For instance, if you are on the green-Y course, the dialogue should go something like this: "Is this the green-Y map?" If the meet official says, "No," then you ask her to find the correct map for you. Competitors have left the start with the wrong map only to discover the error after they are on the clock and in the woods. Clearly, an ounce of prevention is worth a pound of cure.

If you are attending a smaller meet, you may simply be given a start time and handed a map of the area with no course drawn upon it. You then take this map to a nearby table holding master maps of each course and red (or occasionally purple) pens. There you copy your course onto your map. Why red pens? Because red is not one of the five colors used in making orienteering maps, so red lines and circles stand out on the map. Why purple pens? Purple is occasionally provided for people with red–green color blindness. If you are in this group, you should let the course director know well ahead of time to see if a special map can be prepared for you. In drawing your own course, it helps if your orienteering compass has one circular hole for you to mark the location of each control and one triangular hole to mark the start (see figure 10.1). Use the circular hole to mark the finish by drawing a smaller circle inside the one made with the compass.

It is important to draw straight lines connecting each control in the proper sequence so that you do not overlook any of the controls. In most meets, skipping a control disqualifies you, but even if it doesn't, it hurts your score. No matter how fast your time, someone who completes an entire course within the time limit beats someone who does not visit all of the controls. Also, drawing a line between each control assists in finding a heading to that control when you place the compass on the map (see chapter 3).

Occasionally, meets only hand out clue sheets at the start. For those meets, be sure you have some means to secure the clue sheet to your body if you wish to carry it (see chapter 9).

You now have secured your punch card or your e-punch. Your clue sheet is fastened to your arm, your whistle is in your pocket or around your neck, your compass is in your hand, you are wearing your watch, and you're at the start. Your time is called and you are, at last, handed your competition map. What should you do when the starting whistle blows?

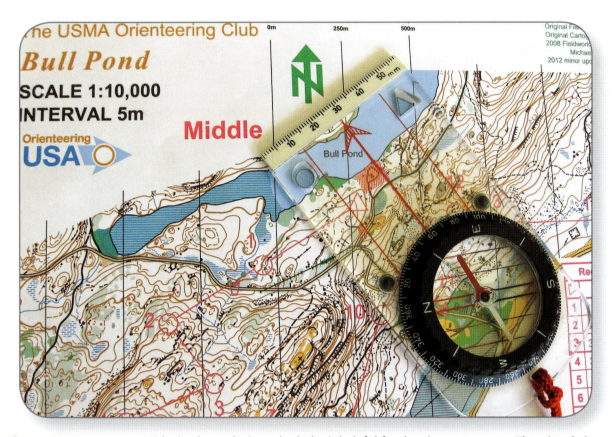

Figure 10.1   A compass with circular and triangular holes is helpful for drawing your course. The triangle is used to indicate the start location, and the circle marks a control location.

Make sure that you number each circle to help you take them in order and to match them to the appropriate clue. Write your numbers in reference to the top of the map (north) so that a nine reads as a nine, not a six. Consider underlining the number six so that if you happen to be running south, the six is obviously not a nine. Also think about putting a slash across the stem of your sevens as most Europeans do so they are not mistaken for ones.

Read and Orient the Map

If you are using electronic punching, insert your e-punch into the timing device at the start. As soon as you hear a beep, immediately turn your map over so you can read it. If you are using manual punching, turn your map over when the starting whistle blows.

As soon as you turn your map over so that you can read it, orient it to north and locate the start triangle. You now know where you are on the map. Next, fold the map so that all of the first leg (called *leg 1*) is shown from the start triangle to control 1. One orienteer I

know, a former North American champion, folds his map just once. I like a smaller package so I fold mine twice. Practice and fold to suit you. With your compass dial in the direction to the first control, use the scale on your compass to measure the distance on the map to the control. Remember collecting features by thumbing along? In this technique, you place your thumb on the map as you progress around the course, but only when you know exactly where you are. You know you're at the start, so begin thumbing along by putting your thumb on the start triangle. Practicing such good habits makes them patterns that eventually you follow automatically.

CAR

Look at the feature that is your first control, comparing it with your clue sheet. Having already found the direction to the first control, measure the distance to that control on the map. Locate an attack point, pick your route, and you're off! Watch people at the start. Few orienteers, especially beginners, fully plan their routes to their first controls before they start to move forward. Instead they will go 20 to 30 meters and stop, intently study their maps, perhaps take a measurement or a direction, and start moving again. For some reason, human nature tells us not to be the last one to begin moving away from the start area, leading to this somewhat wasteful start–stop dance movement. More experienced orienteers tend to move out fast, often because their experience permits them to plan and execute a route on the run, but they rarely do the stop–start routine. Until you get to that level, just ignore your pride and stand there until you have gone through CAR and have a plan of action. Then move forward and execute your plan.

ON THE COURSE

This is an absolute rule: Take your time going to control number 1! Do not blow the first control! Missing the first control makes for heavy mental pressure, often causing you to outrun your orienteering ability in trying to make up the lost time. Outrunning your orienteering ability causes more mistakes and moves you into the luck class of orienteers. Unless you pick winning lottery tickets every time, the hoping-to-be-lucky class is miserable in orienteering. We presented SOFA in chapter 6 because we all get a little mislocated at times, but going to the first control is one of the worst times to wander around because it is such a mental downer.

Manual Punching

As stated earlier, as soon as you see the control marker, slow down, look at your map, pick your next attack point, and plan your route *before* you arrive at the control. This is a good time to slow to a walk, get a distance to the next control, and dial in a new direction. With practice you can do this quickly while catching your breath at the same time. Now recall the code for this control (or look at your clue sheet) and reach for the punch while reading the code on the control. If this is the correct control, punch in the corresponding box on the scorecard. You have already planned your route to the next control, so do not linger around the control you just found but exit quickly so that you do not give the location away to other orienteers.

Start the memorization process by looking at the control code for the next control (easy to do if it is printed in the next box). Drop the punch and move off in the direction you have determined for your route. If you are farther along the course and there is water either at a control or at a nearby point, stop, punch first, and then get a drink. *Never* drink before you punch in. You can guess why you do not drink first: Too many orienteers have done so and forgotten to punch their scorecards.

Electronic Punching

Again, as with manual punching, take your time to the first control. Likewise, when you see the control, look at your map and select your next attack point and route. Consider slowing to a walk so that you can both measure on the map and get a direction. Reach out with the e-punch as you read the code on the control. Read the code on your clue sheet and announce the code and the number of the control out loud (no need to shout) as you place the e-punch into the hole in the timing device. Why say it out loud? You do not have the numbered boxes on the scorecard to help you be certain of the control sequence, so your chances of skipping a control increase when using electronic punching. It doesn't happen often because you also have to misread your thumbing along and your map, but I have done it. So, say the control number and the code out loud to reinforce that you are at the correct control.

Listen for the beep or watch for the light, and move off in the direction you have determined for the next control. If you feel uneasy about the current control—perhaps because it is well off your pace count (too close

Before you start, remember to write the control code in the numbered box for each control. Then all you have to do is look at your scorecard instead of your clue sheet.

Should you help design a course, remember to make the first control straightforward so that your competitors get off to a good start. Make the first control relatively easy with a catching feature close behind it if possible to keep error-prone and overly excited orienteers from going too far past it.

or too far) or because the collecting features along the way did not match up well—then stop and be sure that you did not skip a control. In other words, if the control identifier (code) is correct for, say, the fourth control, be sure you have already visited controls 1, 2, and 3. If the control identifier is not correct but you are certain you are at the correct location based on the map, your distance estimation, and any other clues, then check to be sure your clue card and your map are for the same course. When you pick up your map at the start, someone is usually there to help you select the correct map, but if you also pick up the clues at the start, no one else will check to be sure you selected the correct clues for your course.

I have picked up the correct map (green-Y) and the wrong clue sheet (green-X) and not caught my error until the second control because both green courses used the same first control. After a bit of confusion, I caught my mistake at the second control because I had great confidence that I had come to the correct location on the map (and I'm not always so sure). Therefore, I took the time to compare the clue sheet on the map and the one on my arm, and I saw that the two did not match. Because I had the correct map, I knew I had picked up the wrong clues. From the second control forward, I used the clue sheet affixed to my map.

Water Controls

As with manual punching, when you reach a water control, drink after you have logged in to the timing device, not before. Although we tell you to leave the

The e-punch is inserted into a hole or well in an electronic unit placed at the control location. The electronic unit records the time of insertion on the e-punch. To know the time has been recorded, be sure that a light flashes or a beep sounds before leaving the control. Use the manual punch if it does not!

When you orienteer, you receive lots of information to process, including from your map, your pace, your compass, nearby competitors, the terrain over which you are passing, and more. Likewise you have skills, techniques, and processes to use that data. As you become more experienced, you will learn to differentiate among information that can be ignored, information that is useful, and information that is critical to staying on course.

Chapter 9 gives an example where I misread the contours in one competition, a classic example of ignoring critical information. In that instance, I misread the contours so that I mistakenly ran to a valley instead of to the top of a hill. In order to make this mistake, I had to first run past my pace count (which I blithely did), and I also had to ignore a nearby river that was plainly shown on my map and could not have been so close to where I was searching. The river clue (critical information—the river was not that close to the control) finally woke me up that I had overly depended on my terrain-reading ability (good information that I misused), at which point I also recalled that I had run well past my pace count (another critical bit of information that I had ignored). Looking back I can only assume that I had too much energy and not enough brains at the beginning of the course. And at that time I had never heard of confirmation bias or bending the map (ignoring how close the river was to the control), but you have read about them now and will not, I'm sure, repeat the mistakes I've already made for you.

The lesson here is to become aware of what information is accurate and what information you might be misinterpreting. Combining several pieces of information such as your pace count and the features from your map that you are passing in the terrain as well as their proper relationships (based on the contours or whether the ground goes up or down from where you are) is much more accurate than overly depending on one or two sources of information such as pace and azimuth or terrain association. Depending on limited sources of information also explains why dead reckoning can be so slow and so far off course at times.

control quickly so as not to give it away, water controls are the exception. Water controls are often shared between several courses, so you may see other competitors there. Although you do not want to take up residence, it is a good practice to stop, take a drink, and either place the cup in the garbage bag or, if there is none, throw the cup on the ground by the water for easy cleanup later. Remember, orienteers leave nothing in the woods!

A meet worker will pick up the cups when he returns for the water jugs. You might volunteer to pick up the water jugs—and nearby controls—after the event has ended. Control pickup is great navigation training with no pressure, and it is always appreciated by the people staging the meet. Of course, be sure that you have an appropriate skill level to pick up controls. It is most unpleasant for the meet officials to believe the meet went well, the competitors have gone home and they can soon follow, only to learn that they now have to search for you because you did not have sufficient skill to find the controls you volunteered to retrieve nor to find your way back!

AT THE FINISH LINE

When you arrive at the finish, turn in your scorecard and explain any discrepancies (such as a punch in the wrong box). If using electronic punching, be sure to insert your e-punch into the last timing device at the finish. Later you will download your electronic information on your e-punch to another computer, but if you stop for a few moments, your time will not be affected. At most courses, the finish is where you have to leave your map until everyone has started. If the finish crewmembers ask you for your map, do not give it up immediately (but do not walk off with it, either). This is a good time to review your map for a reasonably short time. While standing at the finish, pay particular attention if you had trouble with any control in order to see if you can determine why you spent more time finding it than you expected. Quickly review your attack points, especially on any control that gave you trouble. Now turn in your map or, if allowed, keep it, and proceed to the download computer if you're using electronic punching. At the download computer, expect to receive a copy of the split times between each of your controls as well as your total time for the course. Comparing splits coupled with route choices has great training benefit. Comparing splits with other competitors can also reveal your comparative fitness and skill levels. Next, find the refreshment area and hydrate.

Rehydrate

If you like electrolyte-replacement drinks and they are available, drink them. If you prefer water, begin to drink immediately. The earlier you put electrolytes and fluids back into your depleted cells, the faster and easier it is to gain a quick and full recovery. Conversely, the longer you wait to drink, the slower the rehydration of cells within your body takes place. You are hit with a double penalty. First, you started later and, second, the body's rehydration process works slower. Therefore your recovery takes longer. Surprisingly, some studies maintain skim milk is one of the best replacement drinks.

Seek First Aid

While you are taking care of your body, it is a good time to clean any cuts or scratches to prevent infection. There is usually a separate first aid station near the finish at big events or a first aid kit at smaller events. In addition, the orienteering supplies in your orienteering bag should include bandages, an antibacterial ointment, and a cleaning agent such as antiseptic wipes that you can use if nothing is available nearby.

RECORD NOTES ON YOUR MAP

Once your map has been returned, take it out of the plastic and record the following information on the back to begin the process of becoming a more effective orienteer. In the spirit of being self-sufficient, carry your own pens in your orienteering bag. I prefer red and black pens, while Coach Turbyfill prefers orange and purple—neither of his conflicts with any map colors. Expect your less prepared buddies to borrow your pens!

At the top of the map, write your name so that if you are in a group comparing maps and routes, you are more likely to get your own map back. Next write the date of the event and your finishing time. When possible, find out the winning time on your course and write the winner's name and time on the back of your map. Repeat this pattern until it becomes a habit after every competitive or training meet. Patterns become habits and habits become patterns.

On the front of the map, using red or another colored ink, place a small mark (called a *tick mark*) on the map at the attack points you planned to use and at the ones you actually used (sometimes they change when you suddenly see a great attack point that you missed on your double-eye sweep). As best you can remember, draw in your exact route in a color such as red or purple (this gets easier with experience) using a dashed line. After some reflection or based on someone else's route, draw in any alternative routes (again using dashed lines) that you think may have been better than the one you executed. Be sure to use other colors so you can tell the routes apart and stick to the same color for your route. When you study your map in a month or in a year, you want to know which route was yours. Use a dashed line for two reasons: first, so as not to completely cover any linear features that you may have followed (such as a path) and, second, if you use a red pen so that you do not confuse the lines already connecting the controls on the map with the lines of the routes you ran.

Now that you've drawn in your route choices, estimate your lost time for each leg. You accumulate lost time when you go off in an incorrect direction, lose track of where you are and have to relocate, or make mistakes such as parallel errors and have to recover. You can even record lost time for those parts of the leg where you were tentative despite being exactly where you thought you were. I tend to slow down when I get within 100 meters of the control. This is a holdover habit from the early days when I read the terrain poorly and had to be overly careful not to pass the control. I'd be faster today if I copied the orienteers who run with confidence, not slowing their pace until they see the control and need to plan their next leg. I've identified this weakness and I'm working on it—especially at local meets.

Note that local meets are an excellent time to work on weaknesses under competitive pressure because you may not be as concerned about having slower times. Train to your weaknesses in local events and run to your strengths in meets that count. In meets that count, if you are good at using attack points but poor at contouring (a form of following handrails), do as much of the first as you can and as little of the second. But when you train, work on contouring a lot more than attack points. Another good practice at local meets is to run the next course up from your age-group course for the fitness and training effect.

Make a column on the back of the map or use the far right column on the clue sheet marked on your map and record your estimated lost time, usually in minutes and tenths of a minute (i.e., .1 equals 6 seconds, .5 equals 30 seconds, and so on). Add up your lost time and subtract it from your total time. Now compare this new potentially error-free time with the winner's time. From this data you get important pieces of information: Did you have a chance to win? Are you getting closer to the winning time? Might you have won without the mistakes and hesitations?

Now you are on your way to analyzing your route choices and comparing them with other possibilities to determine where you can improve. Once you have drawn your routes, ticked off your attack points, and written down any other data, find other orienteers who have completed your course and compare notes on route choices, attack points, and split times. Comparing routes and times is one of the most pleasurable and sociable aspects of orienteering. Be a teacher—if other orienteers have not analyzed their courses as you have, take the time to explain your analysis to them. Not only might they learn from you, but also *your best learning comes when you are teaching*. Regardless, by having actual data you should begin to see which skills and techniques you need to improve in order to become a better orienteer.

AFTER THE EVENT

The race is over and you have put fluids and food back into your body, but you are not yet finished. (That's why this book is a systematic approach to orienteering—completing the course is only part of the system!) Be sure to review whatever time is posted for you, and attend the award ceremony if there is one. Find out if your team or your friends are having a postrace review of maps and courses and put your data into a notebook or online (see the information about Attackpoint in a later section).

Attend the Award Ceremony

Almost all large events present awards as soon as possible after the last competitors finish. Electronic punching even allows the award ceremony to begin while orienteers are still out on the courses. Larger events may present medals on ribbons or small trophies that often reflect the orienteering area. If you won an award, move up to the front and collect it and let the audience applaud. If you did not win an award, clap for those who did.

Awards are presented by age group and degree of course difficulty, usually working up from the least difficult courses to the most difficult. It is polite to applaud all recipients and to stay for the entire ceremony if your travel time allows. It is also helpful for you to pick up the award for someone who lives near you but has already left the event site. Manual punching can lead to long delays and possible math errors

Getting an award for your country feels great!

in determining the order of finish, whereas electronic punching is normally much faster and quite accurate. At most meets, competitor times are posted in a public place as fast as possible after they are computed. Check your posted time against your own watch; be polite and don't block others' view of the times for more than half a minute. If for any reason you think your time is incorrect, report that fact and why you think it is so to a meet official as quickly as possible. The sooner you note a possible error, the quicker the results can be changed so that the proper person gets the right award. Most meets require errors to be reported within an hour of completing your race, so do not hesitate.

Compare Notes

After you have run, it is more fun and generally more productive to go over your course (from route choice to attack points to errors) with someone else who has run the same course. If you do not know anyone, look around for three or four people comparing maps and find a group that ran your course. You can learn a lot

Although you may get excellent coaching on how to improve one or two aspects of your course execution by asking more experienced orienteers, any coach worth her salt will ask to see your training notebook before seriously trying to help you to improve. Back in my pace-and-azimuth days, I approached legendary orienteer Peter Gagarin for help. We were in Scotland and I was constantly drifting off line in my dead reckoning. Peter immediately helped by asking me to show him how and where I held the compass (I was not holding it straight), but even better, he asked, "Why are you using pace and azimuth? These maps are perfect for terrain association" (i.e., rough and precision map reading). His comment was not the answer I was expecting; it was better. I changed my thinking and improved my times. Asking an experienced coach helped me with one problem. With good records to show my trends, he could have helped me improve much more and much faster—which leads us to the orienteering notebook.

by just standing on the periphery and listening, but most people will eventually reach out and ask you how you did. At the larger meets, particularly two-day meets, there is often a dinner on Saturday night open to everyone at a reasonable price. You will find good food for the athlete, but as a bonus, many will bring their course maps. After dinner, individual orienteers who did well on particular courses are often asked to come up front to explain their thinking, attack points, and route selection with the help of a map projected on a screen. (You don't have to do this if you are shy, but it is an honor.) Serious orienteers pay close attention, for there is always something new to learn in orienteering.

ASSESS PERSONAL PERFORMANCE

Now that you've taken the time to write up your orienteering effort on the front and the back of your map, what's next? Take the map home, punch holes in it, and place it in a three-ring binder. See appendix B for a reproducible analysis page. Using this form, begin to accumulate data on your errors and weaknesses, both from training and from competition. Consolidate the data after every six courses (or three two-day events) and look for trends. Do you constantly miss controls to the left? If so, you may have a pronounced drift to the left and should develop training to either curb your drift or to recognize and allow for it. To work on correcting drift, first check out how you hold the compass. Is it centered in the middle of your body, or does it tend to skew to one side? Second, do you almost always go around obstacles such as trees and boulders to the same side? Third, consider shifting tactics. Are you depending too much on your compass when you should be collecting features to stay on course? This is just one example, but the principle is the same for other solutions.

Race-Analysis Assistance

One of the most pleasurable additions to electronic punching is software called *RouteGadget*. When you've run a meet using electronic punching and someone posts the location of RouteGadget for that meet, you simply go to that location on the Internet, find the

Comparing splits: The race is over, but the job's not finished yet. Now it's time to talk over route choices with your team, evaluate the course, draw the path traveled to each control on the map, and record what was done well and what needs improving. Soon patterns emerge that assist in the design of a specific orienteering training program to help you to reach your competition goals.

orienteering map and your course, and use your cursor to trace your routes from control to control. It helps if you have already marked your map by hand and have it in front of you. Once you have drawn your routes, you can activate not only your routes but also all others that have been submitted for your course. Then, watch as the software traces all of the routes simultaneously. Watching the circles chase each other around your course reveals rather quickly which orienteering routes turned out well and which did not. RouteGadget is an excellent visualization of multiple route selections and their success with little effort on your part. It is a good way to compare your route choices and times with others on your course and to consider where you can improve.

Training Assistance

Today's orienteers have access to another high-tech solution: GPS-enabled watches can be a great training aid. All will plot your route and many will also compute your distance and speed. Though the ability to determine split times between controls has vastly improved through electronic punching, there remains the question of where exactly you went in between controls. Wearing a GPS-enabled watch and using the associated software allows both the beginner and the

expert to plot their actual routes with accuracy. Once you can transfer your actual route to a map, you can ask yourself why you chose that route. More specifically, you can see precisely where you drifted off your planned route, allowing better recall of your thinking and your use of skills, techniques, and processes to determine where you lost time. Likewise, you can see where you did well and figure out why that may have happened so you can repeat those actions. Improving your orienteering is so much a matter of knowing your weaknesses so that you can turn them into strengths and knowing your strengths and learning where to use them. GPS-enabled watches are an excellent high-tech training tool for the orienteer, the teacher, and the coach, particularly if you transfer what you observe about yourself to your notebook.

Other Resources

Another source of information, which may not be specific for your particular competition, is DOMAs (digital orienteering map archives), where some orienteers simply present maps of courses they have run while others draw in their routes. With the former, you can view some beautiful maps and plan your own routes. With the latter, you can compare their route choices with ones you might have taken. Remember, though, the excellent advice cited earlier from a North American champion orienteer to decide on a route and then stick to it!

An online program for orienteers called *WinSplits* can be found at www.obasen.nu/winsplits/online/en/about.asp. It is a web-based information service for split times from orienteering events that gets its data from split times uploaded by organizers of orienteering events.

Attackpoint (www.attackpoint.org) is perhaps the best known site in the United States for orienteers to keep online training logs, post and view split times, and discuss training and competition philosophy. It is a great site and probably the most visited by the U.S. orienteering community.

You won't be a top orienteer until you improve your efficiency, your effectiveness, and your fitness. And, much like the near impossibility of trying to find yourself when you are off the map, it is equally hard to improve your orienteering when you have no idea what you are doing poorly or when you are just guessing. Why don't more orienteers keep records and analyze their runs? Probably because they get faster the more often they orienteer whether they analyze their runs or not—up to a point, and then they stop improving and even regress. Because they see some improvement, they don't take the time and effort to know why. Then when they stop improving, they have no data to explain which orienteering skills, techniques, or processes need to be improved. Those who do see their errors, find their trends, and train to hone their skills and overcome their weaknesses will become competitive orienteers much faster than those who do not. Why not keep records, analyze them to find both positive and negative trends (ideally with the help of a coach), and be the best you can be?

Although it may seem painful to write down pertinent information on course execution just as you finish and to transfer it to a notebook at home, it is absolutely the best way to collect the data that should direct your training. Training from data is the fastest way to improve. It is worth repeating that you should train to your weaknesses and compete to your strengths.

600 orienteers. Should you suffer brain freeze or any other malady causing you to forget what you are supposed to do in the start area, at the start line, or on the course, you have two good options. The first option is to look around and see what everyone else is doing and then do the same (but do not follow!). The second option before you go out on the course is to ask someone who is obviously not starting immediately, "Uh, what do I do now? I'm new at this." Most orienteers are more than willing to help in any way, particularly if they sense that this is your first meet. They want you to succeed and enjoy yourself so that you return to the sport that they already love. You can tell who is probably not starting soon because they usually stand well back of the starting line and often are engaging in casual conversations with other orienteers. If all else fails, at least orient the map so that you can start off in the correct direction!

Remember to go safely to the first control so that you began your race with success. Remember also that when you come to a water point, you should always punch your scorecard or use your e-punch before drinking. You know what to expect at the finish line, and you know to start writing down data immediately afterward so that later you can transfer well-remembered information to your orienteering notebook. If you have trouble recalling your routes, train with a GPS-enabled watch and then compare your actual routes with ones you draw first from memory. Eventually both will closely match.

Through these chapters, you now have enough accumulated knowledge to orienteer like a champion. However, that knowledge is no good to you so long as it is theory. You have to go out and gain experience by actually orienteering. Combine knowledge, experience, and record keeping, and fairly soon you will have true orienteering wisdom. Don't forget to learn to map so that you become one with any map from anywhere. Combine your wisdom with fitness training and good nutrition and you can be one of the next world champions, proudly representing your country—and that goal need not be too far down the road!

SUMMARY

The material in this chapter should prepare you for your first meet, whether it is a local meet with 15 competitors or a national A-meet and championship with

Appendix A

Exercises for Teaching Orienteering Skills, Techniques, and Processes

Exercises in appendix A are adapted, by permission, from USOF, 1991, *Coaching orienteering,* edited by M.J. Childs (United States Orienteering Federation).

Activity	Skills, techniques, and processes	Page number
Map reading		
Map Symbol Relay	Quick recognition of map symbols	137
Never a Dull Moment	Map memory	138
Matching Map Pieces Relay	Precision map reading	139
Map Walk: Handrails	Rough map reading, handrail identification	140
Making a 3-D Map Model	Contour recognition, rough map reading	140
Jigsaw Map Puzzle	Precision map reading	141
Corridor-O	Precision map reading, terrain recognition	142
Window-O	Precision map reading, compass bearings, distance estimation	143
Line-O	Precision map reading, distance estimation	144
Quick-Draw McGraw	Map memory	144
Armchair-O	Rough map reading, visualization	145
Map Walk: Contours and Water-Only Map	Precision map reading, rough map reading, contours, distance estimation	146
Map Walk: Estimating Sizes and Shapes	Precision map reading, rough map reading, contours, distance estimation	147
Fruit Relay	Precision map reading	147
Flash-Card Map Symbol Relay	Map reading	155
String-O	Precision map reading, distance estimation	171
Collecting Features by Thumbing Along	Collecting features by thumbing along, map reading	177
Map Memory Under Stress	Rough and precision map reading, map memory	177
Mapping a Classroom	Precision map reading, visualization	178
Map Orientation	Keeping map oriented by precision or rough map reading, precision or rough compass reading	181
Room-O	Rough and precision map reading, map orientation	182
Pace and distance estimation		
Distance Estimation: 100 Meters	Distance estimation	148
Distance Estimation: Variations	Distance estimation	149
Distance Estimation: Running	Distance estimation	149

Activity	Skills, techniques, and processes	Page number
Map Walk: Estimating Sizes and Distances	Size and distance estimation	150
Relocating: Estimating Sizes and Distances	Size and distance estimation	151
Compass and Distance Estimation Course	Precision compass reading, distance estimation	151
Compass use		
Using a Compass as a Protractor	Precision compass reading	152
Bearings: Five-Step Method	Precision compass reading	153
Compass Zigzag Course	Precision compass reading	154
Running on Rough Compass Reading	Rough compass reading, distance estimation	156
Armchair Bearing Quiz	Precision compass reading, map memory	157
Forms of orienteering competition		
Trail-O	Precision map reading, distance estimation, precision compass reading	158
Control descriptions		
Control Symbol Relay	Clues for control symbol recognition	159
Connect the Dots	Control symbol recognition	160
Control Description Quiz	Control symbol recognition	161
Orienteering technique		
Rough orienteering		
Handrail and Large-Feature Course	Rough map reading, terrain interpretation	162
Fine orienteering		
Sprint-O	Precision map reading	163
Attack points		
Finding Attack Points	Precision map reading, attack point recognition and usage	164
Attack Point Course	Precision map reading, attack point recognition and usage	164
Control techniques		
Control Punching Relay	Code memorization, rapid punching	165
Armchair-O: Aiming Off	Rough map reading, rough compass reading, recognizing when to aim off	170

(continued)

Activity	Skills, techniques, and processes	Page number
Control techniques *(continued)*		
Armchair-O: Finding Handrails	Rough map reading, handrail recognition	166
Conspicuous Handrail Course	Rough map reading, handrail recognition and usage	166
Subtle Handrail Course	Rough map reading, handrail recognition and usage	167
Finding Collecting and Catching Features	Rough and precision map reading, recognition of collecting and catching features	168
Collecting and Catching Features Course	Rough and precision map reading, recognition and use of collecting and catching features	168
Control extension		
Extending Controls on the Map	Rough and precision map reading, control extension, visualization	169
Control Extension Course	Rough and precision map reading, control extension, visualization, terrain recognition	170
Map memory		
Map Memory Relay	Map memory, precision map reading	138
Memory-O	Map memory	157
Contouring		
Human Contour Line	Rough map reading, contour visualization	172
Contouring Versus Running a Beeline	Rough map reading (contouring), precision compass reading	172
Projection and visualization		
Map Simplification: Drawing a Course	Rough and precision map reading, map memory, map simplification	162
Control Identification via Slides	Precision map reading, visualization, interpretation	173
Map Walk: Visualization	Precision map reading, visualization	174
Relocation		
Relocation Relay	Rough and precision map reading, terrain recognition, relocation	175
Route selection		
Comparing Route Choices	Route selection	175
Leap Frog	Map reading and route selection at speed	176
Enhancing performance		
Debriefing and Course Evaluation	Rough and precision map reading, analysis	179
Drawing Course in Review	Map reading, memory, analysis	179
Shadowing	All	180

Map Symbol Relay

Objective

To learn the international orienteering map symbols through a relay game

Skills, Techniques, and Processes

Quick recognition of map symbols

Skill Level

Beginner, advanced

Activity Level

Walking or running

Venue

Indoor or outdoor

Time Required

5 minutes

On Map

No

Materials

Index cards (5 × 7 in. [13 × 18 cm]) with a map symbol drawn on one side and a written description of another symbol on the other side. Provide one set of 10 cards per five people. Color-coded cards will keep the sets separate.

Setup

Make cards as shown. Mark a starting line for the teams. At a set distance (10, 20, 30 m), place a set of cards on the ground with symbol side facing up. Place next set of cards about 3 meters away to keep them separate (see diagram).

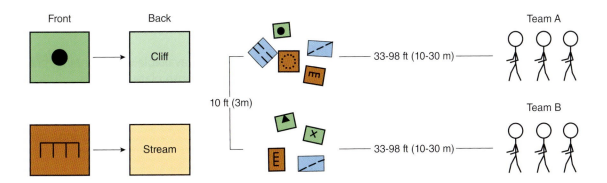

Description

The group is divided into at least two teams of equal size. On "Go," the first person on each team runs a set distance to a group of cards and chooses one card. He races back to his teammates, where he hands his card to the next person in line. This person flips over the card and reads the description of a symbol that she must find. She races to the group of cards and returns with the correct one. Teams repeat the process until all of the cards have been collected. The team that collects all of its cards first wins.

Variations

1. Consider making teams of mixed ability levels.

2. Teams could be arranged by course color, with more advanced colors having a farther distance to run to reach their group of cards.

3. Use the cards as flash cards for a seated audience.

Map Walk: Handrails

Objective

To learn to identify handrails on the map and in the terrain

Skills, Techniques, and Processes

Rough map reading, handrail identification

Skill Level

Beginner

Activity Level

Walking

Venue

Outdoor

Time Required

45-60 minutes

On Map

Yes

Materials

One map per person

Setup

Select an area for a walk where a variety of handrails can be followed from one to the next. Select handrails that are appropriate for the ability level of the group.

Description

As you walk with the group, explain what a handrail is as well as its many forms (e.g., trail, stream, vegetation boundary). Stop periodically and ask the group to identify upcoming handrails. Gradually progress from obvious to less obvious ones.

Making a 3-D Map Model

Objective

To create a three-dimensional model to use in teaching contour interval and terrain variations

Skills, Techniques, and Processes

Contour recognition, rough map reading

Skill Level

Advanced

Activity Level

Sitting

Venue

Indoor

Time Required

2-4 hours

On Map

No

Materials

Corrugated cardboard or Styrofoam, knife, glue, large sheet of paper, pen, scissors

Setup and Description

Draw a simple contour map on the paper, with two to three hills and 8 to 12 contours if using cardboard or one to two hills and 6 to 8 contours if using Styrofoam. Include features such as a saddle, large and small reentrants, steep slopes and gradual slopes, and a depression, if possible. Cut the outermost contour with scissors and then use it as a pattern to mark the cardboard or Styrofoam. Using the knife, cut the cardboard or Styrofoam. Then, cut the paper at the next upper contour. This becomes the pattern for the next level. Glue to the lower level. Repeat until all contours are cut and glued.

Variations

1. Make a model from an actual orienteering map.

2. Provide children with modeling clay and simple contour features to model.

Comments

Store and transport the model in a suitcase or briefcase.

Jigsaw Map Puzzle

Objective

To increase the ability to read maps and make associations between map features

Skills, Techniques, and Processes

Precision map reading

Skill Level

Beginner, advanced

Activity Level

Sitting, walking, or running

Venue

Indoor or outdoor

Time Required

10-15 minutes

On Map

No

Materials

One map per team or group, prepared as a jigsaw puzzle (map, cardboard, hobby knife, glue)

Setup

Select a map with many linear features. Glue the map to cardboard. Using a hobby knife, cut the interior of the map into several irregularly shaped pieces. If desired, glue the outer remaining map border to a second piece of cardboard for a more durable map frame.

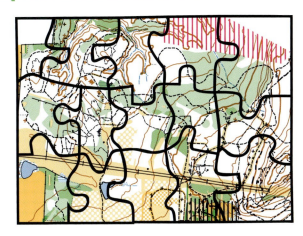

Description

Provide each group of three or four orienteers with a map frame and its pieces. The pieces should be laid out randomly on the table or floor. On "Go," each group begins assembling its jigsaw puzzle. Record the total time for each group to complete its puzzle.

Variations

1. Have groups work all puzzles, combining individual puzzle times for a total time.

2. Set up as a relay with the puzzle frame at one end and pieces at the other.

3. Increase the difficulty by cutting pieces symmetrically or all in squares.

Corridor-O

Objective

To increase skill in reading fine map detail and recognizing such detail in the terrain

Skills, Techniques, and Processes

Precision map reading, terrain recognition

Skill Level

Advanced

Activity Level

Walking or running

Venue

Outdoor

Time Required

30-60 minutes

On Map

Yes

Materials

Maps prepared with only corridors between controls visible on map, additional copies of map, tracing paper, one envelope per person, controls

Setup

Mark a course on the map. Plan legs that do not cross dangerous or impossible terrain (e.g., uncrossable stream). Cover the map with thin white paper (tracing paper) and mark the course with a corridor (6-10 mm wide) between controls. Number controls on the paper. Cut out the corridors. Place the paper over the map and photocopy one map per person. Set controls.

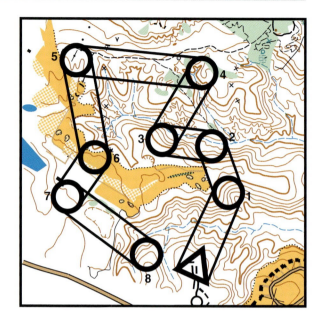

Description

Provide one map per person. Stagger starts. Orienteers navigate using only the information visible in the corridor. Provide orienteers with complete maps to refer to if they get lost.

Variations

1. Send orienteers in pairs.

2. Use a wider corridor for easier orienteering, narrower for more difficult.

Comments

As a competition, place an extra complete map in a sealed envelope. The sealed envelope is necessary at the finish to win.

Window-O

Objective

To learn to move quickly along a compass bearing for a given distance and to then relate terrain features to the map

Skills, Techniques, and Processes

Precision map reading, compass bearings, distance estimation

Skill Level

Advanced

Activity Level

Walking or running

Venue

Outdoor

Time Required

30-60 minutes

On Map

Yes

Materials

One prepared map, one regular map, and one envelope per person; controls

Setup

Mark a course on the map with legs no longer than 400 meters. Plan legs that do not cross difficult or impossible terrain (e.g., dangerous cliff, uncrossable marsh). Place white (tracing) paper over map. Mark a square (1.5 × 1.5 cm) around each control. Connect the squares with a line and number the controls on the paper. Cut out the squares. Place the paper over the map and photocopy one map with windows per person. Set the controls.

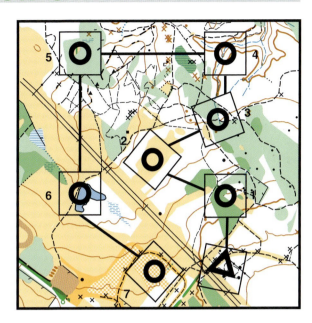

Description

Provide each orienteer with a window map and normal map sealed in an envelope. The sealed map is to be used only if the orienteer gets lost. Instruct orienteers to use the compass to take a bearing and measure distance in meters to the control. While following bearing and estimating distance, they should read the map within the window in order to recognize the area when they reach it. Upon reaching the window, they read the map to the control.

Variation

Make larger windows for easier orienteering.

Comments

Shorter legs reduce the risk of failure due to inaccurate compass routes.

Line-O

Objective

To increase the ability to read fine detail on maps and in terrain

Skills, Techniques, and Processes

Precision map reading, distance estimation

Skill Level

Beginner, advanced

Activity Level

Walking or running

Venue

Outdoor

Time Required

30-60 minutes

On Map

Yes

Materials

One marked map per person, controls or streamers, one pencil per person

Setup

Mark a 2- to 3-kilometer route on the map that begins at a definite feature and traverses the terrain, passing over and along several distinct features. Place streamers or markers along the route with codes that add up to spell a word or phrase. Do not mark the locations of markers on the map.

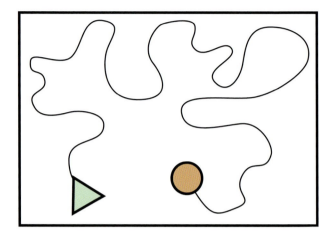

Description

Each orienteer is given a map and pencil. Starting at the triangle, orienteers follow the exact route indicated by the line on the map. If they follow the line, they will encounter all the streamers or controls. Each code is written down and the word or phrase is submitted at the end.

Variation

Orienteers mark the precise location of each control or streamer on their map. (See also String-O.)

Comments

1. Having orienteers mark their maps is good practice in reading map detail.

2. Use more conspicuously detailed locations for novice orienteers.

Quick-Draw McGraw

Objective

To train in quickly recognizing and retaining map detail

Skills, Techniques, and Processes

Map memory

Skill Level

Beginner, advanced

Activity Level

Sitting

Venue

Indoor

Time Required

10-20 minutes

On Map

No

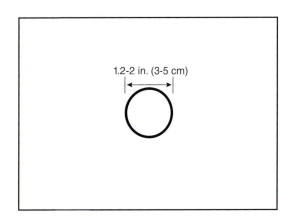

Materials

Five to 10 slides of maps with control circles included, slide projector and screen, one sheet of paper per slide per student with 3- to 5-centimeter circle on each sheet, one set of colored pencils or crayons per person

Setup

Mark maps with control circles. Take close-up photographic color slides. Mark each paper with a control circle approximately 3 to 5 centimeters in diameter.

Description

Pass out one set of colored pencils or crayons and a set of papers to each person. Show the first slide for 3 seconds. Orienteers study the map for 3 seconds; then, while the slide is off, they draw as much detail as they remember over the next 10 seconds. The slide is shown again for 5 seconds and then turned off while orienteers pick up pencils and add detail to the drawing for the next 15 seconds. Discuss the drawings after each slide.

Variation

Show a slide of an entire course in 5-second intervals. Orienteers are given a map and pen to draw the course. The first to complete the drawing wins.

Comments

Demonstrate the process first without regard for time. Use discussion between slides to allow orienteers to give each other feedback, which will help them with most relevant detail on subsequent slides.

Armchair-O

Objective

To learn to visualize contours in the terrain from the map

Skills, Techniques, and Processes

Rough map reading, visualization

Skill Level

Beginner, advanced

Activity Level

Sitting

Venue

Indoor

Time Required

10-60 minutes

On Map

No

Materials

Three to six worksheets with contours and side-view illustrations, pencils

(continued)

Armchair-O *(continued)*

Setup

Make up worksheets that depict a simple contour drawing and one or more side-view drawings to choose from in matching. Or, draw contour images and leave room for orienteers to draw the side view.

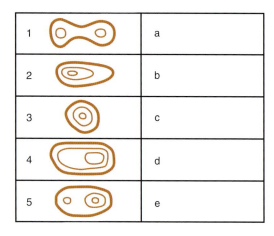

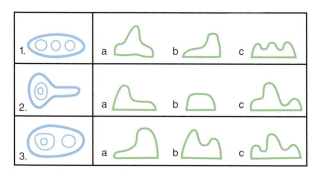

Description

Pass out worksheets to orienteers individually or in pairs. Explain how to do each sheet. Discuss choices and emphasize the correct answer to each. Allow participants to take the worksheets home.

Comments

See *Armchair Orienteering II* by W. Stott (1987, Canadian Orienteering Federation) for a series of excellent exercises of this nature.

Map Walk: Contours and Water-Only Map

Objective

To isolate contours as a map and terrain feature in order to improve the ability to read them

Skills, Techniques, and Processes

Precision map reading, rough map reading, contours, distance estimation

Skill Level

Advanced

Activity Level

Walking

Venue

Outdoor

Time Required

30-60 minutes

On Map

Yes

Materials

Orienteering maps with only contours and water shown (one map per person)

Setup

Plan a map walk that illustrates various contour features and variations.

Description

Walk as a group with maps in hand, reading as you go and stopping to discuss sizes, shapes, and distances of features in view.

Variation

Set a course and race.

Comments

Blue screen on the map (water) is provided for safety rather than navigation.

Map Walk: Estimating Sizes and Shapes

Objective

To increase awareness of how the map depicts the size and shape of features

Skills, Techniques, and Processes

Precision map reading, rough map reading, contours, distance estimation

Skill Level

Advanced

Activity Level

Walking

Venue

Outdoor

Time Required

30-60 minutes

On Map

Yes

Materials

One map per person

Setup

Plan a map walk that will expose orienteers to features of various sizes (e.g., ponds, fields, hills, knolls, bare rock, boulders).

Description

Walk in a group in the terrain, reading the map and pointing out features as you go. Begin by asking participants for dimensions in area as well as height. Emphasize changes in slope. Note the shape of features on the ground versus the map. Point out the orientation of features.

Comments

Encourage participation.

Fruit Relay

Objective

To introduce orienteering and basic map-reading skills to beginners

Skills, Techniques, and Processes

Precision map reading

Skill Level

Beginner

Activity Level

Walking or running

(continued)

Fruit Relay *(continued)*

Venue

Indoor or outdoor

Time Required

5-15 minutes

On Map

Yes

Materials

One orienteering map, schoolyard map, or room map per person; one pencil or pen per person

Setup

Each participant is asked to bring a piece of fruit (e.g., orange, banana, apple). The fruit must be uncut and large enough to fill the palm of the hand (i.e., not strawberries, grapes, and so on).

Description

On "Go," each person leaves the start area with a map, pencil, and fruit and places the piece of fruit in a location that is distinct on the map and on the ground. The location is marked on the map with a circle. Then all participants return and exchange maps. On the second "Go," participants use their map to find the fruit in the circle. On returning, everyone eats their fruit.

Variation

Use holiday treats such as Valentines, Easter eggs, or Christmas treats.

Comments

If a large group is participating, each piece of fruit should have a code on it with a corresponding code placed on the map. This will allow participants to verify that they have found the correct fruit.

Distance Estimation: 100 Meters

Objective

To learn to estimate distance by measuring and using one's pace count while walking and running at race pace

Skills, Techniques, and Processes

Distance estimation

Skill Level

Beginner

Activity Level

Walking or running

Venue

Outdoor

Time Required

5-7 minutes

On Map

No

Materials

Streamers or other means of marking 100 meters, paper, pencils

Setup

Measure or accurately pace a 100-meter line over flat, unobstructed terrain. Mark the start and finish with streamers, flown or by other means.

Description

Have participants line up side by side on the start line. Demonstrate pace counting as double steps while walking. Count out loud. Then explain that they should begin walking from the line while counting silently (beginning with zero) and walk to the finish where you will be standing. Tell them to write down their number but don't speak it. Ask them to raise their hands if their count was between 50 and 70. If not, ask them individually what they got and clarify how to count paces. Have them return and count again. Repeat if necessary. This number is the walking pace. Repeat at race pace (jog or run) and record as the running pace.

Distance Estimation: Variations

Objective

To learn how one's pace is affected by slope and vegetation

Skills, Techniques, and Processes

Distance estimation

Skill Level

Beginner, advanced

Activity Level

Walking or running

Venue

Outdoor

Time Required

15-20 minutes

On Map

No

Materials

Streamers, paper, pencils

Setup

Select two areas: one on a slope through open woods, another on level ground through slow-run vegetation. Use streamers to make a 100-meter line through each area every few meters. Delineate each end with a different color or with a control.

Description

Discuss how distance estimation is affected by slope and vegetation. Then explain the two 100-meter lines that have been laid and give the orienteers the opportunity to check their pace going downhill, uphill, and through slow-run vegetation. Record the pace under each condition to compare with the basic pace count.

Comments

This activity should be delivered only after orienteers are familiar with their pace on trails or roads.

Distance Estimation: Running

Objective

To develop good distance judgment

Skills, Techniques, and Processes

Distance estimation

Skill Level

Beginner, advanced

Activity Level

Running

(continued)

Venue

Outdoor

Time Required

45-60 minutes

On Map

No

Materials

None

Setup

None

Description

This is a training exercise to do while running. Looking ahead, select an object (e.g., telephone pole), estimate its distance from you, and begin pace counting to measure. Continue this process, correcting estimation based on previous measurement.

Comments

This activity is intended for regular running training rather than coaching sessions.

Map Walk: Estimating Sizes and Distances

Objective

To increase the ability to accurately assess the size of features and the distance between them

Skills, Techniques, and Processes

Size and distance estimation

Skill Level

Advanced

Activity Level

Walking

Venue

Outdoor

Time Required

30-60 minutes

On Map

Yes

Materials

One map per person

Setup

Select an area with just enough distinct features to identify specific ones without confusion. Ideally, features should be 50 to 300 meters apart (within visible range) or long.

Description

Walk with the group, pointing out sizes of features and distances between distinct features. Stop frequently and ask the group to estimate a size (e.g., height of a steep slope or ridge, length of a field or pond) or distance (e.g., distance to large boulder, distance to pond), then pace to check accuracy. Continue until accuracy reaches a reasonable level for each person.

Variation

Pick up the pace and do the activity while running.

Relocating: Estimating Sizes and Distances

Objective

To improve the ability to estimate the size of features and the distance between them

Skills, Techniques, and Processes

Size and distance estimation

Skill Level

Advanced

Activity Level

Walking or running

Venue

Outdoor

Time Required

20-30 minutes

On Map

Yes

Materials

Map, cardboard, streamers, knife, controls, paper, pencils

Setup

Select an area with 6 to 10 control features that are 50 to 300 meters long (e.g., fields, thickets, woodlots, ponds, steep slopes, cliffs). Cut out a 2.5- × 2.5-centimeter piece of map showing a control feature, along with two other pieces of map showing a similar feature of a different length or size. Mount all three oriented to north on a card. Repeat for each of the 6 to 10 selected features. Then, use streamers to mark a course from control to control. Hang the card with the three pieces of map at each control.

Description

Orienteers follow the streamers to the first control. Observing the dimensions of the control features, they review the card to select the correct feature and write down their choice before running to the next control.

Compass and Distance Estimation Course

Objective

To increase proficiency with compass bearings and estimating distance by measure and pace counting using a set of bearings and distances

Skills, Techniques, and Processes

Precision compass reading, distance estimation

Skill Level

Beginner, advanced

Activity Level

Walking

Venue

Outdoor

Time Required

20-30 minutes

On Map

No

Materials

One compass per person, streamers, marker, cards with bearings and distances

(continued)

Compass and Distance Estimation Course *(continued)*

Setup

Select an area in open woods. From a marked start point, select a bearing and pace a distance of 30 to 50 meters. Mark the precise location with a streamer, give it a code, and write the bearing and distance on card. Next, hang additional streamers in the area with codes. These should be far enough away (in front, behind, to sides) so as not to be confused with the correct streamer. Select four to six additional points to complete the course, repeating the streamer process at each. Make up one card for each participant with bearings and distances to each point.

Description

Distribute compasses and cards with bearings and distances. Instruct the group to set compass and pace distance. Upon reaching streamers, select the closest streamer and stand by it. When all participants have selected their streamers, reveal the correct one. Discuss ways to improve on the next leg. Everyone then gathers at the correct streamer as the starting point for the next bearing.

Using a Compass as a Protractor

Objective

To explain the logic of the protractor-style compass to beginners

Skills, Techniques, and Processes

Precision compass reading

Skill Level

Beginner, advanced

Activity Level

Sitting

Venue

Indoor

Time Required

15 minutes

On Map

No

Materials

Poster board or flip chart, markers, compass (large teaching compass is helpful but not critical), one compass for every one or two people

Setup

Draw a 120-degree angle to a building on the poster board. Using your compass, show how the angle is set by rotating the baseplate with respect to the bezel—set compass to 120 degrees.

Description

Explain that a protractor-style compass is used to measure an angle. The angle is the location of a feature with respect to north. Have participants set their compasses to 120 degrees. Next, remove the poster board, and holding it level, show how the 120-degree angle can be rotated to face any direction. Explain that the angle should be set with respect to north; therefore, they need to know where north is. Have them use the compass and point to north. Rotate the poster until *N* faces

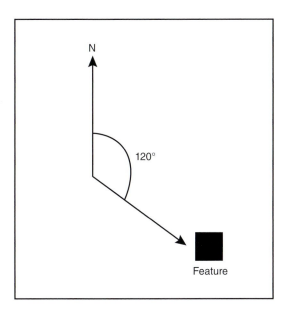

N

120°

Feature

magnetic north. Then, show them how they can use their compass needle to set their 120-degree angle with respect to north by holding the compass level and turning the body until the *N* needle is over *N* on the compass bezel. Have them point to the feature that is at 120 degrees.

Comments

This exercise should only be used with adults and only when enough time is available to then cover the five-step method. Explain that the five-step method does the same thing but in a different order.

Bearings: Five-Step Method

Objective

To understand the five-step method of taking a bearing using a protractor-style compass

Skills, Techniques, and Processes

Precision compass reading

Skill Level

Beginner, advanced

Activity Level

Sitting or walking

Venue

Indoor or outdoor

Time Required

15-20 minutes

On Map

No

Materials

One compass and one map per person (can also be taught to pairs of students)

Setup

Distribute one compass and one map per person.

Description

Review the parts of the compass. Explain and demonstrate each step, and check as you go along that everyone is following.

> Step 1: Line up the long edge of the compass with where you are and where you want to go, ensuring that the direction-of-travel arrow points in the direction you want to go.

> Step 2: Keeping the baseplate lined up, rotate the bezel until the lines are parallel with the north lines on the map, with the north arrow (or cradle) and north magnetic orientating arrow pointing north on the map.

> Step 3: Measure any appropriate distance (e.g., start to control, attack point to control, start to road bend, etc.).

> Step 4: Lift the compass from the map, holding it level and between waist and chest height, with the direction-of-travel arrow pointing away from you. Holding the compass in this position, turn your

(continued)

Bearings: Five-Step Method *(continued)*

body (and your feet) around until the cradle is under the needle.

Step 5: Look up and select an object in the distance that is in line with the direction-of-travel arrow and walk or run to it.

Comments

Repeat this process several times. Ask the participants to state out loud the five steps. This will help them to remember.

Compass Zigzag Course

Objective

To gain confidence in taking compass bearings

Skills, Techniques, and Processes

Precision compass reading

Skill Level

Beginner, advanced

Activity Level

Walking

Venue

Outdoor

Time Required

15-30 minutes

On Map

No

Materials

One compass per person, one card per person with start letter and five bearings, pencils, stakes, 10 index cards (4 × 6 in. [10 × 15 cm]) labeled *A* through *J*, hammer, thumbtacks, pencils

Setup

Select an open area. Make two lines of stakes in an east–west direction. Stakes should be two paces apart within each line and four paces apart between lines. The bearing from *A* to the next stake (*G*) should be 30 degrees. Tack a card to each in the order shown. Make three sets of bearing cards as follows.

(SET 1)

Start at A

30° to ____

130° to ____

90° to ____

330° to ____

210° to ____

(SET 2)

Start at C

310° to ____

150° to ____

30° to ____

180° to ____

50° to ____

(SET 3)

Start at E

330° to ____

270° to ____

210° to ____

90° to ____

310° to ____

Description

Distribute compasses, cards, and pencils. Participants should begin at the stake indicated by the card (i.e., *A*), set the compass to the first bearing (i.e., 30 degrees), and look at the stake on the bearing. They write the letter of the stake next to the bearing, walk to the second stake (i.e., *G*), then take the next bearing. Coach reviews the cards and assists when the series goes awry. Correct sequences should read as follows: set 1: A, G, D, E, I, C; set 2: C, F, B, H, C, J; set 3: E, I, H, B, C, F.

Comments

Check the accuracy of stake placement with bearing cards.

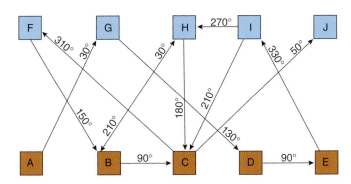

		G	D	E	I	C
1.	A:	30°,	130°,	90°,	330°,	210°
		F	B	H	C	J
2.	C:	310°,	150°,	30°,	180°,	50°
		I	H	B	C	F
3.	E:	330°,	270°,	210°,	90°,	310°

Flash-Card Map Symbol Relay

Objective

To learn the international map symbols

Skills, Techniques, and Processes

Map reading

Skill Level

Beginner, advanced

Activity Level

Walking or running

Venue

Indoor or outdoor

Time Required

10-20 minutes

On Map

No

Materials

Flash cards (index cards, 5 × 7 in. [13 × 18 cm]) with map symbol on front and written description of same symbol on back

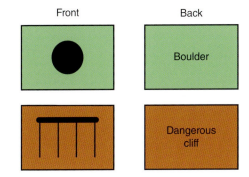

Setup

Make two or more sets of flash cards with 10 to the 20 cards each. Divide participants into two groups (or more if more sets of cards are available) and line them up. Coaches stand across the room (or area) with the cards.

Description

On "Go," the first person on each team runs to the other end, where he is shown the first card. If he correctly identifies the card, the card is placed on the floor. If the guess is incorrect, the card is placed at the back of the pile. In either case, after guessing, he returns to his team and tags the next person. The first team to complete the series of cards wins.

(continued)

Flash-Card Map Symbol Relay *(continued)*

Variation

This can be played while sitting as well. After the student guesses, the teacher uses a signaling technique (e.g., raised hands, thumbs up or down) to indicate agreement or disagreement with the answer. This allows the coach to see who does and does not understand so that help can be given where needed.

Comments

Do not combine these symbols with control descriptions for children; some of the symbols are different, which may be confusing.

Running on Rough Compass Reading

Objective

To learn to run quickly in a given direction without taking a precise bearing

Skills, Techniques, and Processes

Rough compass reading, distance estimation

Skill Level

Advanced

Activity Level

Running

Venue

Outdoor

Time Required

20-30 minutes

On Map

Yes

Materials

One compass per person, list of directions and distances, streamers

Setup

Select an area with good runability and some distinct features. Set a course with 6 to 10 legs using a map to verify compass bearings and distances to features. Each leg should be 50 to 200 meters long and should end at a distinct feature from which a streamer is hung. Record the rough bearing (e.g., *E*, *NE*, *ENE*) and distance (e.g., 75 m) for each leg on a card, as shown, along with the feature on which the streamer is hung.

			Feature:
1.	NE	82 yd (75 m)	boulder
2.	NNW	142 yd (130 m)	saddle
3.	W	109 yd (100 m)	knoll
	etc.		

Description

Distribute one card and one compass per person. Explain that the object is to run as fast as possible on a rough compass bearing for the distance given. Look at the compass often. Upon reaching the area, there will be a streamer hanging from a specific feature. Try to come as close to the streamer as possible. Find the streamer before proceeding on the next leg. Stagger starts.

Armchair Bearing Quiz

Objective

To learn to take compass bearings

Skills, Techniques, and Processes

Precision compass reading, map memory

Skill Level

Advanced

Activity Level

Sitting

Venue

Indoor

Time Required

5-10 minutes

On Map

No

Materials

Maps with courses drawn, one compass per person, pencil, paper

Setup

Select a map and draw a course with 6 to 10 legs.

Description

Distribute maps, compasses, pencils, and paper. Have participants number their papers 1 to 10 (for as many legs as are on the course). Explain to participants how to take a bearing for each leg and write it down. Review and discuss answers.

Variation

Set legs across barriers and have each student draw a possible route and take bearings for the intended route.

Memory-O

Objective

To increase the ability to memorize relevant map detail and use it to read terrain detail

Skills, Techniques, and Processes

Map memory

Skill Level

Advanced

Activity Level

Walking or running

Venue

Outdoor

Time Required

30-60 minutes

On Map

Yes

Materials

A number of maps equal to the number of controls, map cases, string, one map and one envelope per person, stopwatch, control cards

Setup

Select an area with distinct features and handrails. Design a simple course and then draw one leg of the course on each map (e.g., start triangle to control 1, control 1 to control 2). Legs should be fairly easy, using handrails and distinct features. Write the control description on each map. Place an unmarked map in each envelope and seal it. Hang controls.

(continued)

Memory-O *(continued)*

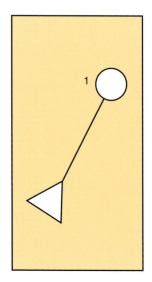

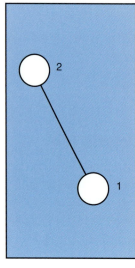

Description

Distribute control cards and sealed envelopes containing unmarked maps. Explain that the envelope is only to be opened if absolutely necessary—a penalty will be given for a broken seal. Emphasize the need to take time at each map to memorize a desired route and the control location. Look for the simplest route using handrails and distinct features. Stagger starts and time runners.

Comments

Sealed envelopes with maps are not essential. They can provide assistance if any orienteer becomes disoriented and needs help to continue.

Trail-O

Objective

To provide the mental challenge of orienteering for all participants, while specifically designed for people in wheelchairs, who are allowed to receive any necessary physical assistance to traverse the course

Skills, Techniques, and Processes

Precision map reading, distance estimation, precision compass reading

Skill Level

Beginner, advanced

Activity Level

Sitting, walking, or running

Venue

Outdoor

Time Required

60 minutes

On Map

Yes

Materials

One map per person, three or more control markers and three punches per control station, punching platform, cards with control codes, control cards

Setup

Select an area with a paved nature trail. Design courses with controls on distinct features within 50 meters of the paved path. Course difficulty is based on the difficulty of reading the precise location of the control at a feature. Set up a punching platform aside the path with a punch and code for each control. Mark the maps.

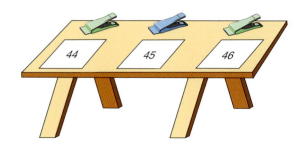

Description

Each competitor is assigned an assistant to help the competitor proceed physically through the course. Distribute maps to competitors (maps may be placed in map holders attached to wheelchairs). Competitors read the map and proceed from control to control. (Note: Other control locations from other courses will be along the path as well.) When they reach what they believe to be the proper control location (punch stand will be at each control location), they study the three or more controls in the area to determine which one is in the precise location as indicated by the exact center of the circle on the map. The assistant may clarify which block to punch for which control. The competitor decides on the correct marker and punches the card with the punch in the correct spot on the scorecard, then proceeds to the remaining controls. Competitors are timed and control cards are checked for correct punches.

Control Symbol Relay

Objective

To increase familiarity with code symbols in order to quickly and correctly identify control descriptions

Skills, Techniques, and Processes

Clues for control symbol recognition

Skill Level

Beginner, advanced

Activity Level

Walking or running

Venue

Indoor or outdoor

Time Required

5 minutes

On Map

No

Materials

Index cards (5 × 7 in. [13 × 18 cm]) with a control description pasted to one side (use 8-column IOF symbol clue sheet). Only one control description should be on each card. The precise interpretation of the symbols should be written on the other side (underline the key words). Make one set of 10 cards per five people.

Setup

Mark a starting line for the teams and a designated distance where the controller of the exercise has the flash cards.

Description

At one end of the area, one person for each team (neutral party) stands with cards. On "Go," the first person from each team runs to the other end. Upon reaching it, the neutral person holds up a card and the runner interprets the columns. The card holder refers to the back of the card and tells the runner if she is correct or not. In either case, the runner returns and tags the next team member. If the card is correctly read, it is set aside. If incorrectly read, it is placed at bottom of the pile. The first team to correctly identify all cards wins.

(continued)

Control Symbol Relay *(continued)*

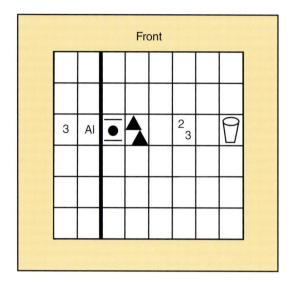

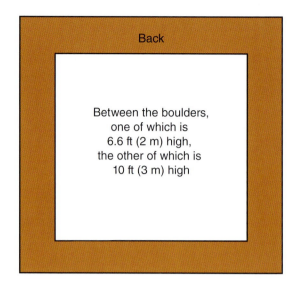

Variation

When beginning, work on only the control feature (column D) description, then gradually add the other columns.

Comments

Use colored index cards to distinguish control symbol cards from map symbol cards, if both sets are available.

Connect the Dots

Objective

To increase the ability to quickly interpret control symbols on the clue sheet and control appearance on the map

Skills, Techniques, and Processes

Control symbol recognition

Skill Level

Beginner, advanced

Activity Level

Sitting

Venue

Indoor

Time Required

10-15 minutes

On Map

No

Materials

One map per person with a course of appropriate difficulty (circles only, no lines or control numbers), pens

Setup

Design courses (all the same for the group or multiples of a few courses of appropriate difficulty). Each control location must be unique in terms of description. Mark the maps with circles and start triangles only. Do not add lines between controls or numbers. Make up an IOF control description (clue sheet) for each map.

Description

Distribute a pen, map, and clue sheet to each person. On "Go," each person uses the clue sheet to figure out which circle is the first control. Upon selecting it, a line is drawn from the start triangle to control 1. Repeat the process until all controls have been identified and marked. Label each control. The first person to finish wins.

Variation

Can be done as teams.

Comments

To increase the difficulty, use similar but slightly different control features (e.g., middle reentrant, shallow versus lower reentrant, overgrown).

Control Description Quiz

Objective

To increase the ability to recognize IOF control description symbols

Skills, Techniques, and Processes

Control symbol recognition

Skill Level

Beginner, advanced

Activity Level

Sitting

Venue

Indoor

Time Required

10-20 minutes

On Map

No

Materials

Flash cards with control descriptions displayed in 8-column IOF format, paper, pencils

Setup

Using index cards (5 × 7 in. [13 × 18 cm]), draw a control description using IOF symbols. It should be large enough to see at 10 meters. Write the interpretation on the back. One set of 10 to 15 cards will do.

Description

Distribute paper and pencils. Explain that the paper should be numbered 1 through 10 (or 15). Show a flash card and hold it in view while participants write the description. Repeat for each card. When finished, review cards and answers and discuss, if necessary.

Variation

When just learning symbols, use only column D (control feature), then gradually add other columns. When the group is proficient, have them each make a card to use in the flash-card set.

Handrail and Large-Feature Course

Objective

To learn to move quickly through the terrain by using handrails and large features

Skills, Techniques, and Processes

Rough map reading, terrain interpretation

Skill Level

Advanced

Activity Level

Running

Venue

Outdoor

Time Required

30-60 minutes

On Map

Yes

Materials

One map per person, control descriptions, control cards, control markers

Setup

Select an area with both obvious and subtle handrails and large features. Design a course that enables runners to follow handrails and use large features for the greater part of each leg. Controls should be easy to find. Set markers. Mark maps and control descriptions.

Description

Review the definition of *handrail* and discuss variations (e.g., contour differences, linear patches of green). Emphasize the use of handrails and large features in course design. Distribute maps. Stagger starts.

Variation

Have assistant coaches (or athletes) position themselves along the course and evaluate orienteers' use of handrails and large features.

Comments

Have participants mark their own maps. Courses should be designed using handrails and features of appropriate difficulty.

Map Simplification: Drawing a Course

Objective

To learn to view the larger features of the map and commit them to memory in order to quickly move through the terrain and not get bogged down by map detail

Skills, Techniques, and Processes

Rough and precision map reading, map memory, map simplification

Skill Level

Advanced

Activity Level

Walking or running

Venue

Outdoor

Time Required

60-90 minutes

On Map

Yes

Materials

One map per person, paper, colored pencils or crayons, control markers

Setup

Design a short (3 km) course with four to five legs in an area with both large features (e.g., hills, streams, clearings) and fine detail (e.g., boulders, small marshes, thickets). Legs should allow the use of large features to navigate.

Description

Distribute the maps with courses. Discuss map simplification. Distribute paper and colored pencils. Direct the group to use the paper and pencils to draw a simplified version of its course. When finished, send orienteers out with the hand-drawn, simplified maps to use in finding controls.

Comments

Orienteers may take the map along to use in case of serious disorientation.

Sprint-O

Objective

To learn precision map reading and use of attack points when approaching controls

Skills, Techniques, and Processes

Precision map reading

Skill Level

Advanced

Activity Level

Walking or running

Venue

Outdoor

Time Required

20-30 minutes

On Map

Yes

Materials

One map per person, control descriptions, control markers

Setup

Select an area with a lot of detail. Design a short course (2 km) with 6 to 10 controls placed 200 to 300 meters apart. Hang controls. Mark maps.

Description

Review the importance of precision map reading between attack point and control. Distribute maps. Explain that orienteers should use each control as an attack point for finding the next control. Go as fast as possible while reading the map. Stagger starts. Review when finished.

Comments

Have participants draw their own courses.

Finding Attack Points

Objective

To learn to recognize attack points

Skills, Techniques, and Processes

Precision map reading, attack point recognition and usage

Skill Level

Beginner, advanced

Activity Level

Sitting

Venue

Indoor

Time Required

15 minutes

On Map

No

Materials

One map per person, pencils

Setup

Design a course on a map with many possible attack points. The course should have 10 to 15 legs with distances of 150 to 700 meters each. Select control locations that have route choices plus one or more attack points. Attack points should be within 150 meters of the control.

Description

Distribute maps and pencils. Review attack points. Instruct participants to plan each leg by selecting an attack point and circling it. Then they select the route to reach the attack point and pencil it in. When all courses are completed, discuss.

Variations

1. Do the activity in pairs or groups.
2. Make slides of the course and allow participants to illustrate their attack points and route choices.

Attack Point Course

Objective

To learn to recognize attack points and use them to quickly get within 150 meters of a control

Skills, Techniques, and Processes

Precision map reading, attack point recognition and usage

Skill Level

Advanced

Activity Level

Walking or running

Venue

Outdoor

Time Required

30-60 minutes

On Map

Yes

Materials

One map per person, control markers

Setup

Select an area that has enough detail to provide nearly all legs with an attack point. Design a course (3-4 km) with an attack point for all but one or two controls. Hang markers. Mark maps. Orienteers should see the attack point before the control feature.

Description

Review attack points. Distribute maps. Explain to orienteers to look for the attack point (if there is one) and navigate to it, then use fine orienteering to reach the control. Stagger starts. Review when finished.

Variation

Have an assistant coach on legs without attack points to observe route choices.

Comments

Have participants mark their own maps.

Control Punching Relay

Objective

To develop a method of remembering the control code and punching quickly

Skills, Techniques, and Processes

Code memorization, rapid punching

Skill Level

Beginner, advanced

Activity Level

Running

Venue

Indoor or outdoor

Time Required

15 minutes

On Map

No

Materials

Ten control markers with codes and punches, cards with control codes listed, punch cards, stakes (may not be necessary)

Setup

Label controls in the following (or similar) pattern: NA, NB, NC, ND, NE, SV, SW, SX, SY, SZ. Select an open area approximately 10 by 30 meters, bordered by fences or other objects from which to hang controls. Hang controls in two rows in order (i.e., NA through NE and SV through SZ). Make up 10 to 15 index cards (3 × 5 in. [8 × 13 cm]) with a random assortment of these codes.

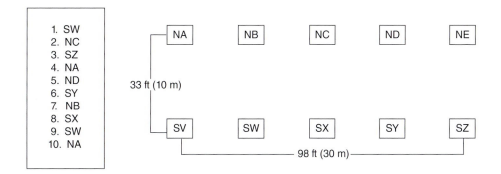

Description

Divide the group into two or three teams. On "Go," the first member of each team selects a control code from the coach along with a punch card, then quickly runs from control to control, punching in the designated order. When finished, he returns and tags the next member, who selects a new card and repeats. Used code cards are returned to the coach for reuse. The first team to run the course twice wins.

Armchair-O: Finding Handrails

Objective

To improve the ability to recognize handrails on the map

Skills, Techniques, and Processes

Rough map reading, handrail recognition

Skill Level

Beginner, advanced

Activity Level

Sitting

Venue

Indoor

Time Required

20-30 minutes

On Map

No

Materials

One map per person with a white, yellow, orange, and brown, green, red, or blue course; purple or red pens

Setup

Select a map on which four courses can be drawn that have plenty of handrail opportunities as route choices.

Description

Distribute maps and pens. Discuss handrails, both conspicuous and subtle. Have each person draw an optimal route on the white course, using any handrails available. Review participants' choices. Proceed through yellow, orange, and advanced courses, discussing handrail opportunities between courses.

Variations

1. Make slides or colored overheads of courses to aid in group discussion.

2. Do the activity in pairs.

Conspicuous Handrail Course

Objective

To improve the ability to recognize and use conspicuous handrails

Skills, Techniques, and Processes

Rough map reading, handrail recognition and usage

Skill Level

Beginner, advanced

Activity Level

Walking or running

Venue

Outdoor

Time Required

20-40 minutes

On Map

Yes

Materials

One map per person, control markers

Setup

Select an area with many conspicuous handrails (e.g., trails, streams, power lines, fences, distinct vegetation boundaries) that ideally intersect. Design a short course (2-3 km) that uses conspicuous handrails to reach controls (or their attack points, for higher-level orienteers). Mark maps and hang controls.

Description

Review handrails. Distribute maps. Explain to participants that they should move as quickly as possible through the course using conspicuous handrails. Stagger starts. Discuss routes when everyone has returned.

Variation

Have assistant coaches or athletes along the course to observe and critique use of handrails.

Comments

Have orienteers mark their own maps.

Subtle Handrail Course

Objective

To improve the ability to recognize and use subtle handrails

Skills, Techniques, and Processes

Rough map reading, handrail recognition and usage

Skill Level

Advanced

Activity Level

Walking or running

Venue

Outdoor

Time Required

30-40 minutes

On Map

Yes

Materials

One map per person, control markers

Setup

Select an area with many subtle handrails (e.g., pond or marsh margins, chains of small marshes, thickets, clearings, noticeable changes in slope). Design courses that use subtle handrails as a possible route choice. Mark maps. Hang controls.

Description

Review handrails. Distribute maps. Explain to participants that they should move as quickly as possible through the course using subtle handrails, even if the handrails are not the optimal route choice. Emphasize that this is a handrail training exercise. Stagger starts. Discuss routes when everyone has returned.

Variations

1. Have assistant coaches (or orienteers) along the course to observe and critique.

2. This exercise can also be done in pairs, with the pair discussing the subtle handrails. On each leg, one person takes the lead, running along the handrail, while the other follows, reading the map.

Comments

Have participants mark their own maps.

Finding Collecting and Catching Features

Objective

To increase the ability to recognize collecting and catching features

Skills, Techniques, and Processes

Rough and precision map reading, recognition of collecting and catching features

Skill Level

Beginner, advanced

Activity Level

Sitting

Venue

Indoor

Time Required

10-15 minutes

On Map

No

Materials

One map per person, one highlighter per person

Setup

Select a map with many linear features. Design white, yellow, orange, and brown, green, red, or blue (advanced) courses that have collecting features and catching features on most legs.

Description

Review collecting and catching features. Distribute maps and highlighters. Tell the group to study the white course, highlighting collecting and catching features on each leg. Discuss leg by leg or when the course is completed. Progress through the other courses, discussing each course before moving on to the next.

Variations

1.   Make slides or overheads to assist in group discussion.

2.   Do the exercise in pairs.

Collecting and Catching Features Course

Objective

To increase the ability to recognize and use collecting and catching features

Skills, Techniques, and Processes

Rough and precision map reading, recognition and use of collecting and catching features

Skill Level

Advanced

Activity Level

Walking or running

Venue

Outdoor

Time Required

30-45 minutes

On Map

Yes

Materials

One map per person, control markers

Setup

Select an area with many linear features. Design a 2- to 3-kilometer course with legs that have a conspicuous collecting feature (e.g., trail, stream, reentrant, large clearing), catching feature (e.g., trail, stream, ridge, pond edge), or both. Obvious route choices should take advantage of these. Mark maps.

Description

Review collecting and catching features. Distribute maps. Explain that participants should look for an obvious collecting feature or catching feature and run as quickly as possible to it (even if it is beyond the control, as in catching features). Then, they should slow down and carefully read the map to the control (red-light, green-light orienteering). When everyone has returned, discuss routes.

Variations

1. Have assistant coaches (or athletes) along the course to evaluate orienteers.

2. This activity can also be done in pairs, where the pair discusses the collecting or catching feature on each leg and then takes turns taking the lead running to the control.

Comments

Have participants mark their own maps. Emphasize the use of collecting and catching features rather than finish time.

Extending Controls on the Map

Objective

To increase the ability to recognize and visualize the larger feature upon which the control feature is located

Skills, Techniques, and Processes

Rough and precision map reading, control extension, visualization

Skill Level

Beginner, advanced

Activity Level

Sitting

Venue

Indoor

Time Required

10-15 minutes

On Map

No

Materials

One map per person, one highlighter per person

Setup

Select a map (most maps will do). Design a course with controls on point features that lie on larger features such as spurs, reentrants, semi-open areas, and so on.

Description

Distribute maps and highlighters. Review control extension. Do the first leg as a group, discussing the larger feature and highlighting it. Explain to orienteers that they should look at the next leg, find the control, and find a larger feature and highlight it. Have someone explain how she expects the larger feature to look and how she would get to it and then to the control. Repeat for each leg.

Variations

1. Make slides or overheads of maps to aid in discussion.

2. Do the exercise in pairs.

Comments

Have orienteers draw their own courses.

Control Extension Course

Objective

To learn to recognize, visualize, and use control extension to quickly reach the vicinity of the control

Skills, Techniques, and Processes

Rough and precision map reading, control extension, visualization, terrain recognition

Skill Level

Advanced

Activity Level

Walking or running

Venue

Outdoor

Time Required

45-60 minutes

On Map

Yes

Materials

One map per person, control markers

Setup

Select an area with good possibilities for control extension. Design a 4- to 5-kilometer course using a variety of large features on which the control features are placed. Legs should be 500 to 800 meters long, with the extended feature out of view from the previous control. Mark maps. Hang controls.

Description

Distribute maps. Review control extension and visualization. Begin with a map walk, discussing how to extend the feature around control 1. Have athletes silently visualize the area, and then have someone describe it verbally. Walk to the area, pointing out the feature as it comes into view. Upon reaching it, discuss how its appearance differs from expectations. Have athletes figure out next the extension feature, describe it, and walk to it as before. As athletes become proficient, pair them up and have them proceed ahead of the group through the course. Each pair should discuss the extended feature. They visualize it and then one person (alternating) takes the lead and runs to the feature.

Comments

Have athletes mark their own maps.

Armchair-O: Aiming Off

Objective

To increase awareness of uses of aiming off

Skills, Techniques, and Processes

Rough map reading, rough compass reading, recognizing when to aim off

Skill Level

Beginner, advanced

Activity Level

Sitting

Venue

Indoor

Time Required

10-15 minutes

On Map

No

Materials

One map per person, one pen per person

Setup

Select a map with many linear features. Design a course or two (one simple, one advanced) with linear features near controls that can be used for aiming off.

Description

Distribute maps and pens. Review aiming off. Explain to orienteers that for each leg, they should look for a feature near the control to which they can aim. Have them draw a line showing how they would proceed to the feature and where they would expect to intersect it. When finished, discuss routes. Evaluate how well they did and give constructive suggestions to individuals and groups.

Variation

Make slides or overheads of maps to aid the group discussion.

Comments

Have participants mark their own maps. Tie in collecting and catching features with this exercise.

String-O

Objective

To increase the ability to read fine detail on maps and in terrain

Skills, Techniques, and Processes

Precision map reading, distance estimation

Skill Level

Beginner, advanced

Activity Level

Walking

Venue

Outdoor

Time Required

30-60 minutes

On Map

Yes

Materials

One map per person, 500- to 1,000-meter string, one pen per person

Setup

Place string in terrain over and along distinct features.

Description

Provide each orienteer with a map and a pen. Identify the start of the string on the map and in the terrain. Orienteers may go as a group or individually but must work independently. They follow the string, marking the map as they go with a continuous line indicating the exact placement of the string.

Variation

Set markers along the string. Orienteers must also indicate the location of each control.

Comments

String placement should be appropriate for the skill level of the group (e.g., on handrails for novices, over intricate terrain for advanced students).

Human Contour Line

Objective

To enable novice orienteers to see contour lines in the terrain so as to better understand them on the map

Skills, Techniques, and Processes

Rough map reading, contour visualization

Skill Level

Beginner, advanced

Activity Level

Walking

Venue

Outdoor

Time Required

2-5 minutes

On Map

No

Materials

None

Setup

Select an area with small and medium-sized reentrants.

Description

Review contour lines. Assemble a group of orienteers. Select one and instruct him to walk away from the group while remaining on the same contour as the group. He should be careful not to go downhill or uphill. Group members can help by observing if he is walking level and telling him when he begins to go up or down. Tell the walker to stop after he has covered 10 to 15 meters and then send another walker out 10 to 15 meters beyond the first. Continue until each member of the group has become part of the human contour line.

Contouring Versus Running a Beeline

Objective

To learn the advantages of running on a contour versus running a beeline

Skills, Techniques, and Processes

Rough map reading (contouring), precision compass reading

Skill Level

Advanced

Activity Level

Walking or running

Venue

Outdoor

Time Required

20-30 minutes

On Map

No

Materials

Control markers, paper, pens, two stopwatches, streamers (if necessary)

Setup

Select an area with a large hill, a small hill, a large reentrant, and a small reentrant. Set a control marker on either side of the hill and either side of the reentrant. Place streamers along the route if necessary.

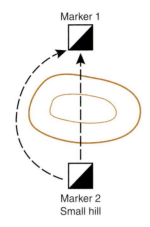

a
Marker 1
Marker 2
Small hill

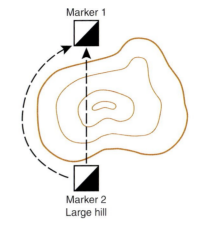

b
Marker 1
Marker 2
Large hill

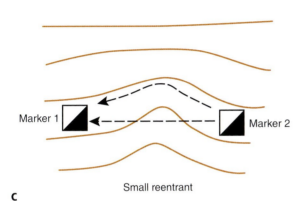

Marker 1
Marker 2
Small reentrant

c

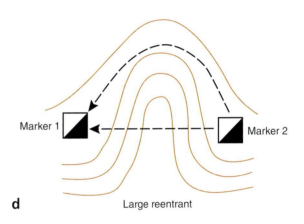

Marker 1
Marker 2
Large reentrant

d

Description

Walk the group from the first to the second control marker on the contour in order to familiarize them with the terrain. At the second marker on the other side of the obstacle, explain that each runner will get a start time, and on "Go" they will run back to the first marker on the other side, staying on the contour. An assistant coach times each athlete at the other side. The athlete then walks up and over the hill, returning to the second marker. When rested, she gets a start time, and on "Go," she runs over the hill back to the first marker where her time is again recorded. Each route (over versus around) should be run two or three times. Compare times. Repeat for the small hill, large reentrant, and small reentrant. Determine whether it is better to run straight or on the contour for each type of terrain.

Control Identification via Slides

Objective

To improve the ability to relate terrain features to map symbols

Skills, Techniques, and Processes

Precision map reading, visualization, interpretation

Skill Level

Advanced

Activity Level

Sitting

(continued)

Control Identification via Slides *(continued)*

Venue

Indoor

Time Required

20-30 minutes

On Map

Yes

Materials

Slides of control features, stopwatch, one map per person, paper, pencils, compass

Setup

Select a map with 10 distinctive control locations. Control features should have other identifiable features nearby (e.g., vegetation differences, trails, streams). Photograph each control (with marker) while showing other features as well, and create slides from the photographs. Record the location and compass bearing from the photo site to the control. Mark the maps with 10 photographed features and 5 additional features. Label the slides with the bearing.

Description

Distribute paper and pencils to the group and have them number their papers 1 through 10. Distribute maps upside down. Explain that each slide will be shown for 15 seconds and the bearing will be given. They have 15 seconds to look at the slide and another 15 seconds to determine which control it is on the map and write it down. Repeat for 10 slides and review when finished.

Variations

1. Have the group run laps between each slide, but give more time to observe the slide and decide.

2. Print photographs instead and clip them to cards with a bearing. Have athletes run a lap with each photo card and a map, recording the control at the end of each lap and picking up the next photo. Organize it as a relay to increase speed.

Map Walk: Visualization

Objective

To improve the ability to create a mental picture of an upcoming feature or area

Skills, Techniques, and Processes

Precision map reading, visualization

Skill Level

Beginner, advanced

Activity Level

Walking

Venue

Outdoor

Time Required

30-45 minutes

On Map

Yes

Materials

One map per person

Setup

Select an area with a variety of features. Mark a short (3 km) course with 6 to 10 controls, with each control out of sight of the previous one. (Control markers need not be hung.)

Description

Distribute maps. Review visualization. Have the group select a route to control 1. Then have the group silently visualize how the area should look, and ask a few to describe what they picture. Proceed to the control, stopping when it comes into view and discussing how its appearance compares with expectations. Repeat for each control.

Relocation Relay

Objective

To increase awareness and memory of features in the terrain in order to determine one's location on the map

Skills, Techniques, and Processes

Rough and precision map reading, terrain recognition, relocation

Skill Level

Beginner, advanced

Activity Level

Sitting, walking, or running

Venue

Outdoor

Time Required

45-60 minutes

On Map

Yes

Materials

One map per person

Setup

None

Description

Divide athletes into small groups (three to four people) with a similar level of technical and physical ability. Identify the start location on the map. Explain that each group should select a leader who runs for 300 to 500 meters while reading the map and then stops at a distinct feature. Others follow the leader without looking at the map but while observing the terrain. When the leader stops, everyone looks at the map to determine the precise location. The leader checks with each person and indicates if the location is correct. When the whole group has found the location, a new leader is chosen. Give a time for all to return to the start.

Variation

No one looks at the map until the leader stops, and then everyone decides.

Comments

Those with fewer technical map-reading skills should run along handrails.

Comparing Route Choices

Objective

To determine when to use trails and when to run cross country

Skills, Techniques, and Processes

Route selection

Skill Level

Advanced

Activity Level

Running

Venue

Outdoor

Time Required

60-75 minutes

On Map

Yes

Materials

One map per person, control markers, pens, stopwatches, numbered index cards for number of controls

(continued)

Comparing Route Choices *(continued)*

Setup

Select an area with a simple trail network. Design a short (2-3 km) course in which, for each leg, there is a choice between running cross country and running a trail. The course should start and end at the same location. Mark maps. Set controls.

Description

Explain to the group that the course is to be run twice. First, run the course cross country. At each control, record the time of arrival on the card. Immediately leave for the next control. At the finish, record the time and initials and rest. Then, take a new card and repeat the course, running trails instead. Mark the time and initials on the card at each control. Stagger starts, and provide a map on "Go." When finished, compare cross-country running times with trail times on each leg. Compare times with the map to determine situations when it is better to go cross country and when it is better to take trails.

Leap Frog

Objective

To increase the ability to plan a route while on the run

Skills, Techniques, and Processes

Map reading and route selection at speed

Skill Level

Advanced

Activity Level

Running

Venue

Outdoor

Time Required

20-30 minutes

On Map

Yes

Materials

One map per person, controls

Setup

Select an area and design a short course (2-3 km) with 8 to 10 legs with choice of routes. Set controls. Mark maps.

Description

Divide the group into pairs of similar technical and physical ability. Explain that one person will lead to control 1, running continuously and map reading on the run. The second person follows, planning the leg from 1 to 2 on the run. At control 1, the second person takes the lead and the first person follows, planning the leg from 2 to 3. Repeat for the entire course. When finished, discuss route choices. Stagger starts. On "Go," distribute maps.

Comments

This tends to be a fast drill because each new leader already has a route planned and simply needs to execute it.

Collecting Features by Thumbing Along

Objective

To learn to maintain awareness of one's position on the map

Skills, Techniques, and Processes

Collecting features by thumbing along, map reading

Skill Level

Beginner, advanced

Activity Level

Walking or running

Venue

Outdoor

Time Required

10-20 minutes

On Map

Yes

Materials

One map per person with course of appropriate difficulty, map case

Setup

Provide maps with courses or master map and pens.

Description

Do the course as a group, beginning at a walk and progressing to a run if appropriate for the group. Begin by demonstrating how to fold the map small enough (approximately 4 × 4 in. or 10 × 10 cm) for the thumb to reach the center. Demonstrate placing the thumb on the start. Walk along and note distinct features that indicate the current position. Demonstrate how the thumb moves to each new identifiable location. Check all thumbs for the correct position. Proceed through the course, frequently checking location, thumb position, and map orientation.

Map Memory Under Stress

Objective

To exercise map memory during physical stress, such as running

Skills, Techniques, and Processes

Rough and precision map reading, map memory

Skill Level

Advanced

Activity Level

Running

Venue

Indoor or outdoor

Time Required

10-20 minutes

On Map

No

Materials

Maps, place to run a loop (e.g., woods, field, track, road), paper, pencils

Setup

Maps should have a number of legs drawn on them (not necessarily connected).

(continued)

Description

Subjects are allowed time (10, 20, or 30 seconds) to study a leg. They then run a loop (300-500 m) and return to draw what they remember of the leg. Then they run another loop and return to study another leg. If fitness level is known, running pace can be adjusted to a specific level of effort. Also, running tempo can be varied to see where proficiency falls.

Mapping a Classroom

Objective

To learn how maps present a two-dimensional top view of a space

Skills, Techniques, and Processes

Precision map reading, visualization

Skill Level

Beginner, advanced

Activity Level

Sitting or walking

Venue

Indoor

Time Required

20-30 minutes

On Map

No

Materials

One large sheet of paper or poster board and one 8.5- × 11-inch (22 × 28 cm) piece of paper per group of three or four students, pencils, markers

Setup

Draw the perimeter of the room on the poster board, indicating locations of windows, doors, and so on.

Description

Display the poster of the room perimeter. Explain top view and have participants identify the windows, doors, and other landmarks you have drawn. Divide the participants into groups of three or four, giving each group a section of the room to map. Distribute paper and pencils to each group. Explain that they should map their area in top view, trying to keep objects to scale. (Do not map the ceiling.) When finished, have groups transfer their section drawings to the poster board using the marker.

Comments

Divide the room area unevenly so that the groups do not all finish at the same time. Use the map for games and exercises.

Debriefing and Course Evaluation

Objective

To determine which techniques worked well at a race and to discover a pattern to determine which skills need emphasis in training

Skills, Techniques, and Processes

Rough and precision map reading, analysis

Skill Level

Beginner, advanced

Activity Level

Sitting

Venue

Indoor

Time Required

15-20 minutes

On Map

No

Materials

Training diary, competition analysis form (see appendix B)

Setup

Obtain competition analysis forms. See appendix B for a sample form.

Description

Assemble the athletes after the training course or race. Discuss how to record comments in a training diary. Distribute competition analysis forms and discuss how to record information on the form. Have athletes evaluate their races. Periodically review diaries and competition analyses privately with athletes.

Drawing Course in Review

Objective

To systematically evaluate performance in order to determine which skills, techniques, or processes need improvement

Skills, Techniques, and Processes

Map reading, memory, analysis

Skill Level

Beginner, advanced

Activity Level

Sitting

Venue

Indoor

Time Required

10-15 minutes

On Map

Yes

Materials

Course map, training diary, red or purple pens

Setup

None

Description

Have athletes draw their actual route on their course as soon after the race as is convenient. Mark every stop. Make notes on the back of the

(continued)

Drawing Course in Review *(continued)*

map, leg by leg. Note whether attack points were used, whether catching or collecting features were used, and whether the route choice was the best. Describe errors and how to avoid repeating them. Make notes in the training diary on patterns noted and skills that need to be improved.

Comments

File maps and use notes before competing in the same area again.

Shadowing

Objective

To obtain feedback on orienteering technique and to learn how to evaluate another athlete's performance

Skills, Techniques, and Processes

All

Skill Level

Beginner, advanced

Activity Level

Walking or running

Venue

Outdoor

Time Required

30-45 minutes

On Map

Yes

Materials

One map per person (runner and shadow), pens, control markers, stopwatches

Setup

Design short (3-4 km) courses of appropriate difficulty. Hang controls. Mark maps.

Description

Divide the group into pairs, matching a more experienced orienteer (shadow) with a less experienced orienteer. The orienteer is given a map and runs the course. The shadow follows with the map. The shadow makes notes on time for each leg, time spent stopped, locations on the map where stops occurred, errors, and evidence of good technique. Stagger starts. When finished, the shadow gives constructive criticism on the orienteer's course.

Variation

Have the group shadow an experienced orienteer to observe good technique in action.

Comments

Have athletes mark maps.

Map Orientation

Objective

To learn to orient the map to north and to reorient it as one changes direction

Skills, Techniques, and Processes

Keeping map oriented by precision or rough map reading, precision or rough compass reading

Skill Level

Beginner

Activity Level

Walking

Venue

Indoor or outdoor

Time Required

5-10 minutes

On Map

Yes

Materials

One map per person, *North* sign, red marker

Setup

Post the sign on a wall or on the ground in the appropriate position. Mark the north edge of each map with a conspicuous red line.

Description

Have participants stand one arm's-length apart. Distribute maps to the participants and have them place their maps on the ground at their feet and face you. Tell them which way is north. Then tell them to face north, then east, then south, then west, then north again. Explain, "You moved in relation to land around you." Ask, "What happened to the land?" Tell them, "Pick up the map and orient it, then put it back on the land at your feet." Explain, "The land did not move; the map moved." Have them pick up their maps. Tell them to watch you. Turn the map (with your thumb on it) while moving around. Have them do this two or three times. Then have them wander randomly through the area, keeping their maps oriented as they walk. Observe for problems (red edge of the map should always face north). Assist where necessary. Repeat in woods.

Variation

Use the compass needle to stay oriented to north.

Room-O

Objective

To learn to relate to a two-dimensional map of a three-dimensional space

Skills, Techniques, and Processes

Rough and precision map reading, map orientation

Skill Level

Beginner, advanced

Activity Level

Walking

Venue

Indoor

Time Required

10 minutes

On Map

No

Materials

Poster board, marker, 7 to 10 small orienteering stickers (or other stickers), paper, pencils

Setup

Draw a map of the room. Write a letter on each sticker and place stickers on the mapped features. Each sticker should have a letter to eventually spell a word when all stickers have been found. Some word suggestions are *attack point, collecting features, Bulldogs, Boy Scouts, be prepared,* or any other appropriate phrase for the group.

Description

Distribute paper and pencils. Introduce the map of the room. Explain that the object is to look at circles on the map and seek the stickers on those features. When all stickers have been found, unscramble the letters to make a word. On "Go," all begin. Periodically rotate the map so that participants find it necessary to reorient it when they return to view it between sticker searches.

Comments

Add interest by placing stickers anywhere between the floor and ceiling.

Name of Exercise

_____

Objective

Materials

Skills, Techniques, and Processes

Setup

Skill Level

Beginner, advanced (circle appropriate levels)

Description

Activity Level

Sitting, walking, running (circle appropriate levels)

Venue

Indoor or outdoor (circle one)

Variations

Time Required

Comments

On Map

Yes or no (circle one)

Do you have an idea for an exercise that you would like to share? Please copy this form and fill it in with the workings of your idea. Send it to: OUSA, Coaching Certification Committee, P.O. Box 1444, Forest Park, GA 30298.

From _Discovering orienteering_ by C. Ferguson and R. Turbyfill (Orienteering USA, ed.), 2013 (Champaign, IL: Human Kinetics).

Appendix B

Competition Analysis Forms

The following competition analysis forms will help you analyze your errors and weaknesses so that you can train for them, and they will also help you identify your strengths. Fill out the forms immediately after each event, and consolidate the data after every six courses (or three two-day events). It is important to fill out all three sheets to give the coach a clear picture of the type, quality, and condition of all events.

Competition Analysis: General Course Information

Date	Location	Organization	Class	Map quality	Scale	Terrain	Weather

Notes:

1. In column 1, enter the date of the event—you should have also put it visibly on the map.

2. In column 2, give the name of the map.

3. In column 3, give the club name that is responsible for organizing the event.

4. In column 4, put the class you competed in.

5. In column 5, put your best estimate of the quality of the map based on your previous knowledge.

6. In column 6, put the scale of the map you competed on.

7. In column 7, describe the majority of the terrain as you found it on your course.

8. In column 8, describe the weather conditions during *your* run.

Competition Analysis: Times and Placement

Course length	Winner	Winner's time	Min per km	Own time	Min per km	Number of competitors	Your place

Notes:

1. In column 1, put the length of the course as printed on your clue sheet.

2. In column 2, put the name of the winner on *your* course in *your* category.

3. In column 3, put the winner's time in hr:min:sec.

4. In column 4, calculate the winner's minutes per kilometer in min:sec.

From *Discovering orienteering* by C. Ferguson and R. Turbyfill (Orienteering USA, ed.), 2013 (Champaign, IL: Human Kinetics).

5. In column 5, put your own finish time in hr:min:sec.

6. In column 6, calculate your minutes per kilometer in min:sec.

7. In column 7, put the number of competitors on *your* course in *your* category.

8. In column 8, enter what place you finished in this event.

Competition Analysis: Detailed Breakdown of Problem Controls

							Sum	%
Date								
Number of controls							6	100
Number of problem controls								
First leg								
Second leg								
Third leg								
Fourth leg								
Fifth leg								
Sixth leg								
Seventh leg								
Eighth leg								
Ninth leg								
Tenth leg								
Eleventh leg								
Twelfth leg								
Thirteenth leg								
Fourteenth leg								
Fifteenth leg								
Sixteenth leg								
Seventeenth leg								
Eighteenth leg								
Nineteenth leg								
Twentieth leg								
Finish								
Total estimated time lost								100
Placement								
Minutes behind winner								
What went wrong?								
Lack of concentration before starting (US)								

From *Discovering orienteering* by C. Ferguson and R. Turbyfill (Orienteering USA, ed.), 2013 (Champaign, IL: Human Kinetics).

(continued)

									Sum	%
What went wrong? *(continued)*										
Leaving the control point (LC)										
Map memory (MM)										
Misunderstanding the map (MU)										
Pacing (P)										
Precision map reading (PM)										
Precision compass (PC)										
Planning of route choice (PR)										
Rough compass (RC)										
Rough map reading (RM)										
180 out (OO)										
Problem caused by . . .										
Being too hurried										
Parallel error										
No sure attack point										
Taking a chance										
Underestimating										
Lack of concentration										
Seeing other runners										
Being overexcited										
Not reading the description										
Being too slow										
Unusual terrain										
Fatigue										
Hesitation										

Notes:

1. In row 1, enter the date for each event you are logging.

2. In row 2, enter the number of controls for each event you are logging.

3. In row 3, enter the number of problem controls you encountered (any leg on which you lost time).

4. In rows 4 through 24, enter the amount of time you lost in min:sec.

5. In row 25, enter the total amount of time that you lost (i.e., add up rows 4-24).

6. In row 26, enter your placement in the standings.

7. In row 27, enter how far behind the winner you finished in min:sec.

8. In the "What went wrong?" section, enter the number(s) of the leg(s) at which the item listed occurred. If the occurrence was on more than one leg, follow the preceding number with a comma. Do *not* put a comma *after the last number* you list in each box.

9. In the "Problem caused by . . ." section, use the same procedure as you did for the "What went wrong?" section. Do not use *0* for any occurrence.

From *Discovering orienteering* by C. Ferguson and R. Turbyfill (Orienteering USA, ed.), 2013 (Champaign, IL: Human Kinetics).

Index

Note: The letters *f* and *t* after page numbers indicate figures and tables, respectively.

About Orienteering USA

Founded in 1971, **Orienteering USA** is a volunteer-run organization dedicated to promoting orienteering as a viable and attractive recreation choice for outdoor enthusiasts; increasing awareness of orienteering as a tool for education, personal development, and environmental awareness; and improving the competitive performance of U.S. orienteering athletes to world-class levels.

About the Authors

Charles Ferguson, PhD, served as president of the United States Orienteering Federation (USOF) from 1999 to 2007. A former colonel in the Air Force Reserve, he became the initial vice president of academic affairs at Marine Corps University at Quantico Marine Base, Virginia, until retiring.

A member of the U.S. CIOR team and an expert orienteer, Colonel Ferguson represented the United States as a competitor in eight competitions. In 1977, he led his team to the first U.S. win in the over-35 (veteran) category in the CIOR military competitions in the United Kingdom. His team again won the over-35 category in 1982 in the United States.

Colonel Ferguson later served as orienteering coach for the U.S. CIOR team for 2 years and with his wife, Linda, as orienteering coach for the Canadian CIOR team for 3 years. Canadian teams finished 11th in orienteering their first year, in the top 10 the next year, and in first place their third year. He also served for 13 years on the NATO CIOR competition commission, leading the rewrite of the orienteering rules of the competition. At the summer military competitions, he was elected to the CIOR orienteering technical jury for 5 years, serving as chair for 3.

Along with Coach Turbyfill, he teaches the beginning orienteering course, Zero to Orange in Three Days, and he holds OUSA Olympic Level I and Level II orienteering coaching certificates. A frequent orienteering competitor in the United States, he placed second in his age group in the 2007 U.S. individual championships.

Dr. Ferguson currently serves USOF as a director of the OUSA Endowment Fund (EF) and EF liaison to the OUSA board of directors. He is also a member of the executive board of the Adventuresports Institute.

LTC Robert Turbyfill works as an analyst for the Department of Homeland Security in Washington, DC. He has served as a United States Marine Officer for 11 years and as an Army National Guard Officer for 14 years.

He is a former all-Marine, interservice, United States, and North American orienteering champion. He has represented the United States 11 times at world-class competition (8 times as a competitor and 3 times as the coach of the U.S. orienteering team).

A graduate and faculty member of the Marine Corps Physical Fitness Academy, he coached the 1977 and 1978 CIOR navigation event. The U.S. CIOR team won that event for the first time in CIOR history.

In Army ROTC he has coached the Brigham Young University (BYU) Ranger Challenge Team for four seasons to national titles. His record was third, first, third, and first in the nation by comparative score at the Fourth Army ROTC Region at Fort Louis, Washington.

As a team consultant, he is coaching and teaching orienteering to the USMA orienteering club cadets at West Point. He is the current coaching certifier for Orienteering USA. He teaches a college-level orienteering course and an Olympic Level 1 coaching course at West Point in conjunction with the Adventuresports Institute at Garrett College in western Maryland. He has developed navigation certification standards approved by the OUSA board of directors in November of 2006.

Discover Orienteering. Discover Yourself.

Orienteering is more than a sport in wilderness navigation. It is more than you, a map and a compass. It is a chance for you to spend a day in the woods, to learn a new skill and to learn more about yourself. Join us.

To find an orienteering event close to you, join Orienteering USA, or make a donation, visit www.orienteeringusa.org.